THE WALDEN<

Persecution and Survii

The Poor of Lyons, called by their detractors 'Waldensians' after their founder Waldo or Vaudès, first emerged in about 1170. Like other groups of the period, they formed a religious community founded on the strict observance of the gospel, preaching and poverty. Defying Church rulings stating that the laity had no right to preach and applying the scriptures to the letter, in particular denying the existence of purgatory and refusing to take oaths, they were condemned as heretics. The community was forced underground and dispersed widely; but through a unique, organised body of itinerant preachers they nevertheless managed to maintain links throughout the whole of Europe, from Provence and Dauphiné to Calabria and Apulia, Austria and Bohemia, Pomerania, Brandenburg and Poland.

Of all the medieval dissenters, the Poor of Lyons were alone in surviving to the dawn of modern times. They were then swept up in the great wave of the Reformation: by adopting Protestantism in the sixteenth century, they gave up their separate, ancestral identity.

This book is less a history of Waldensianism than an account of men and women who, remaining true to an ideal, lived in anxiety and under suspicion, often fearful and sometimes in blind terror. Theirs is a tale of people great and small. Proclaiming their faith timidly, yet with an astounding – sometimes dogged – tenacity, they hold up a mirror to us today.

GABRIEL AUDISIO is Professor of Early Modern History at the University of Provence. He has published widely on the history of Provence and Piedmont, and on sixteenth-century religious history; he is also the author of a handbook of palaeography, *Lire le français d'hier* (1991).

Cambridge Medieval Textbooks

This is a series of specially commissioned textbooks for teachers and students, designed to complement the monograph series Cambridge Studies in Medieval Life and Thought by providing introductions to a range of topics in medieval history. This series combines both chronological and thematic approaches, and will deal with British and European topics. All volumes in the series will be published in hard covers and in paperback.

For a list of titles in the series, see end of book.

THE WALDENSIAN DISSENT

Persecution and Survival, *c.* 1170–*c.* 1570

Gabriel Audisio

Translated by Claire Davison

PUBLISHED BY THE PRESS SYNDICATE OF THE UNIVERSITY OF CAMBRIDGE
The Pitt Building, Trumpington Street, Cambridge CB2 1RP, United Kingdom

CAMBRIDGE UNIVERSITY PRESS
The Edinburgh Building, Cambridge, CB2 2RU, United Kingdom
http://www.cup.cam.ac.uk
40 West 20th Street, New York, NY 10011–4211, USA   http://www.cup.org
10 Stamford Road, Oakleigh, Melbourne 3166, Australia

Originally published in 1989 as *Les 'Vaudois': naissance, vie et mort d'une dissidence*
(xiie–xvie siècle)
by Albert Meynier Editore
and © Gabriel Audisio

First published in English by Cambridge University Press 1999 as *The Waldensian Dissent:*
Persecution and Survival c. 1170–c. 1570
English translation © Cambridge University Press 1999

Printed in Great Britain at the University Press, Cambridge

Typeset in Bembo on 10/11.5 pt   [CE]

A catalogue record for this book is available from the British Library

Library of Congress cataloguing in publication data
Audisio, Gabriel.
[Vaudois. English]
The Waldensian Dissent: Persecution and Survival, *c.* 1170–*c.* 1570 / Gabriel Audisio;
translated by Claire Davison.
p.   cm. – (Cambridge Medieval Textbooks)
Includes bibliographical references.
ISBN 0 521 55029 7 (hardcover). – ISBN 0 521 55984 7 (pbk.)
1. Waldenses.   1. Title.   11. Series.
BX4881.2.A8313   1999
273'.6–dc21   98–49526   CIP

ISBN 0 521 55029 7 hardback
ISBN 0 521 55984 7 paperback

To Protestant friends from Provence, from Piedmont and else-where, descendants of the former Poor of Lyons, who honour the memory of their forebears, who courageously reject legends and who are never loath to put received notions into question; whose quest for the truth is insatiable. To those whose love of history is such that they will never distort its meaning. They have under-stood its true aim: to understand.

'And further, by these, my son, be admonished: of making
many books there is no end'
(Ecclesiastes, 12: 12)

'Prove all things; hold fast that which is good'
(I Thessalonians, 5: 21)

CONTENTS

MAPS

x

PREFACE

It is quite a hazardous undertaking to seek at the same time to take into account the most recently published research by historians on a particular question and also to present it in as simple and honest a manner as possible to an inquiring but generally non-specialist reader. The difficulty becomes even greater when the domain in question is so vast, chronologically and geographically speaking, and so varied and complex in theme that it would be rash indeed for anyone to claim to be an authority on the entire history of the Waldensians. Who could maintain that they had read and studied the entire corpus of available sources written in various languages and scattered throughout Europe?

It would be presumptuous indeed for me to claim that this work presents an overview just of my own research into such varied aspects of the Waldensians' history across the centuries. My aim, rather, has been to make accessible to the 'enlightened amateur' the results of the latest research on the question, both my own and that of other specialists in Waldensian history. I have purposely omitted those works which I consider unreliable. I believe I have mentioned all those which I deem important. All works and articles which provided me with information have been cited: the reader will find relevant publications and other sources listed at the end of each chapter. It is only just that proper acknowledgement should be made where it is due, for we all benefit from the work of those who went before us, in the distant or the recent past. I have never ceased to be moved by the words that John of Salisbury attributed to Bernard of Chartres who, as early as the twelfth century, was perhaps aware that he could see further than his masters, to whom he paid the following homage: 'We are dwarfs, set upon giants' shoulders.' But this does not mean the work is only a compilation. Its composition was shaped by a structured line of thought, reflections on methodology concerning the sources and how to use them, and a personal inclination to honesty, accompanied by my uncompromising will to 'overlook' no document, even those that disturb rather than enhance my argument.

Specialists, however, should not expect to find in these pages echoes of the often heated debates that have animated academic gatherings. There may be just a veiled allusion here or there. But if they cannot find any reference whatsoever to one debate or another, let me reassure them. If I have not evoked their theory, opinion or position, it is generally not because I am unaware of it, certainly not because I have dismissed it. Quite simply, I felt that it would be pointless to try to sum up the various theses for a public generally unconcerned by such matters. Let me be perfectly clear about this: when one specialist has appeared more convincing to me than another, I have inclined to their point of view and presented it here. Where the debate would still seem open, I have chosen either to offer a middle way, or not to refer to it at all if it concerns a question of secondary or at least inessential importance. Let me give an example. In the first chapter, which deals with the origins of Waldensianism, a polemic (in the scientific sense of the term, of course) set Christine Thouzellier against Kurt-Viktor Selge. Thouzellier believed that Vaudès's primary vocation was poverty, which led inevitably to preaching. The German scholar, on the other hand, argued that the cornerstone was preaching and that Vaudès and his companions opted for a life of poverty in order to dedicate themselves entirely to their mission as preachers. At a certain level of specialisation, I do not hesitate to accept the importance and the relevance of the debate. In the circumstances, however, I have chosen to ignore the matter and the reader will not find the slightest reference to their 'dispute'. To my mind, both historians were equally convincing. The question is thus still undecided. I consider that preaching and poverty both constituted original and fundamental aspects of Waldensianism. The reader wanting to know more can always examine the question in greater detail, using the bibliographical references provided.

It should therefore be clear that this work is not addressed to my colleagues, who have no need of it. It is intended as a guide for those little or unacquainted with Waldensianism. For this reason, the critical apparatus has been kept as light as possible. Footnotes have been avoided to facilitate reading. A reader wishing to trace a quotation, the author of which is always given in the text, will easily be able to do so by consulting the bibliography at the end of each chapter. When a work has figured once in an end-of-chapter bibliography, it will not appear again, even if it is used subsequently in later chapters. The reader will find all the titles, organised in what is intended to be a practical manner, as well as manuscript sources and related publications, in the general bibliography, which has also been limited to essential works, at the end of the book. Similarly, to bring the reader into contact, as far as it is possible to do so, with the men and women of those distant times who have aroused our interest here, it is indispensable to quote from original documents; these have always been translated. We all know the Italian saying, *Traduttore, traditore*. Should one present extracts from documents in the Latin in which they were written, from a legitimate desire to be faithful to source material? It was indeed the language used in most texts from that period, being not only the language of the Church but also of science. Such a hardline position did not seem tenable here, considering the objective of the work. Once again, anyone wishing to do so can refer to the original documents. If the manuscripts have been published, they will figure in the end-of-chapter bibliographies. Those still unpublished are given at the end of the book.

Using the much-used terms of the misleading, traditional dichotomy of Pythagoras – a duality cherished by medieval scholars in the west and from which we have yet to free ourselves – I would say that the present work aims to be solid in matter and accessible in form. It has always been my belief that the work of a historian was complete only when it was published in a manner which brought the underlying research to the greatest number of people. It is a worthy ambition both on a scientific and a pedagogical level. Will the history told here have succeeded in fulfilling this two-sided aspiration? The reader is ultimately the only judge.

ACKNOWLEDGEMENTS

This English edition of my work would never have materialised without the good will and determination of Peter Biller, my friend and colleague at York University. I am sincerely grateful to him. In addition I would like to thank Miri Rubin, and also the publishers for agreeing to commission and publish the translation.

I am particularly grateful to Claire Davison, my colleague at the University of Provence, for the meticulous care and the intelligent sensibility of the language with which she has set about rendering all the nuances of the French text.

I hope that this version will enable the English-speaking readership to become better acquainted with the Waldensian dissent which never ceases to surprise and affect us.

INTRODUCTION

'Another history of the Waldensians!', certain readers, specialists in particular, might be thinking. 'Is it called for? What is the use?' Similar endeavours have become increasingly frequent since the sixteenth century. A minority religious dissent has intrigued those who have studied religious history in Europe to such an extent that an alarming wealth of bibliographical documentation awaits the neophyte. Acquainting oneself with it is not only a time-consuming task, it is also fastidious, for the works are repetitive and the authors have sometimes plagiarised one another shamelessly. The latest synthesis, by Giorgio Tourn, appeared in 1980, if we discount those works which have been published on the question but which cannot really be called historical studies, whatever their authors may think. Has our knowledge on the matter progressed sufficiently to justify a new update for a readership beyond the limited circle of Waldensian specialists?

There are several reasons which can plead in favour of a new version of Waldensian history. First, it must be acknowledged that important results from research carried out and published in the 1970s and even the 1960s have yet to be taken into account by the authors of recent, general histories of the Waldensians intended as broad surveys addressed to the general public. For instance, although their work is well known and much appreciated, little or no reference has been made in recent general studies to Kurt-Viktor Selge, Alexander Patschovsky, Dietrich Kurze and Grado Merlo or even Amadeo Molnár and Romolo Cegna to some extent. And yet history has advanced considerably, and it is somewhat frustrating to read contemporary authors who blithely continue writing as they did thirty years ago, as if no historian had done any work since.

Furthermore, even in the last ten years, important new work has become available which not only enriches our knowledge of previously neglected areas, in spatial or temporal terms, but which also throws new light on certain outdated notions, challenging issues that had too hastily been considered complete, and revealing new documents or new methods of approach. For these reasons, results made available by Peter Biller, Martin Schneider, Pierrette Paravy or myself should quite naturally find their way into new histories of the Waldensians.

There have been relatively important discoveries in recent or less recent times illuminating obscure matters and bearing out hypotheses; certain former debates have been brought to a close. But this is not all. There have been real changes in the way the Waldensians have been taken up, for a historian is above all a man of his time; the history he writes therefore depends on the society in which he lives. I would not be so naïve as to suggest that we have become more 'objective' in the way we consider those dissenters who challenged the Roman Church. Everyone knows how necessary, honourable and illusory the ideal of objectivity is. And yet, if history in general is subject to the partiality of judgements, because history is human and those who make and write history are human too, how much more sensitive to bias and prejudice is religious history, for it harks back to mostly bygone times when religion played a decisive role in European society. The weight of time, tradition and custom proves all the more burdensome in this domain. It is certainly the case for the Waldensians.

Even today, historians, as well as those who claim to be historians, are rather too hasty to make value judgements more or less implicitly concerning the dissenters who later became Protestants. Two major tendencies can be traced in the reams they have published. The first, which can be found in the works of Catholic and Protestant authors alike, sees the movement as a kind of religious community that was ultimately little removed from the Roman Church, the beliefs and rites of which it never fully rejected. In other words, it was not as heretical as one might think. The other tendency, which can equally be found amongst Catholics and Protestants, sees the Waldensians as real 'heretics', or even in some case as authentic 'holders of the truth' and harbingers of the Reformation. For writers subscribing to this approach, theirs was a bastion which stayed true to its religious precepts, opposing Rome for four hundred years, in spite of the assaults directed against it.

It may come as a surprise to learn that in both historiographical traditions there are Catholic and Protestant authors. One perhaps tends to expect that denominational differences will find expression through diverging or even opposing approaches, as is often the case. It is true that, if we look closely, the denominational divide is indeed present. And yet, a rather unexpected and certainly unintentional ecumenism has meant that the varying positions are not ultimately so far removed from one another, whatever the denominational origins of the author; they even converge in the end because on either side they derive from the same, well-known *a priori* – that of using history to serve other aims. It comes down to using the past to serve a thesis, an opinion or a cause. This 'utilitarian' approach to history proves, in the present case, detrimental to the Waldensians, even when it is adopted by those who claim to honour their memory. Neither side really attempts to under-stand the minority which, I emphasise, was neither Catholic nor Protestant. How much more simple to adopt a reductive, frequently used approach whereby the unknown is drawn within the sphere of the known. It is more disturbing by far to become acquainted with otherness on its own territory. And yet it is only by casting aside one's own judgement that one can understand Waldensianism and the Waldensians. Should the reader of the present work have already made up his mind about the Waldensians or about the author; should he be convinced of the soundness of his knowledge and his judgement to the extent that he has no intention of looking anew at the minority dissent; in short, should he be unwilling to listen and feel disinclined to consider an approach which, in all lucidity, might appear better adapted to the facts; then may I quietly suggest that he read no further.

I could replace the term 'Waldensian' in the title by the expression 'the Poor of Lyons'. The term 'Waldensian', in fact, was coined by those who persecuted them, designating the heretics by the name of their founder, as is so often the case. The 'heretics', however, never used this name. On the contrary, they claimed they had but one master, Jesus Christ. In no document issued from within the community is the term 'Waldensian' used. They distinguished themselves from other Christians by saying they were 'Brothers', 'Poor of Christ' or 'Poor of Lyons'. By using these names, we can avoid one label which was pejorative at the time and came to be synonymous with 'heretic'. It also suggests that we are adopting a more favourable approach when trying to understand these men and women who put their lives in peril and for generations chose to live their Christianity differently and not according to Rome. The choice of one name or another may seem somewhat trifling. I am, however, convinced that it is not an insignificant detail. But there is neither time nor space to talk about such matters here.

For the same reasons, I have adopted the chronological limits given in the title, that is, from the twelfth to the sixteenth century. The starting date is absolute, for no-one today would claim that the Waldensians' origins date back to the apostles or even to the time of pope Sylvester (314–35). The closing date is equally definite to my mind, but certain historians think differently. There do, admittedly, still exist 'Waldensian valleys' in Piedmont and a 'Waldensian Church' (*Chiesa valdese*) in Italy and certain other countries. Moreover, some people descended from the former Waldensians continue to consider themselves as Waldensians. This is a mistake. Waldensianism was a religious movement with certain quite precise characteristics. These were almost entirely lost when it was decided to join the Reformation in the sixteenth century. From that point on, Waldensian and Protestant became completely separate, if not absolutely contradictory, terms. For this reason, I consider that Waldensianism came to an end at the time of the Reformation and I bring the history of the Waldensians to a close in this period, adding an epilogue at the end to account for the existence of a region, a descent and a Church which still bear the name 'Waldensian' to this day. Speaking of the Poor of Lyons, rather than the Waldensians will probably make the situation clearer and avoid any misunderstandings.

As for the geographical scope of the work, it covers Europe with one or two exceptions. England, the Iberian Peninsula and Scandinavia were the only lands in Europe where the dissenters were not to be found. A basic characteristic of the community was its life as a diaspora, subjected as it was to incessant persecution and forced to flee in various directions to ensure its survival. From southern Italy to the Baltic Sea, from the Atlantic Ocean to Poland, the Poor of Lyons lived paradoxically as a tiny minority with followers in a great many nations. There can be no doubting that the situation created serious problems concerning the unity of the movement and made it necessary for them to organise themselves efficiently. But it also enabled them to escape excessively narrow considerations by tackling and resolving problems in a broader perspective that could take local differences into account. No other medieval dissent managed to cover so vast an area or to live so long.

Many obstacles lie, however, in the path of the writer setting out to retrace the history of the Poor of Lyons. The Waldensian people left few direct testimonies. They were peasants, not scholars or men of influence who cultivated the written word. They were also dissenters living in hiding, doing their best to pass unnoticed; they therefore tried to leave as few traces as possible. Most documents about them were the work of those who fought them, writing treatises and essays or recording trials. As is the case for all clandestine minorities, a major drawback is that our source material is mostly indirect, requiring particularly careful analysis to see through its potentially biased nature. How to interpret such sources creates a real methodological problem. There is no easy answer and it would be wrong to pretend to the reader that such problems do not exist. But there is no reason to be discouraged, either. While difficulties do arise, they can, as we shall see, be overcome. One's efforts are well rewarded.

It is time, then, for me to invite my reader on a voyage of discovery. Let us cast our prejudices aside as best we can. Our quest will lead us towards a people in our own image, with their high aims and low quarrels, who, even as they evolved, adapted, accepted compromises and risked betrayals, managed to refuse assimilation, protect their group identity and preserve the major tenets of their faith for four hundred years. Does this in itself not make them worthy of our attention, our respect and even our affection?

I

1170–1215: DECISIVE AND
PURPOSIVE ORIGINS

The early days of the Poor of Lyons, as is the case for many other movements, be they anti-establishment, minority, religious or otherwise, were so unassertive that they were hardly noticed at all. Later, faced with the movement's survival and endurance, partisans and antagonists vied imaginatively with each another – for the notion of historical precision was not an issue in the middle ages – in some cases admittedly with the best of intentions, to explain and thus describe the origins of this curious group.

For this reason, within the group from Lyons the myth grew up that their origins dated back to apostolic times, a belief that was to persist for centuries. To understand their reasoning, it must be borne in mind that the worst criticism that could be addressed to Christians appearing not fully to respect the faith or the moral doctrine of the Church was that of being innovatory. Like all revealed religions, Christianity is built around a canon to be conserved and a message to be transmitted. This was the role both of the 'Tradition' in the true sense of the term and also of the Roman hierarchy which had every intention of controlling the transmission of the message and, as doctrinal authority, supervising its authenticity. They reasoned that God had spoken once and for all through his son Jesus Christ and that his Word addressed to mankind was entirely contained in the bible. Innovation therefore amounted to making a stand not only against the Church and the church hierarchy, but also against mankind by degrading the divine message and compromising the promise of salvation, and ultimately against God himself.

To rebut the accusation of being innovatory, the Poor of Lyons set about tracing back their origins as far as possible. Ancient times were a guarantee of authenticity, of intrinsic truth. As we know, both Luther and the sixteenth-century Protestants took the same step, refusing to be suspected of innovation. And how much further can one go than the apostles, the founding fathers of the Church? This was illustrated by Pierre Griot, who, when questioned in 1532 by the inquisitor as to the authors of 'this law', replied that they were the apostles. This was certainly what the community members told one another. Two of Griot's superiors, whom we will have occasion to return to further on, wrote in 1530 that their people had survived in spite of hardship 'for four hundred years and even, as our elders tell us, since apostolic times'. This legend persisted until the nineteenth century but no-one today could take it seriously.

Without wishing to assert direct links with the apostles, another opinion was also held among the Poor of Lyons which was taken up and challenged by their adversaries; this alleged that their origins dated back to the time of pope Sylvester. It was he who, by accepting the famous donation of Constantine I at the beginning of the fourth century, had led the Church away from its mission by making it not just a spiritual but a temporal power. The dissenters from Lyons were said to be the descendants of the first opposers of the Roman Church's historical deviation. This belief may have become common within the group in the fourteenth century, but even from the first half of the thirteenth century, anti-Waldensian polemicists had set about refuting it. No-one today can subscribe to this point of view either. Such debates are no longer valid; it is now unanimously accepted that the Poor of Lyons date back to the twelfth century. If, however, it appears simple to agree on the century of their origin, the shadows of doubt are far from having been lifted altogether.

VAUDÈS

In spite of a great number of scholarly studies, we know no more today than we did around thirty years ago about the founder, the key figure in this spiritual adventure. No new document has come to light since then, and a great many uncertainties persist about the man from Lyons, for it was indeed in Lyons that it all began. In the first place, his name. What was he called? Elementary as the question may be, it is not easy to answer. If we turn to original documents from within the community, we only come up with three, one of which is rather late. The first is the confession of faith that the group's leader is thought to have signed in about 1180; the second is the account of a conference held in Bergamo in 1218 between the ultramontane and the Lombard divisions, the two groups the movement was composed of at the time. The third piece of documentary evidence is a series of letters exchanged between the Lombards and their Austrian brothers but these date from 1368. It is here that we can find reference to their legendary origins dating back to pope Sylvester and also to a certain Peter the Waldense, or 'from the valley', who was supposed to have reinstated the movement at the end of the twelfth century. We have already dismissed the legend, but let us consider the name. The Christian name Peter first appeared in the fourteenth century, that is, 150 years after the man's death. If, however, the followers needed to select a Christian name, what better choice could they have for their founder than naming him after the apostle on whom Christ had founded his Church? But since no contemporary reference exists to confirm the name's authenticity, it may consequently be dismissed. Opinion is now unanimous on this matter too.

As for the surname, many people are doubtless familiar with the one traditionally employed which can still be found in recently published works. The founder of the Poor of Lyons was supposedly called Peter Waldo. The Christian name has been dropped; can the surname at least be maintained? We may leave aside those polemicists who were the man's contemporaries, or who came just after him, who tended to go round and round in etymological circles in their attempts to explain the term *vaudois* – in Latin, *valdenses*. They all agreed, however, that the generic term should be linked back to the founder of what was called a sect or a heretical tendency. This would indeed appear to be the case. If we turn to the aforementioned original documents, they would appear to employ only the adjectival form which in Latin, the language used exclusively for writing, gives, for instance, *societas valdesiana* (the Waldensian group). There is just one instance where the noun form of his name is used. In the confession of faith of 1180, the man in question wrote of himself *ego valdesius*. This does not, however, tell us what the founding figure was called in the spoken language of the time, nor does it help us to decide what we should call him. We do not know the exact form of his name, that used by his family, friends and neighbours in the Franco-Provençal vernacular used in Lyons in the twelfth century. Since we only have the Latin translation, we have to try to work back to the original. If we leave aside the Italian form 'Valdo' for which there is no evidence, our choice is limited to two alternatives: 'Valdès' or 'Vaudès'. In 1980, Gonnet showed convincingly that 'Valdo' should be abandoned in favour of 'Vaudès'. In a note published in 1982, Thouzellier explained why she preferred the other form, 'Valdès', which seemed to her better to conform to the Franco-Provençal employed in Lyons at the time. The detail is a minor one. Respecting these recent publications, the present study will use either Valdès or Vaudès, even if I have a slight inclination for the meridional ring of the latter term, for French was not spoken at that time in Lyons.

We now have a man whose surname we know but who lacks a Christian name. We must be satisfied with this. Little else is known of the man Vaudès. He lived in Lyons and belonged to the city's elite. He was most likely a merchant, which comes as no surprise considering the flourishing commercial status of the city which was an international crossroads on the river Rhône. It was not for these reasons that Vaudès remained famous. His renown derives from his religious conversion. This wealthy figure, who apparently handled business investments for the archbishopric (which was, incidentally, suspected of practising usury towards the poor), one day decided to give up his worldly life and his family and to 'strip himself bare of all his possessions to follow the bare Christ', as Walter Map wrote.

How and why did Vaudès make up his mind to change his life? The exact circumstances are unclear since several accounts exist of this incident, the repercussions of which were to extend well beyond the man himself. The most endearing version tells how Vaudès was enthralled by the story of St Alexis, sung by a minstrel. This legend belonged to the tradition of popular medieval tales which inspired the piety and imagination of congregations and clergy alike. According to the *Golden Legend*, Alexis, the son of a rich noble Roman prefect in the fourth century, decided to give up his life of ease on his wedding night. Having persuaded his bride to remain chaste, he fled to Asia Minor. 'On his arrival, he distributed amongst the poor all the goods he had brought with him, then, clad in rags, he went to join the poor gathered beneath the porch of the Church of the Virgin Mary. Of the alms he collected, he kept just what he needed, the rest he gave to the poor.' The story of St Alexis does not end here. Years later, he returned by chance to his father's house where his father and the other members of his household did not recognise him. He thus finished his life collecting alms in his own home. The details are not of great importance; the meaning of this edifying tale is clear and Vaudès hearkened to it: it was the call to poverty.

The other version is less spectacular and perhaps more plausible. Vaudès was asking questions about his eternal salvation, which he feared might be jeopardised by his great wealth. Listening to the gospel, he is said to have been very moved by the story of the rich young man to whom Jesus replies: 'If thou wilt be perfect, go and sell that thou hast

and give to the poor and thou shalt have treasure in heaven; then come
and follow me.' What doubtless struck the rich merchant from Lyons
even more were Jesus' remarks once the young man had left, for his
words are indeed very strong if taken literally: 'Verily I say unto you. It is
easier for a camel to go through the eye of a needle, than for a rich man
to enter the kingdom of God' (Matthew 19: 21–4). From this moment
on, as Vaudès put this evangelical advice strictly into practice, radically
changing his life and exhorting a group of people around him to do the
same, the adventure of the Poor of Lyons had begun.

As has already been seen, the texts issuing from the group are few and
far between and, what is more, very short on information concerning
the first years of their existence. More is to be found written by their
adversaries and in particular the inquisitors. This is how one of them,
Bernard Gui, evoked the origins of the Waldensians in his work *Practica
inquisitionis heretice pravitatis*. Although it was compiled later, at the
beginning of the fourteenth century, the inquisitor's manual written by
the Dominican friar merits our attention. Indeed, the chapter dedicated
to the Waldensians is largely inspired by, if not in many places directly
copied from, another inquisitor who lived in the thirteenth century,
Stephen of Bourbon. He was virtually a contemporary of Vaudès and
had written *De septem donis Spiritus Sancti* between 1250 and 1261. Let us
then turn to Bernard Gui's treatise at the chapter bearing the title *De secta
valdensium*:

The sect or heretical movement of the Waldensians or Poor of Lyons began in
about the year of our Lord 1170. Its author was an inhabitant of Lyons, one
Valdesius or Valdensis from whom the name of the sect's members derives. He
was rich but having given up all his worldly goods, he set about observing a life
of poverty and evangelical perfection, following in the steps of the apostles. He
had the holy scriptures and other books of the bible translated for his own use
into the vernacular, along with a collection of maxims of St Augustine, St
Jerome, St Ambrose and St Gregory which were distributed bearing titles that he
and his followers called *sententiae*. They read them frequently but barely understood them; they were self-infatuated, although they were of little education, and
usurped the function of apostles and dared preach the gospel in the streets and in
town squares. The above-mentioned Valdesius or Valdensis encouraged a
number of accomplices of both sexes in this presumption, sending them out to
preach as disciples.

Let us stop reading for a moment. If we overlook the inquisitor's
value judgements, which an unbiased, elementary sense of historical
criticism requires us to do, what may still be retained from this account?
It can be seen that three basic elements are established from the outset:
poverty, preaching and the holy scriptures. These are the three struc-

turing pillars of Vaudès's inspiration which are both essential and inseparable. If only one or another is retained, or if one is overlooked, what remains could still characterise some religious order from the Church of Rome, or some dissenting group, but certainly not the Poor of Lyons. In their initial movement, in the first drive inspired by their founder, as in their history over the centuries despite its evolutions and adaptations, they were always to preserve these three defining characteristics, even if these too, as we shall see, were to be subjected to reorientations, reinterpretations and modifications over the centuries.

THE FOUNDATIONS

The bible

The bible, and more precisely the gospels, represented the original, fundamental basis of Vaudès's beliefs. As we saw above, it was after listening to the striking words of Jesus that Vaudès made up his mind to change his life so abruptly. This attitude is highly indicative. In Vaudès's opinion, which was later shared by his brethren, the Word of God was to be heard precisely and wholly. His Word was clear; there was no need whatsoever to interpret it. What mattered, so that they might apply it, was to understand it, but this the Church's official version, the 'Vulgate', rendered impossible because it was written in Latin. Hence the necessity to have the bible translated into the vernacular, starting with the gospels. Vaudès commissioned two clergymen from Lyons to do this, one of whom translated, while the other wrote the translation down. Once translated into a comprehensible language, the Word of God had to be applied to the letter. As we shall see later, this attitude was sometimes to have absurdly exacting consequences in practice. In this way, after reading from the Book of Matthew, Vaudès set the example of practising what was preached by giving up his belongings to make himself poor – in other words, a beggar.

Poverty

There are no grounds for doubting that at the basis of Vaudès's original inspiration is the call to poverty. All the contemporary writers agree on this point, from the inquisitors such as Stephen of Bourbon and Bernard Gui, the adversaries and contradictors, to the upholders of the Poor of Lyons. Indeed, the very name chosen by Vaudès's disciples, the Poor of Christ, or the Poor of Lyons is sufficiently revealing: it was through poverty that they chose to define themselves. There was nothing really original in this, as we shall see further on. Particularly since the Gregorian reforms in the eleventh century, many church people had espoused a life of poverty in one way or another, and urged the clergy to do likewise. Seeking a return to evangelical poverty, Vaudès was in keeping with a trend that was quite powerful at the time. Begging, however, was a delicate topic. Society might feel threatened by idlers who, for allegedly religious reasons, claimed the right to live at its expense, giving nothing in return. Vaudès countered this objection with his own example. He began to preach.

Preaching

Like poverty, the need to proclaim the Word of God derived from clear evangelical instructions: 'Go ye therefore, and teach all nations ... teaching them to observe all things whatsoever I have commanded you' (Matthew, 28: 19–20). This was Jesus' last message to his disciples. To Vaudès's mind, the duty to spread the good news was therefore imperative. The merchant from Lyons and the group that formed around him, following him and doing as he did, were, however, laymen. In the Roman Church, only clergymen could preach, as they had been trained for that mission. By challenging the clergy's monopoly of the Word, the Poor of Lyons provoked first astonishment, then reprobation and finally the condemnation of the Church hierarchy. But now let us get back to reading Bernard Gui:

Although they were ignorant and unlettered, these people, both men and women, went from village to village, going into people's homes and preaching in public squares and even in churches, the men in particular leaving behind them a host of misunderstandings and mistakes. The archbishop of Lyons, Jean aux Belles-Mains, commanded that they abandon such a presuming mission, but they flouted his authority, maintaining, in order to disguise their delusions, that one should obey God rather than men. God had ordered the apostles to preach the holy scriptures to all, they argued, taking upon themselves what had been said to the apostles, even having the audacity to declare themselves their imitators and successors on the grounds of their false profession of poverty and disguised by a mask of saintliness. They did indeed despise prelates and the clergy, claiming that they possessed abundant wealth and lived a life of pleasure.

The decisive issue was therefore that of preaching. The other matters – translating the holy scriptures and the life of poverty – were all rather edifying in the end, even if they unsettled those affluent clerics who came thus to be pointed out and denounced. For this reason, in the early years, there was no open conflict. Vaudès and his followers corresponded to the needs of both Christians and the clergy at the time. It is indeed important not to lose sight of the context in which the events were taking place.

THE FIRST COMMUNITY

Vaudès's example and his preaching aroused interest and encouraged certain people to imitate him because his contemporaries were receptive to his ideas. Within a few years, by 1170–75, we can assume he had gathered a group of disciples, men and women, referred to in some texts as a *societas*. As poor, itinerant preachers, with the holy scriptures in their hands, they encouraged those they met to repent. They were neither the first nor the last to do so at the time. A trend of preaching had developed, recalling the poor, humble lives led by the first Christian community; sometimes overtly anti-clerical, it appealed to the population who often welcomed the attacks. In the twelfth century, groups of itinerant preachers had multiplied, all more or less accepted by the Church hierarchy. The call to poverty had been heard from the Petrobrusians, the Arnaldisti, the Henricians and the Humiliati. If the Roman Church was sometimes reluctant to analyse too closely the individual doctrines being taken into the streets or to check their orthodoxy, it was because a far greater threat, that of the Cathars, was growing in the south of France. This movement of dissent had also met with local approbation, the population being shocked by the lives led by the clerical orders and receptive to the ideas expressed by the Cathar itinerants whose lives were obviously in greater conformity with those of the apostles than were those of the clergy. It was because of the peril represented by the Cathars that the Church also delayed dealing with Vaudès and his preachers.

Even today, some people see little difference between the Cathars (or Albigensians) and the Waldensians (or Poor of Lyons) or even fail entirely to distinguish them. The truth of the matter is that the two religious groups only resemble each other in form. The fundamental difference between them is the Cathars' manichaean doctrine which maintains that there are two equally powerful divine principles, one good, the other evil. Strictly speaking, the Cathars cannot be regarded as Christians. Is there any need to insist that such a conception of the world, of the creation and of salvation was completely anathema to Vaudès and his men? Besides, the Poor of Lyons renounced all personal possessions in the name of poverty, believing that a preacher who was dedicated to his mission did not have the time to concern himself with his own belongings. The holy scriptures said he should live by his ministry. This asceticism held no appeal for the Cathar dissenters who did not push strict obedience to that degree. The opposition between the two movements was such that the Roman Church did not hesitate to play on it. Not only did some members of the Lyons group go and preach against the Cathars in the south-west of France in the years 1175–84, taking part in controversies against them, but after Vaudès was excommunicated in 1184, many bishops continued to turn a blind eye, so content were they with their anti-Albigensian preaching which was effective because the local people hearkened to it.

Vaudès and his friends were thus favoured by the people and relatively well thought of by the Church hierarchy. The only contention remained the question of preaching. No-one was allowed to appropriate for himself the role of preacher without official permission. It is highly likely that the men from Lyons had several wrangles with the archbishop of Lyons, the Cistercian Guichard. Whatever the case, a small delegation of members, probably led by Vaudès himself, set off for Rome in 1179 to petition the Third Lateran Council. It was in this city, after all, that they could find the supreme authorities of the Church: the pope and the Council. As a result of their supplication being examined, general approval was expressed, albeit only orally, of their life of poverty and they were given the permission, again not in writing, to preach so long as they first presented themselves to the local priest so that he could issue the appropriate licence. Pope Alexander III was so moved by the leader inspired by personal saintliness and the mission of the Church, that he is said to have kissed him.

CONFLICT

The archbishop of Lyons was left with the task of settling the issue in judicial terms, with the help of another Cistercian, Henry of Clairvaux, who had recently been made a cardinal and sent to France as a papal legate to fight against Catharism which the Lateran Council had just condemned. It was at this time, in March 1180, that the formal judicial pronouncement took place, known as Vaudès's 'Profession of Faith'. In this declaration, Vaudès and his gathering of followers attested their anti-Cathar orthodoxy, for this was the great preoccupation at the time, following a protocol issued in Rome. In return, the ecclesiastical authorities granted him the right to lead a life of itinerancy and poverty within the community, without worrying about tomorrow (referring to Matthew 6: 34), but having to beg for their daily bread. As for preaching, while it was not authorised in writing, it was accepted orally, following the decision made in Rome, providing they sought the local priest's agreement. So far, the Poor of Lyons would appear to have committed no 'error' since they had been examined in Rome and granted the right to preach, albeit on certain conditions. It is thus clear to what extent the inquisitors and unfavourable chroniclers, and Bernard Gui in particular, maligned the 'sect' in its early years.

The two or three years which followed were marked by growing difficulties, which are hinted at rather than openly recorded in the texts. It may be that some Waldensian preachers, choosing to be demagogic, played on the anti-clerical sentiments of the people. Certain priests may have refused to grant them the right to preach, inspired by a vague feeling of jealousy towards these people who had chosen to be poor and whom the people often preferred to the priests themselves. Or again, it may be that some Waldensian preachers failed to get the essential local permission or even decided not to apply for it. What is certain, however, is that a number of women who had also been converted by Vaudès and who became his disciples also began to speak in public. This originality was unacceptable to the Church powers. Whatever happened, complaints from both sides must have reached the new archbishop, Jean aux Belles-Mains. He was doubtless irritated by the ill-defined movement over which he held little sway and probably sought to bring it under his control. In any case, he withdrew the verbal agreement and forbade preaching. Vaudès refused to obey, drawing confidence from the agreement accorded by the pope in Rome and from the words of the holy scriptures. Convinced he had been invested with a divine mission, he cited the proud reply given by Peter and the apostles: 'We ought to obey God rather than men' (Acts 5: 29) which amounted to considering his vocation to be superior to canon law.

His attitude can be understood by bearing in mind that he and his companions believed they had been specifically chosen and invested with a precise mission. The bible itself had taught them that people were responsible for the salvation of their fellow sinners. This unshakeable belief in their duty to spread the Word of God is clearly expressed by Vaudès's companion, Durand of Huesca, who described thus the Waldensians' mission in his treatise against the Cathars: 'To preach with the grace that God has accorded to us'. As Selge wrote thirty years ago, 'ardent faith and a sense of responsibility for the salvation of their neighbours: such was the essence of the Waldensian movement from its very origins'. If Vaudès did not submit to the prelate, it was because his conscience could not allow him to renounce his mission.

EXCOMMUNICATION

When they refused to comply, Vaudès and his friends were condemned and hounded from Lyons. The community sought refuge in other places where they could preach: Languedoc, where Catharism was widespread; northern Italy where a host of spiritual movements were active; then other French-speaking regions and the borders of Germany. Lucius III pronounced, and the emperor confirmed, the papal condemnation in Verona in 1184, directed against the Waldensians and also the Italian Humiliati for having usurped the ministry of preaching without a mission. The excommunication marked them as 'schismatics', in other words they had disobeyed Church laws, but not as 'heretics'. It was to be reworded on several occasions on a local scale. Nothing appeared at that time to be definitive. Vaudès and his fellows continued to hope the sanction would be lifted. Excommunication orders indeed often went unheeded. The Poor of Lyons continued to preach against the Cathars and to appeal to people to be converted by good works and poverty. Even as late as 1190 and 1207, some bishops agreed to join in debates with them, proving that they did not see them as staunch heretics who should simply be eliminated.

Drawing on Durand of Huesca's treatise *Liber antiheresis*, which I referred to above, K.-V. Selge has clearly shown that Vaudès and his fellows did not only remain orthodox, but also had no intention of doing otherwise. The preachers were indeed fully accountable to Christ, Lord of the apostles. Vaudès himself was not the community's sovereign. His authority was that of founder, of the first man to be called. The only canon was that they should live like apostles by their ministry of preaching, according to the New Testament. This constitutional precept, immediate and unquestionable, did not imply disobedience to the Roman hierarchy. There is one limit to the obedience due to bishops: that of obedience to the mission of Christ. 'We ought to obey God rather than men' does not mean God alone should be obeyed, not men, but rather that God should be obeyed more. The Poor of Lyons therefore considered the excommunication to be unjust. But they had to continue obeying those priests whose sins did not call into question their function. The entire Church hierarchy was still to receive all due honour, so long as it did not contradict their mission held from Christ. Such was the conception of authentic Waldensianism from its origins until the middle of the thirteenth century, when, in around 1240, Moneta of Cremona could still witness to this ecclesiastical obedience under certain conditions. The situation had nonetheless seriously degenerated in between. The decisive era was between two crucial dates: 1184, the excommunication of Verona; and 1215, the anathema pronounced by the Fourth Lateran Council.

How can the final, definitive condemnation be explained? What happened in those thirty years? During this period, and even beyond, as we have seen, the Poor of Lyons still considered themselves to be faithful to the Roman Church, in spite of their condemnation. How was this possible? The answer is partially to be found in the fact that, as has been seen, some prelates continued to discuss with them, in no way treating them as excommunicates. The judgement remained theoretical to some extent. Moreover, the Poor of Lyons were in constant contact with the people and lower clergy who considered them to be Catholics, that is to say anti-Cathars; this was also their own opinion. Last but not least, the preachers, who were dispersed in different regions, had no real, central organisation. Nor did they need one, since they had no particular doctrine to spread or uphold other than the holy scriptures themselves. Although they were dispersed in distant lands, the Brothers do not appear to have encountered any difficulties due to diverging opinions or feelings. There are, at least, no traces of any such tension. Yet difficulties did exist. The fact that the people and a good number of the clergy took the Brothers for good, devout Catholics gave them unity and helped prevent their relations with Rome becoming too strained. The situation reached breaking point after 1200.

EVOLUTIONS

Before this date, the movement had already evolved in different ways. Waldensianism in itself did not constitute an act of heresy. The followers were, however, guilty not only of disobedience towards the Church hierarchy. By acting as preachers 'as a direct result of the need for good works to attain salvation' (Selge), they found themselves preaching doctrines and encouraging practices considered heretical but which to their thinking were deeply rooted in the New Testament. Durand of Huesca, for example, rejected moderate predestination as taught by the Church. He continued to justify suffrage, or prayers, for the dead, which others rejected. Similarly, a new tendency emerged which inclined towards rejecting oaths and the death penalty, based on a literal interpretation of the holy scriptures (called biblicism or evangelism). This was a result of the Poor of Lyons being influenced by other dissents with which they had come into contact, notably in Lombardy after their first condemnation.

The other question, which was condemned as heresy, concerned the sacraments. The Poor of Lyons acknowledged them of course, particularly favouring baptism, the Lord's Supper and penance, and considered them necessary for salvation. They encouraged the sacrament of penance, insisting on it in their preaching, inciting their audiences to confess when most people considered it sufficient to meet the minimum annual requirements for confession as defined by the Church hierarchy. But seeing how Christians held the clergy in contempt, giving them the pretext for shunning penance, the Poor of Lyons began to commend confession to laymen. Those listeners who had been moved by their preaching were therefore offered a form of spiritual direction. Furthermore, they had begun to organise their own holy communion on the model of the Last Supper. This innovation was doubtless not intended to oppose the Roman Church directly, but rather had a pastoral function prompted by the care of souls. Christians living in regions where heresy was widespread, notably the Cathars, were actively encouraged by heterodox preachers to neglect the sacraments, particularly renouncing the Lord's Supper. This was what the Poor of Lyons sought to remedy. Their practices, which the Church was not slow to deem 'heretical', had only been intended as an answer to a critical situation and to pressing needs. This was the first form of Waldensianism, which Selge called 'authentic Waldensianism'.

It is hardly surprising that within the group from Lyons divergences should have appeared. Indeed, preachers enjoyed great autonomy, and at the time there was neither a co-ordinating body nor a doctrinal authority. Certain trends thus led to schisms within the community. In Metz, for instance, in 1200 or thereabouts, a group of preachers siding with popular anti-clerical sentiment denied ministerial power to those members of the clergy whose lives did not conform to the apostolic model. Two of the community's founding principles came thus to be deformed. 'You shall obey God rather than men' became 'You shall obey God alone.' The original doctrine, claiming that those who lived apostolic lives had the power and the right to preach the gospel and consecrate the sacrament, was also overthrown. Those priests leading sinful lives were denied all their rights; any act realised under their responsibility was invalidated. This 'donatist' tendency only affected certain groups, however, and was in no way a reflection of the movement as a whole.

TENSION FROM WITHIN

The internal crisis may have been deferred for some time, but it nonetheless came to a head at the beginning of the thirteenth century. It was to last for ten years or more. On this matter let us again turn to Selge whose conclusions concerning the beginnings of the movement the present author shares, as the reader has doubtless realised:

It should be understood that the distinction we have highlighted between the Waldensians' original position and Waldensianism as described by Alain of Lille does not imply we are dealing with two separate groups or two distinct orders. Nor are we facing two doctrinal systems which two professors might have presented and discussed in some theology department. Far from it. Rather, there was a fair number of isolated, revivalist preachers, all belonging to a community that had no fixed constitution and who crossed the country converting people. Some were more vigorously committed than others to criticising the Church: the theologian Alain of Lille brings to light their severest tenets and treats them as if they constituted a theological system of doctrine. In the Waldensian community itself, people were probably less sensitive to theological nuances: they were not always discussing doctrine, but they had to preach.

Vaudès thus came up against false brethren whom he dismissed unhesitatingly, as his confession of 1180 shows; at this time it was doubtless just a precautionary measure. The first reference to a separation from such followers can be found in Languedoc in around 1200. This concerned preachers who maintained that they alone had the right to baptise, denying the right to Cathars or priests of the Roman Church. They therefore rebaptised people. Anabaptists of this kind were also to be found in Provence, in Italy and in Trier. Greatly influenced by Catharism, which sanctioned the distribution of *consola-mentum*, they claimed that only those in a state of total poverty when they died would find salvation. They insisted upon this drastic conversion before death. It was they who were 'excommunicated' by Vaudès in around 1200.

Discussions with the Lombardy Poor on the one hand, and with the Roman Church on the other, were far more awkward. The mission of the Poor of Lyons in Lombardy dated back to 1184 or before. The situation there was particularly propitious, despite language differences which were in fact minor. The Waldensians might even have been welcomed by the Humiliati. The tenets of this group were, however, much more extreme, with hints of 'donatism'; moreover, they allowed manual labour. Some of them were reconciled with the Church in about 1200, while others attempted to draw closer to the Poor of Lyons. The essence of the debate concerned the compatibility of manual labour and preaching. Vaudès's reply was unequivocal and negative: the apostolic preacher had to devote himself wholly to his mission. Those Brothers who failed to accept this could not belong to the Lyons group.

The second contention was over an institutional issue. The Lombardy Brothers elected one member as an 'intendant'; first, there was Jean of Ronco, then Oto of Ramazello. As far as Vaudès was concerned, Christ was their only leader. The donatist trend was at the core of other heated discussions: could the acts of an apostolic ministry be invalidated if its members failed to live up to the apostolic model? In the end, when

Vaudès had defined the grounds for exclusion, two independent groups co-existed in northern Italy: the Poor of Lyons and the 'Lombardy Poor'.

A CRITICAL SITUATION

Relations with the Roman Church were quite curious in the end. As far as Rome was concerned, the Waldensians had been condemned as schismatic from 1184 and had to be defeated if they would not listen to reason. This was, however, a purely theoretical stand and in practice things worked quite differently. Their staunchest and most intransigent opponents hunted down the Waldensians; those most sensitive to their mission left the self-appointed bearers of the Word of God to do their work and some were willing to exchange ideas with them or even help them in their apostolic duties. Vaudès and his group held that the preachers had been invested with a divine and therefore inalienable mission; as a consequence their excommunication pronounced in Verona was unjust. They hoped and even expected it would be lifted, so sure were they that their movement was still orthodox. But as time went by, their excommunication became more effective. Some members gave up hoping for an imminent reconciliation with Rome and rejected the Church hierarchy. Vaudès had actively devoted himself to maintaining orthodoxy and faithfulness to the Church according to his conception of it, in other words on certain conditions, and his death, which was apparently around 1205–7, certainly hastened the division.

In 1207, the Council of Pamiers spurred the movement on again. It was during this 'disputation', in other words a discussion according to the ecclesiastical model of the times, that Durand of Huesca, Vaudès's companion, although never once calling into question the divine mission with which Vaudès had been invested, was reconciled with Rome along with several of his friends. The 'Poor Catholics' thus came into existence. Durand doubtless expected the other Poor of Lyons to do likewise for it would have been the best means to protect them from slipping into heterodoxy – in other words, heresy. But Durand was soon disenchanted. Giving in to the local hierarchy would have signalled the end of the apostolic mission. Few men therefore followed Durand of Huesca; the last opportunity to unite had passed. They therefore needed to get organised to survive. It was decided that an annual synod uniting all the Brothers would be held, during which two 'rectors' from amongst the assembled members would be elected to hold office for one year. They would be responsible for controlling the preachers' mission. At the following assembly, they would have to account for their activities before new elections were held to replace them. Selge writes:

The second reorganisation concerned the *fractio panis*. It was decided that ministers would have to be elected for this. These ministers were not selected from among the preachers but from the novices, the *nuper conversi*, or from the *amici*, the followers who had heeded the preachers' spiritual guidance or *consilium spirituale*. This meant the Brothers' sole task continued to be their mission as preachers. It therefore solved the crisis which had grown from the fact that the Roman Church was no longer distributing the eucharist to the Waldensians. But it did not imply that a distinct hierarchy was created, vying with the hierarchy of Rome. The ministers were appointed for a period of service. Moneta of Cremona also testifies, after 1240, that even in his era, Waldensians would receive the eucharist from priests in the Roman Church if the latter were prepared to give it.

We may thus suppose that the Poor of Lyons had realised that their excommunication was effective, that they had to organise so as to cope with their most immediate needs and that, while they could continue hoping to be reconciled with Rome, it became less and less likely as time went by that a reconciliation would occur. The Poor of Lyons therefore maintained their original midway situation. They had not been swayed by the Lombardy Poor who deemed that the Roman priesthood was unjust and that the Roman Church was false (*ecclesia malignantium*). Nor had they been persuaded that when the Poor Catholics were reconciled with Rome, Rome had recognised the apostolic vocation of the Poor of Lyons. They were still waiting for this recognition; they had not given up hope, at least not entirely; some still remained hopeful. Their position was that of Vaudès: obedience on certain conditions. As Selge has demonstrated, the bone of contention was clear: had God entrusted a mission to the Poor of Lyons or not? Traditionally, the theological criteria enabling a divine mission to be identified were well established. As far as the Church hierarchy was concerned, a virtuous life and the biblical passages cited by the Waldensians were insufficient proof; in the eyes of the Poor of Lyons, they were perfectly adequate. Their opinion was shared by a considerable number of Christians and the clergy. Who was right?

The Poor of Lyons' apostolic vocation was never to be recognised by Rome, just as their excommunication was not to be lifted. On the contrary, the situation degenerated. As a result of being progressively and lastingly marginalised, the Poor of Lyons gradually hardened their positions, adopting tenets of other dissents that had not previously been theirs. In this way, they came increasingly to be charged by the Roman hierarchy with being mistaken and were judged to be tainted with heresy. The outcome was that the excommunication of Verona was confirmed and even extended. In 1215, the Fourth Lateran Council condemned the Poor of Lyons and a number of other dissents not only as schismatic as had been the case in 1184, but as heretical: in other words, heterodox – erring in the ways of the faith. The anathema was pronounced against them and the rupture with Rome was complete. The hope of a reconciliation had been illusory.

Let us complete here the reading of the passage by Bernard Gui which we began earlier:

> By arrogantly usurping the office of preachers, they became masters of error. When they were forbidden to preach, they disobeyed and were declared guilty of contumacy and were subsequently excommunicated and chased away from their home towns and their country. In the end, as they remained impenitent, a council held in Rome, before the Lateran Council, declared them schismatic and condemned them as heretical. Thus as their numbers grew on earth, they dispersed through the province, into neighbouring regions as far as the frontiers of Lombardy. Separated and cut off from the Church, associating instead with other heretics whose errors they adopted, their own deluded imaginings became mixed up with the errors and heresies of earlier heretics.

Whilst the inquisitor's obviously biased comments can be left to one side, we must accept that it was the most radical tendency within the Poor of Lyons, that which had remained a minority for a long time, which benefited from the definitive separation from Rome and came to dominate. From this point on, their history was to begin anew, telling of a dissenting religious minority that was organised, persecuted and dispersed.

A CONTEXTUAL EVALUATION

Before examining how the fate of the Waldensians was to be determined during the following two centuries, we should try to understand the sense of such a movement, bearing in mind its context. As was said earlier, there is nothing surprising in the fact that towards the end of the twelfth century there was an increasing number of calls for evangelical poverty. This is not to say they were banal, but many others before Vaudès had made their protests heard during what is known as the Gregorian reform of the eleventh century. Nor is there anything particularly original in the fact that the call for reform gave rise to an irrepressible need to preach. After Vaudès, Dominic of Guzman and, some years later, Francis of Assisi were to speak out in the same way. The former, who was sent to preach against the Albigenses (or Albigensians) in 1205, was the founder of the order of preaching brothers, the Dominicans; the latter, known as *il poverello*, was founder of the order of mendicant friars, the Franciscans. Even the association of wandering preachers and poverty can be seen as a sign of the times. It is surely striking to notice that within half a century three strong voices of reform should have made themselves heard, all three urging changes in the same direction and originating in three Latin countries: Spain, France and Italy. There is no doubting the fact that the regrettable experience of the Waldensians, at least from the Roman Church's point of view, served as a lesson to the papacy when dealing with Dominic's and Francis's disciples later on. How can the uncompromising attitudes on both sides, which ultimately led to the breach, be explained?

Vaudès's real originality lies elsewhere. He was a layman and wished to remain so. He refused either to enter an existing religious order or to found a new one. He rejected the idea of a mould in which his own inspiration would lose its uniqueness. This attitude should be understood as an expression of the laity's desire to play a different, more important role in a Church which had become too clerical. The vindication can be interpreted in the same way as that of the newly emerging middle classes demanding a better status in the medieval society of the time. But the fact that laymen – and women, a matter which tends to be overlooked – should have taken up preaching threw into question the very foundations of the Church and society as they were defined then. We should remember that only about 10 per cent of the population was literate and that, even in a city as big as Lyons, the proportion can hardly have been more than 20 per cent, although the lack of dependable statistical evidence makes it absolutely impossible to offer even approximate figures. Reading therefore constituted a form of real power in this oral civilisation where hearing and memory played an essential role.

In such a context, the clergy enjoyed unequalled prestige. Overall, the clergy represented by far the best educated class of society. In social, cultural and religious terms, their status was outstanding. In their hands were concentrated all the powers that gave access to both reading and writing. They were the official bearers of the holy scriptures and represented the one and only means to have access to them. They alone could correctly interpret the Word of God. As a result, they also monopolised public speaking – in other words, preaching. When one bears in mind, firstly, the importance of the spoken word in such an oral world; secondly, the role that a literate class could play; and lastly, the esteem the clerics enjoyed (in spite of traditional, good-natured anti-clericalism) within this society shaped by and dependent on the religious orders, only then can one assess the importance of Vaudès and his followers and the challenge they, perhaps unconsciously, represented.

The reaction of the Church can now be understood. Internal quarrels were set aside. The clerical class as a whole put up a common, united front before this attempt to break its monopoly over the spoken and written word. It is therefore hardly surprising that preaching became the core of the conflict. Neither the Roman Church nor even medieval society itself could accept Vaudès's 'alleged mission' without running the risk of undermining the very structures which made it function. The polemicists who were Vaudès's contemporaries, and the inquisitors who came after, all referred to his 'pretence', 'presumption' and 'usurpation'. They seized every opportunity to maintain that Vaudès's mission could not be genuine for the very reason that he had not been sent by the Church hierarchy. Furthermore, they did not hesitate to scoff at him and his companions who were deemed *idiote et illiterati* (ignorant and illiterate) by Stephen of Bourbon and Bernard Gui, for example. What was the truth of the matter?

We know that some genuine men of letters were to be found amongst Vaudès's first companions. Bernard Prim, Guillaume of Arnaud and especially Durand of Huesca whom we evoked earlier, the author of *Liber antiheresis*, were perfectly capable of engaging in theological discussions, contradictory debates and verbal fencing matches; they had excelled in such skills during the struggle with the Cathars. As for Vaudès himself, we know he did not understand Latin because he had a cleric translate the gospels. On these grounds alone he could be condemned as unlettered, since all literature was written in Latin, which was the language of the sciences, including religion. Vaudès, however, certainly knew how to read which, for a merchant, was to be expected. Even if Lyons was behind the times in terms of the commercial techniques and banking systems of the Italian cities, there can be no doubting that the merchants of the Rhône valley knew how to read and sometimes write for negotiating purposes.

Whatever the case may be, the mission that Vaudès undertook, proclaiming the Word of God and gathering together for this purpose biblical texts translated into the vernacular, was to lead him and his companions to read in private and in public. Certainly, this veneration of the holy scriptures would not transform the Poor of Lyons into refined men of letters, sages or Byzantine theologians. But this was not their intention either. Not being or wishing to be clerics, the Poor of Lyons found themselves rejected by a class of educated men who reacted as a privileged caste anxious not to lose its power based on the divine monopoly of the oral and the written, the Word and the holy scriptures. This is where Vaudès's prophetic naïvety lies and where the real originality of his movement can be situated. This finally explains why he was the victim of excommunication. And so it was decreed that the history of the Poor of Lyons would be written outside the Roman Church.

BIBLIOGRAPHY

Durand of Huesca, *Liber antiheresis*, ed. K.-V. Selge. In *Die ersten Waldenser*, vol. ii (see below).
Gonnet, G., *Enchiridion fontium valdensium*. 2 vols., Turin, 1958 and 1998.
'Pierre Valdo ou Valdès de Lyons?' *Bulletin de la Société de l'Histoire du Protestantisme Français* 135, 1980, pp. 247–50.
Gui, B., *Manuel de l'inquisiteur*, ed. G. Mollat. 2 vols., Paris, 1926–7.
Patschovsky, A. and Selge, K.-V., 'Quellen zur Geschichte der Waldenser'. *Texte zur Kirchen und Theologie Geschichte* 18, 1973.
Selge, K.-V., *Die ersten Waldenser*. 2 vols., Berlin, 1967.
'Caractéristiques du premier mouvement vaudois et crises au cours de son expansion'. *Cahiers de Fanjeaux*, no. 2 (see below), pp. 110–42.
'Discussions sur l'apostolicité entre vaudois, catholiques et cathares'. *Ibid.*, pp. 143–62.
'La figura e l'opera di Valdez'. *Bollettino della Società di Studi Valdesi* 136, 1974, pp. 4–25.
Thouzellier, C., *Catharisme et valdéisme en Languedoc à la fin du XIIe et au début du XIIIe siècle*. Paris, 1966; reprinted Brussels, 1969.
Hérésie et hérétiques. Rome, 1969.
'Considérations sur les origines du valdéisme'. In *I Valdesi e l'Europa*. Torre Pellice, 1982, pp. 3–25.
Vaudois languedociens et Pauvres Catholiques. *Cahiers de Fanjeaux*, no. 2, 1967.

THE THIRTEENTH CENTURY: THE NEED TO ADAPT

The faltering beginnings of the Poor of Lyons and their first efforts to find a new place within the Church and the society of the time gave way to a situation they were not prepared for and which they had not foreseen. Once rejected by a Church hierarchy they had tried to appease, they were left with the choice either of retracting by giving up their evangelical mission to preach, or of going into hiding to remain faithful to their apostolic vocation. As has been seen above, however, their position was not as straightforward as this, nor was the situation so clear at this point, even after the anathema of 1215. As the reader will have realised, the date of 1215 has been taken as a pivotal point between the two chapters mainly for practical reasons. This is not to deny the significance of the official, solemn and definitive condemnation of the Poor of Lyons; it did indeed change the fate of the Waldensian movement altogether. But it is too easy to overlook the fact that, essential as laws, regulations and other normative texts may be, the difference between theory and practice can be great. It should be recalled that after the Council of Verona in 1184, and even after the Fourth Lateran Council in 1215, many Christians continued to listen in public to the preachers of poverty, many clerics went on discussing and debating with them, even going so far as to defend them, and many Poor of Lyons considered themselves not only to be members of the Church of Christ but also faithful to the Church of Rome.

THE MEETING IN BERGAMO

We have accounts of this episode in the Waldensians' early years thanks to one of their own documents which, as was stated in chapter 1, are extremely rare. There is thus less need for caution when studying this account than we will need later with the inquisitorial trials. The document is a letter from the Italian Brothers to their German counterparts in which they compile an account of the discussions they have had with the ultramontane (that is, French) division in Bergamo in 1218. This meeting brought together six French and six Lombard representatives in an attempt to resolve a certain number of differences then dividing the two groups, one from either side of the Alps. A schism had already occurred in about 1205 between Vaudès and Jean of Ronco. At the Bergamo meeting, there is no mention of the latter and Vaudès is reported to have died. If a decade or so before, the Poor of Lyons were not threatened by internal divisions, it was no longer the case after the anathema of 1215. We may easily understand the concern which reigned at this attempt to unify the two sides.

Seven of the nine issues dividing the two groups within the Waldensian movement were resolved. Were provosts or rectors to be elected to head the movement? Should ministers chosen from the *nuper conversi* (newly converted) or the *amici* (friends) be ordained? Could a labouring congregation be accepted? This was a principle which Vaudès had always refused to consider, on the grounds that the apostle must live from his preaching. Vaudès's disciples had always voted against these questions. In Bergamo, however, in a clear attempt to reconcile the two sides, it was decided that each case would be examined individually, bearing in mind the shared interests of those concerned and the need for peace. Was baptism effective and could marriage be dissolved or not? Here a consensus was reached, stating that no-one could be saved who had not received the holy water at baptism, and that husband and wife could be allowed to separate only by mutual agreement or in the case of infidelity. As for ecclesiastical discipline, this was the responsibility of Brothers from within the communities who were aware of their members' failings and misdemeanours, hence the need to set up some sort of internal tribunal. Finally, they agreed unanimously that the holy scriptures were their ultimate source of reference; the supreme rule of faith and morality was the bible, the authority of which would prevail when judging any rule or tradition whose legitimacy appeared doubtful.

Two outstanding issues remained divisive. What was the eternal fate of Vaudès and his companion Vivet? What conditions decided whether the consecration of the sacrament was valid or not? These were the two questions to which the representatives failed to reply unanimously. The Ultramontanes maintained without a doubt that the two founders had been saved; the Lombards tempered this assertion with a condition: they were saved if, before their deaths, they had confessed all their sins to

God. Their division over the sacraments derived from different concep-
tions of the eucharist. According to the Ultramontanes, the words of the
priest were entirely effective; in no case was the validity of the sacrament
dependent on the man who had pronounced it (corresponding to the
Catholic conception of *ex opere operato*). On the other hand, the Italian
Lombards held that only a worthy minister could consecrate the body of
Christ; if this were not the case, his words were vain and the sacrament
ineffective (this was the donatist trend, the conception of *ex opere
operantis*). The two groups were intransigent on these questions and the
division defied all attempts at reconciliation. Whatever the results, it was
not a major disagreement if we bear in mind that only the divisive issues
between the Brothers were studied at this meeting.

   This account provides us with essential information about the Waldensian brotherhood at the time. Communities existed in France, Italy
and Germany; their doctrine was not clearly structured and they were
divided on certain matters. It is also clear that they were beginning to
consult with one another and felt the need to organise a co-ordinating or
even ruling body. By refusing discussion, the Roman Church had surely
made this inevitable. The Waldensians were forced to admit that they
were, at least temporarily, rejected. They had to draw up a pastoral
definition that reinforced their mission but protected their clandestinity.
The two concepts were not easily compatible.

THE BELATED ENFORCEMENT OF THE LAW

The task of abandoning their legitimate, effective campaign of preaching
against heretics (meaning primarily the Cathars) in which they enjoyed
popular support and official favour, to adopt a mission that was first
discreet and finally clandestine was certainly a great upheaval for the
Waldensians. The preachers were doubtless profoundly troubled, so
ardent were they in their zealous devotion to the Word of God, aware of
the urgent dominical duties to be carried out, yet forced to go into
hiding, concealing 'a candle ... under a bushel' (Matthew 5: 15), which
meant, although they were the imitators of the apostles, disobeying the
words of the gospel. The process was gradual, which at least allowed the
preachers to adapt progressively to their new situation. But it must
equally have troubled the Christian population as a whole, so avidly did
they welcome the preachers' words. In the 1240s, inhabitants of the
south-west of France who were charged by the Inquisition with heresy
reminded the judge that the Waldensians themselves had not yet been
charged. Raymond Hugues, for instance, questioned in 1244, declared
that 'about forty years ago, he had on more than one occasion seen

Waldensian Brothers preaching in the church of Aiguesvives [in the department of the Aude] after the gospel reading, before a large congregation'. In 1243, a certain Arnaud Combarieu maintained that twenty years before, he had seen members of the Waldensian community proceeding in public through the streets of Montauban. In the same year, the court heard a statement from a knight, Sais of Montesquieu: one night, sixteen years before, when he was approaching Lacroisille near Puylaurens, he had encountered at the town gates a group of local men and the parish priest. He asked what they were doing gathered there and they replied that a Waldensian Brother was speaking and they were listening to him. The knight then remonstrated with them for listening to the man at such an hour, but the men replied that their priest was with them. In 1244, a certain Peregrina, a former servant to the countess of Toulouse declared to the inquisitor that 'once she had given food to four Waldensians after the harvest in the house of P. Ortola, since dead; but in those days, the Church did not persecute the Waldensians, and she herself had learnt a prayer from those Waldensian preachers'. When asked to give a date to this event, she added, 'it was less than twenty years ago, perhaps fifteen or sixteen'. Such testimonies as these provide considerable proof of the unease felt by local populations faced with the persecution of preachers who had formerly been officially recognised and esteemed by the people. They also reveal that in 1204, as far as the first document is concerned, in other words twenty years after Verona, and in 1223, 1227 and 1228 as regards the other documents, that is between eight and thirteen years after the Fourth Lateran Council, preachers from the Poor of Lyons were still speaking in public, in spite of official condemnations and prohibitions.

Such a situation could not last. This raises the question as to when law became fact, or, to put it another way, when the parish priests began applying the conciliar decree. By analysing the small number of testimonies, two examples of which have been examined above, it would appear that after 1230 there was no longer any trace of Waldensians preaching in public. Until this time there is proof of their activities in the streets and on public squares, and even of their having access in a town such as Montauban to a private home, hospice or cemetery, giving them a public base to some extent. They were then plunged into obscurity, preaching by night in the homes of those whose good will towards them was unchanged, or concealing their function by assuming the identity of itinerant workers to justify their travels.

The year 1230 is of particular significance. The year before, in 1229, the Treaty of Meaux-Paris was signed, bringing an end to the crusade against the Albigensians. In the light of this, matters fall into place. Until

that date, the Church had been uniting all its forces in the fight against
the Cathar heresy, considering it to be the major threat. It could not
afford to reduce its strength in any way by launching a second offensive
at the same time, that is, against the Waldensians. The Catholic hierarchy
had, for that matter, perhaps with more than a little cynicism, preferred
to take advantage of the Waldensian preachers to whom the people
listened and whose voice against the Cathars was so effective. Once the
Cathar threat had been effaced, there remained that of the Waldensians
who had been condemned at least twice by the official authorities of the
Church nearly half a century before. It was an aberration, indeed a
scandal the control of which was long overdue, considering that heretics
who had been duly excommunicated and anathematised were continuing to spread their errors with complete impunity while Church
decisions remained a dead letter. Such was the new vision of the Roman
Church, and such was its reaction.

THE INQUISITION

It is noteworthy that, after slowly evolving, the Inquisition, or Holy
Office, was formally to come into existence in 1231. By Inquisition was
meant 'the special jurisdiction exercised by delegates of the pope for the
repression of heresy'. After the reforms of the eleventh century, the Latin
Church had been confronted by an ever-increasing number of doctrinal
deviations which were difficult to contain using traditional means. The
Church needed a new judicature to enable it to put up an effective fight,
particularly against Catharism and Waldensianism, the two large-scale
heresies which threatened it in the eleventh and twelfth centuries. It was
to take years for the Church to forge this tool to be amenable, firm and
efficient at the same time. In 1184, it was decreed that impenitent
heretics and 'relapsers', or recidivists, should be burnt at the stake; in
1199, the confiscation of goods was included as an additional sentence.
From 1180 to 1250 or thereabouts, a whole series of measures defined
inquisitorial proceedings to deal with heresy: torture was authorised
(known as 'the question'); the names of witnesses were kept secret to
avoid reprisals; legal proceedings were simplified; the use of 'the secular
arm', that is to say, lay power, was acquired during the crusade against
the Albigensians (1212–29). The Church lacked a specialised tribunal.
The bishop's tribunal (or *officialité*) was often overwhelmed by a great
variety of tasks and its legal proceedings often lacked continuity for this
reason; competent officers for these duties were also lacking. As for the
secular judges, they all too often displayed alarming zeal, as was the case,
for example, during the war against the Albigensians in the south-west of

France where collective burnings bore witness to their cruelty. An exceptional court of law was therefore set up, answerable directly to the pope. In 1231, he appointed his first delegate, in Germany; the year after, the system was extended to France. The Inquisition had begun.

Inquisitors settled like conquerors in the south of France. Three permanent seats were established, in Toulouse, Carcassonne and Provence. The fight against heresy was entrusted to the Dominicans who were particularly well trained in theology, controversy and preaching. Their labours, however, proved arduous. Religious dissent was so deeply rooted in the region that their proceedings often instigated riots and conspiracies. After complaints were received, the Dominicans were sent away, to be replaced in 1249 by Franciscans. This order was no more successful than the first and the Black Friars were reinstated as inquisitors by 1256. The second half of the thirteenth century can be held as the golden age of the Inquisition in the south of France. By this time, the machinery was functioning well. Manuals circulated, aiming to help inquisitors in their delicate duties, such as that by Raymond of Peñafort in the thirteenth century or by Bernard Gui in the early fourteenth century which we have referred to several times above. With such a judicial body at its disposal, the Church could launch a systematic attack against the Poor of Lyons, and against other dissenters wherever they had been detected, even beyond the south of France. Drawing up a map of inquisitorial activities in the thirteenth and fourteenth centuries amounts to locating areas where a 'heretical' presence was also active.

JUDICIAL SOURCES

Commentators, and particularly historians, can sometimes be heard rather cynically remarking, 'Thank goodness for the Inquisition; had it not existed we would not have its precious archives teaching us virtually all we know about those whom the Church hounded from its doors.' It is certainly true that the documents gathered together by the inquisitors over the centuries constitute one of the most remarkable resources available to historical research; there are numerous outstanding publications, many of them very recent, bearing witness to this. It is equally true that these archives provide a unique source of information about specific heretics, dissenters and clandestine dissentients. But it is also more than likely that had these various 'heretics' not been persecuted, they themselves would have left us traces of their beliefs, their way of life and their implantation within a given time and society. Moreover, we would not be faced with the deformations which the inquisitors more or less consciously imposed on reality, forcing us to play a subtle, awkward game of textual criticism in order to be able to discover if not the truth, at least what was most probable, reading through their deviations and duplicity.

Judicial sources in general, and inquisitorial sources in particular, do indeed pose a real problem to the reader. Anyone who has had to submit to a police or court cross-examination will understand what I mean. At such a session, or rather such an ordeal, the rules of the game have been defined beforehand and the positions of the two parties are completely unequal. One of them is self-assured and confident in the legitimate, albeit ephemeral, authority that his power over the other bestows on him. He interrogates. The other party is in a state of absolute inferiority, feeling more or less guilty; he is interrogated. At the end of their dialogue or confrontation, a statement is drawn up. What would we make of someone who assumed the right to speak of us, our tastes, our values, in short who claimed to know us, after reading nothing other than such a document? Would we not denounce their conclusions as caricatures, as deluded and unspeakably pretentious? And yet this is the situation of the historian working with such judicial documents. It is in fact far more delicate since the position of the accused, with his life at stake before the inquisitor, is only vaguely comparable to that of our hypothetical position at the police station or in court.

How can we reinstate the truth, the words the witness or the defendant really spoke? This is not to say the inquisitor purposely falsified declarations, but he did orientate and induce answers, whether consciously and deliberately or not. And he might do this to such an extent that the accused was led, for all sorts of reasons, to maintain the very opposite to what he believed or intended. Carlo Ginzburg has indeed clearly demonstrated how, at the end of the sixteenth century, the inquisitor of Friuli distorted the words of the Benandanti whom he had before him. While these country folk, brought up in a world of rural folklore, spoke to him in traditional terms of popular culture, he, a man of refined education accustomed to scholastic theology and convinced of the veracity of his own fixed beliefs, understood witchcraft. He succeeded in making them confess to this crime, which was also a heresy. How often must such dialogues at cross-purposes have taken place between a cleric convinced of the legitimacy and truth of his own position and members of an underground dissent from a different culture? They can indeed have barely understood each other even if they did speak the same language. Is the only solution, then, to give up in despair and conclude once and for all that there is nothing to be gleaned from such judicial sources? The answer is obviously no. Excellent research based on them shows that history can find what it is seeking, provided a certain number of precautions are taken.

Inquisitorial sources require special critical treatment. The first precaution, which applies to any document, is to discount anything for which there is only one witness. An occurrence which seems strange in context or in view of other facts and for which only one witness exists must be overlooked. Here, the guiding principle of the law remains as valid for history: *testis unus, testis nullus* (one witness, no witness). In any case, the occurrence cannot be taken as certain. The first rule in historical method is to compare and contrast statements. Furthermore, in matters of religion and clandestinity in general, in other words all the causes examined by the courts of the Inquisition, a distinction should be made between doctrine and the concrete forms of 'heresy'. As far as the concrete forms are concerned, it is likely that the information gathered by the inquisitor is perfectly correct. This includes people known to the accused, where and when he met other heretics, what practices he has seen or followed, and so forth. It was in fact in the interests of the organs of justice to record the most detailed and accurate information possible so as to track down the other followers and eventually wipe out the heresy itself. The same cannot be said of declarations about faith and morality. In this domain, the judge tended all too often to bring all possible evidence against the accused, making him admit to errors or greatly exaggerating them by his questioning tactics in which all sorts of traps were hidden. Such cases call for the utmost caution. Lastly, a difference should of course be established between revelations made spontaneously, declarations drawn out by leading questions, agreements given in answer to closed questions or questions implicitly leading to the expected answer, and avowals elicited by torture. Now, bearing in mind these provisos, we will turn in earnest to the inquisitorial trials.

THE MOVEMENT DISPERSED

The Poor of Christ expounded new ideas and a new approach to faith directly linked to the apostolic mission with which they believed they had been invested. Having originated in Lyons, and then hounded from the city between 1185 and 1190, they recruited new devotees in the south-west of France in the following two decades during their zealous anti-Cathar crusade, and also in northern Italy and in Burgundy and Lotharingia near the linguistic frontier with the German states. It was in these regions that the densest populations were to be found when, in 1230–40, systematic persecution was organised against them as the documents from the inquisitorial trials testify. It was also during the two previous decades that the Poor of Lyons had gone underground. The judicial evidence enables us not only to locate 'heretics' when the statements were being made but also to draw up a map of their implantation up to forty years previously by drawing on the accounts given by witnesses and those being charged and tried. It therefore becomes possible for us to follow the evolution of the group over nearly a century, going back as far as the era when the Inquisition had not yet begun and when the Poor of Lyons were not persecuted by the law.

It becomes apparent that at the beginning of the thirteenth century one of the Waldensian bastions was the Quercy and Albigeois region and more particularly the towns of Moissac, Montcuq, Gourdon and Montauban, where their presence was particularly felt: in 1241, out of the 200 heretics quoted, 80 were Waldensians. It is clear that the Brothers sought above all to settle in towns. However, from the middle to the end of the century, a second migration took place eastwards. The first regions to be settled were clearly those where their anti-Cathar preaching took place. We can also understand that when they were persecuted alongside the Cathars, the Poor of Lyons were obliged to leave a region that the ecclesiastical courts supervised and ordered most efficiently; hence the new settlements in Rouergue and Castres, and then Narbonne, Carpentras, the Franche-Comté and in the Viennois. The inquisitorial registers drawn up by Jacques Fournier, the bishop of Pamiers, containing statements from 1318 to 1325, record the activities of fifty Waldensians between 1275 and 1320. Half of them come from Burgundy; the others are from other regions including Italy, Lotharingia, Champagne and Provence. Gascony is also mentioned as an area under Waldensian influence.

As far as Italy is concerned, we know only that there were Brothers in Lombardy, by which is probably meant the Po valley. It may have been during the thirteenth century that the Poor of Lyons reached the Cottian Alps and the Piedmont valleys. No other information has so far come to light concerning the Italian division between the Bergamo meeting in 1218 and the Giaveno trials in 1335 led by Albert of Castellario. We have to accept more than one century of silence. However, we are better informed about the Germanic regions. The mission into Germany set off from the borderlands, as mentioned above. The first testimonies date from 1231–33, as a result of severe persecution in the Rhineland and in Trier. There were also Waldensians tried in Bavaria towards the middle of the century. The worst persecutions were, however, in Austria between 1259 and 1266. During a visitation in the diocese of Passau, a note was made of Waldensians being present in at least forty parishes. Their settlement in Austria was to prove solid and lasting. Until the end of the fourteenth century at least, Austria was to remain the region where the densest populations of Brothers were to be found. From this stronghold, the expansion eastwards was to continue after 1260. Communities from the Poor of Christ were to reach and settle as far as Thuringia, Bohemia, Moravia, Silesia, Brandenburg, Pomerania and Poland. In the early fourteenth century, Waldensians were prosecuted in cities such as Prague, Vienna, Breslau and Stettin. In 1315, an inquisitor declared, 'There may be more than 80,000 heretics in Austria, but in Bohemia and Moravia, their number is infinite.'

The movement's prodigious spread eastwards clearly represented a major event in the history of the Poor of Lyons in the thirteenth century. From this point on, they could no longer be considered a small insignificant group. The major drawback of this was that as they grew in appeal, they appeared all the more dangerous in the eyes of the Church hierarchy. Prosecutions were therefore stepped up, becoming more inclusive, more intense and better co-ordinated. Their other essential displacement during the century was thus underground.

CLANDESTINITY

The urgent need to go underground was to change not only the lives of the Brothers in general, as was only to be expected, but also the ways in which their movement was to evolve. Their primary mission, the very reason for which they existed, was to announce the Word of Christ. This obviously implied the duty to preach in public. Suddenly, they were forced into hiding, labelled and hunted down as heretics; their Brothers were designated as partners in crime, their books and sermons dismissed as erroneous. The initial goal of converting others to evangelical poverty could henceforth be maintained only in an indirect, moderate way since fear of being denounced compelled them to be silent. Public gatherings in churches and on public squares came to an end. A new era began, characterised by hasty meetings at dusk, limited circles of friends gathering by night around the hearth, veiled allusions, covert glances and signs known only to themselves. The only way to meet the Brothers was to be introduced by a friend. This is illustrated by the following statement from a widow in the diocese of Castres in 1327. One of her neighbours came to her and said, 'If you wish to believe in a good man, that I'm sheltering at our house, and hear him preach and say his good words, I'm sure you'll like him very much.' The curious widow asked what it was about and was told, 'He's a good, upright man ... He dare not be seen in public, because he is one of those persecuted by the Church.' The woman went and met two men and heard them speak, but she did not see them; she heard them pronounce 'many good words ... but nothing against the faith'. In other words, these missionaries came gradually to give up converting new followers; their duties gradually altered. Rather than going to seek new sheep who had wandered from the flock, they devoted themselves to looking after the converted, maintaining them in their faith in the face of outside pressure and persecution. The thirteenth century marks this new approach for the Poor of Lyons.

The systematic persecution organised against them had another significant and lasting consequence. It considerably modified the group's social composition. As we have seen, the movement originated in quite a major city. Vaudès recruited his original followers from amongst the urban elite that he himself came from. There is nothing surprising about this. It was the new, fast-developing towns that generated the economic and social dynamism of the twelfth century. It was also in urban areas that the most wealth was to be found, and equally the outrage stemming from the shocking contrast between flaunted affluence and relentless poverty. This, then, was where the call to poverty was to strike a chord. It was on urban soil that the early movement of the Poor of Lyons would take root and develop. After the towns in the south-west of France, it was in the cities of central Europe that the missionaries of poverty found their ideal preaching ground during the era when they were still allowed to speak. In the towns, they found the biggest gatherings of Christians – or indeed Cathar heretics – ready to hearken to their call and be converted. The Poor of Lyons, like the Dominicans and Franciscans after them, also settled in urban areas because, as beggars living from alms, it was in the towns that their chances of finding subsistence were the greatest. Moreover, the new urban elites, the merchants and the clerks, answered their appeals not only by giving them charity, but also by being converted, giving up their possessions and following them, thus swelling their ranks. In the most natural manner possible, they thereby highlighted the great hold clerics and the Church in general had over the urban world, which was already considerably stronger than elsewhere.

By the middle of the thirteenth century, however, and certainly in the early years of the fourteenth, the Poor of Lyons had fled from the towns. The movement eastwards, already signalled above, was also accompanied by a new tendency to prefer the country to the town. In France, for instance, after 1250, there are no traces of Waldensians living in towns in Burgundy, Gascony or Rouergue. In other words, when they departed from their initial urban bases, they did not settle in towns in the new regions to which they migrated. In 1250, they can be traced to small neighbourhoods near Châlons-sur-Sâone and to the south of Lons-le-

Saunier. In the south of France, they settled in Castelnau-Barbarens, Mirande and Marciac, and even in villages smaller still such as Mazères, Saint-Jean-le-Comtal and Bars. Their newly redefined mission took them to small market towns, villages or even hamlets and it was in such modest areas that they were to stay. The reasons for their mission's success in the town were also the reasons for which they fled. The town had ensured them crowds of eager listeners, but later multiplied the risks they ran. Urban areas had particularly efficient Church networks, whose zealous justice would threaten them. The first converts were townsmen; by necessity, their successors turned to the rural world; later generations became country folk themselves.

Such developments in their geographic orientation could not but have far-reaching social consequences. Hence the men charged with Waldensian heresy, caught in the mesh of the inquisitorial net in the second half of the thirteenth century and the beginning of the fourteenth, did not belong to the same social class as their predecessors. When documents state their professions, they were, in France, carders, carpenters, tailors or blacksmiths; in other words, skilled labourers, or, in the majority of cases, simple peasants. For the rest of their history, the Poor of Lyons inevitably became and were to remain crofters and herdsmen. The Germanic countries were to witness a similar ruralisation of the movement. As a result, their way of life, and in particular the relations between the Poor of Lyons and the wealthy and lettered classes of society, were considerably altered. The latter ceased to be attracted by their ideas; they even became oblivious to them. The Waldensians' preaching, which had become discredited, no longer moved them, nor indeed did it reach them. By turning away from the urban world, albeit under duress, the Poor of Lyons lost contact with the most dynamic sector of society. By becoming ruralised, they were also marginalised to some extent. By choosing the country, when indeed they had little choice, they also opted for the world of the past.

Going into hiding induced certain modifications in their behaviour and psychology. Not that any tangible proof can be given of this, but tell-tale signs can be picked up, often barely perceptible, but revealing nevertheless. The Brothers began to live in a state of permanent fear, reacting like wanted men, forced to hide and to be prudent in everything they did to avoid being identified or denounced. Entire communities were seized by a feeling of guilt behind their instinctive fear. On the other hand, however, their situation also promoted a kind of superiority complex amongst them, as is frequently the case for persecuted minorities. Since the world was against them, since justice was unjust, their sole refuge was in God alone, in whom they put their exclusive trust.

They became convinced that they were the 'last sons of Israel', alone
worthy of the wrath, perhaps, but also the love of God. The essential
question was that of survival; new followers no longer counted. This
changing mentality coincided with their changing mission, as described
above. Finally, the fact of being hunted down, the feeling of belonging
to the elect and the need to hide inevitably inspired a sense of tenacious
solidarity and a satisfying conviction that they belonged to the same
family whose members, in the face of adversity and general misunderstanding, had to rally together and provide one another with unfailing
mutual support. It may well be that, in a paradoxical, unforeseeable
manner that is still quite easy to explain, the sight of this real brotherhood, the appeal of shared secrets and the attraction of what is forbidden
actually contributed to the movement's expansion after it had been
completely proscribed. Thus poetic justice reasserts itself, for persecution
does not always wipe out what it seeks to destroy; it may, unwittingly of
course, help the ideas it tracks down to propagate.

On the threshold of what was to prove a very dark fourteenth
century, marked by the Black Death, the Hundred Years War, and the
Great Schism during which as many as three popes vied for power at the
same time, the Poor of Lyons had lived through remarkable changes.
From choice or by force they had adapted to a completely new situation
compared to their beginnings over a century before. Their public
preaching had become private, as a result of the excommunication the
Church had declared against them, which really became effective with
the Inquisition. They consequently fled from the towns, where the
religious and civil authorities were particularly well organised, to take
refuge in the countryside. The same exodus carried their ideas to the
rural populations in the east so that, thereafter, their main bastions were
situated in central Europe. Well before this, internal differences had
surfaced in the community of Brothers. How much more would the
movement's unity be threatened by their dissemination in geographic
terms?

We now have to turn to a question that has so far been left to one
side, because of the very fragmentary nature of available documentation
and also for practical reasons, to avoid repetition. We shall consider the
organisation of the Poor of Lyons, their ideals, their message – in other
words the specificity of their religious sensibility for which they would
be persecuted and many of them burned at the stake for heresy. In the
fourteenth century, the documentation is richer both in France and Italy
and also in the Germanic countries. Our approach can thus be more
detailed and more concrete.

BIBLIOGRAPHY

Dedieu, J.-P., *L'inquisition*. Paris, 1987.
Ginzburg, C., *I Benandanti*. Turin, 1966.
Merlo, G. G., 'Les origines: XIe–XIIIe siècles'. *Colloque international d'Aix-en-Provence: les vaudois des origines à leur fin (XIIe–XVIe siècles)*, April 1988.
Schneider, M., *Europaïsches Waldensertum im 13. und 14. Jahrhundert*. Berlin, 1981.

3

THE FOURTEENTH CENTURY: THE CHALLENGE OF BELIEVING DIFFERENTLY

The wealth of documentation from the fourteenth century is, for the most part, available to us due to the fact that the Inquisition was being stepped up. It has already been stated that there remains only one document from the era issuing directly from the Poor of Lyons themselves, this being the exchange of letters between the Lombard and Austrian Brothers dating from about 1368. Other than this, the mass of documents consists of polemical treatises, and manuals of inquisitorial procedures and trials. Jacques Fournier, to whom we referred in the previous chapter, the bishop of Pamiers and the future pope Benedict XII, led proceedings in the south of France between 1318 and 1325, at the same time as the Dominican inquisitor Bernard Gui. In northern Italy, the Inquisition led by Albert of Castellario was set up in Giaveno in 1335, while in the same region of the Alps, Thomas of Casaco led the trials in the Lanzo valleys in 1373 and Antony of Settimo led those in western Piedmont in 1387. On a much larger scale were the proceedings led by Henry of Olomouc in Styria between 1360 and 1370 – which prompted the exchange of letters between the Italian and Austrian Brothers in 1368 – and especially those headed by Gallus of Neuhaus, another Dominican inquisitor, who led a ruthless campaign in Bohemia for twenty years, from 1335 to 1355. Lastly, in Stettin, Pomerania and Brandenburg, the Celestine monk Peter Zwicker interrogated nearly 200 people suspected of Waldensian heresy from 1392 to 1394. As well as what the inquisitors' records, which are particularly rich in information, teach us about the Poor of Christ during this era, we know that many other delegates from Rome were also appointed to join in the campaign against the heretics, particularly Waldensian heretics, although few traces of their activities have survived. For instance, in 1318, pope John XXII sent inquisitors to the dioceses of Prague (Bohemia) and Olomouc (Moravia); Benedict XII did the same in 1335. In the last years of the century, Peter Zwicker and a certain Martin devoted themselves to hunting down Waldensians in Erfurt in 1391, Pomerania and Brandenburg in 1393, Styria in 1395 and Hungary in 1400–4. It is thus clear that the Inquisition covered almost the entire century, and most of the territory where the Poor of Lyons had settled. How much can we learn from these documents deriving primarily from repression?

THE DIVERSITY OF DISSENT

Reading accounts of how the inquisitors tried the 'heretics' and extracts of confessions made by defendants of their own free will or under torture, the lasting impression is one of astonishment considering how many heretical movements there were scattered throughout the whole of Europe, and to what extent non-conformist religious groups had multiplied. Clerics drew up catalogues of heresies and their leading characteristics. Lest one should be overlooked, conciliar decrees listed them painstakingly in Verona in 1184 and at the Fourth Lateran Council in 1215 when the Cathars, Patarins, Humiliati, Poor of Lyons, Passagins, Josephins and Arnaldisti, among others, were condemned. For judicial reasons, of course, the inquisitors' manuals drew up lists intended to be exhaustive. The manual by the Dominican Nicolaus Eymericus, for example, issued in Avignon in 1376 and revised and updated by Francisco Peña in 1578, listed ninety-six categories of heretic, from the best known to the most obscure. As for Bernard of Luxembourg, another Dominican friar, he displays skills for classification which verge on the obsessional when, in his *Catalogus haereticorum* issued in 1522, he managed to quote a total of 432 categories of present or former heresy, to which he conscientiously added twenty-six unclassified heresies. It becomes clear that the professional investigations undertaken by the courts of faith were confronted by a complex web of unorthodoxy. As the inquisitors sought to see their way through this mesh, to link a particular error to a duly identified heresy, they came up against innumerable obstacles. We can at least understand them on this point, since our difficulties are very much the same.

The inquisitors' first stumbling block was the population's ignorance of religious matters. A good many Christians passed off as 'mysteries' various theological subtleties that were beyond them: the Trinity, incarnation, redemption, the double nature of Christ, the sacraments and the eucharist, for example. Their faith was often completely erroneous compared to Roman dogma, but upheld with the purest of intentions and a perfectly clear conscience. They had no dissenting or controversial intentions. Their beliefs were misguided simply because they had misunderstood what they had heard or been taught. The situation persisted in Europe well beyond this epoch. In the sixteenth century, both Erasmus and Luther were to speak out against the ignorance of the people, which they attributed to the ignorance of the clergy. A century later, certain religious orders began to specialise in the 'inner mission'; they felt no need to go and evangelise populations overseas since there were pagans to be found in their own lands in Europe. In conditions such as these, it was hardly difficult for the judges of the Inquisition to make those suspected of heresy admit the error of their ways; either they did so of their own accord, out of pure naïvety, or they fell without difficulty into the traps set for them. When the theologian judges heard their gross mistakes and put on indignant, sententious airs, the simple man being charged was quickly convinced he had erred and recognised his mistake, doubtless thinking the cleric was making mountains out of molehills.

Another difficulty arose from the misunderstanding which reigned between the courts and the suspects. Culturally speaking, the two sides obviously came from different worlds. Since all that remains of the judicial proceedings is the account by the court clerk, we can rarely assess to what extent intentions were betrayed by words. One admittedly late example exists, but judicial procedures and proceedings were much the same from the fourteenth to the sixteenth century. During a cross-examination led by a Dominican in Provence in around 1530, a woman charged with Waldensianism declared that the Virgin Mary was a prostitute who was impregnated by Satan after going round the world seven times. In his report, the inquisitor quotes her words to show how perverse the heretical sect had become in that region. If we had access only to his report, we might be perplexed and, rather like the Dominican in question, have trouble deciding under which category of error such ravings should be listed. A complaint was, however, lodged against the inquisitor. In this we learn that the woman was simple-minded (although this cannot be taken as certain) and, more importantly, that she was speaking of Mary Magdelene, the fallen woman of holy scriptures, whereas the inquisitor was thinking of Mary, the mother of Jesus. Was the friar being scrupulously honest? We do not know, but nor do we know the intentions of the defendant. In the absence of absolute proof, the friar should be allowed the benefit of the doubt. The case is comparable with that of the Dominican from Friuli studied by Carlo Ginzburg to which we referred above. It is clear that the misinterpretation of words, resulting from mutual incomprehension, is an additional obstacle when classifying dissenters.

In other cases, it was the suspect himself who deliberately confused issues, particularly if he was the leader of a persecuted group. Relatively well educated, with a passing knowledge of the law, he therefore tried to save himself by resourcefulness. In such cases, he used mental agility, answering questions by questions, claiming ill health and the need for rest, or again ignorance of what was right and wrong; but by doing so, he risked saying anything, and possibly making mistakes, to satisfy the inquisitor. Unless he was a beginner, however, the inquisitor was rarely taken in by such ploys; his handbook, indeed, cited the various stratagems and taught the inquisitor how to defeat them. It is, however, not impossible that certain suspects managed to dupe the courts. In this case, their declarations are vague enough to resist being classified with any certainty.

A fourth difficulty is linked to the inquisitor's mentality; indeed, the same can be said of the researcher or historian. The inquisitor, motivated by judicial zeal and we, trained in Cartesian analysis, share the same need to clarify, classify and label. The dissenters' world, however, appears particularly vague, shifting and multifaceted. There may have been different groups, autonomous and organised, but these groups were in permanent contact with one another. Numerous points in common created a sense of complicity, even fraternity, between them: their opposition to the Church was always based exclusively on reference to the bible; they wanted to recreate a Christian community like that founded by the apostles; they generally tended to consider Rome as an illegitimate Church; finally, their persecution inevitably brought them together, for they shared a common enemy. In this way, various aspects of dissent passed easily from one community to another. The situation was such that their members were often prepared to participate in the clandestine meetings of one or another movement. They were all convinced they were good Christians, even the real Christians. The judicial proceedings launched against them did nothing to alter this belief; on the contrary, they consolidated them, for had not the apostles, the first Christians, also been persecuted? Persecution, indeed, became the reason justifying their existence, the act that gave authenticity to their mission. Furthermore, the margins of the various groups were ill defined: there was a 'hard core' of leaders; then came the more or less solid ranks of the faithful; next, the regular supporters; and last of all the more fainthearted sympathisers. The truth of the matter is that we are dealing with quite an adaptable, even nebulous body, which is consequently difficult to define.

It is equally difficult to give a theological definition of these groups. Easy as it may be for the expert in canon law (that is, Church law, as opposed to common law or Roman law) to identify and classify individual instances of deviation from the faith, the various ways these errors came together and mixed and the unexpected ways in which one deviation took precedence over another tended to create a religious landscape that confounded the canonist of the era as much as it does the historian of today. This is yet another instance of both inquisitor and researcher, either from methodological zeal or from too hastily comparing a heretical tendency with the Roman model, expecting to find a perfectly clear doctrinal corpus, in which the truth is precisely set down and whose orthodoxy is accurately defined. This is not the case at all. Within a given group of dissenters, opinions could vary considerably from one member of the same community to another, except on a few fundamental principles which, in many instances, did not constitute a 'doctrine' anyway. Even as far as the leaders were concerned, their beliefs in theological terms generally appear not to have been co-ordinated and organised into a hierarchical, coherent system of doctrine. There are just a few major points on which the dissent was based. It is for this reason that it is preferable to refer to it as a religious sensibility rather than as a particular theology or even a doctrine. Just as members could pass easily from one group to another, so too their ideas evolved as they came into contact with others. Various ideas were shared; certain notions inherent in one community could later appear elsewhere. In short, the dissenters seem not to have been disturbed by the syncretism which so confounds inquisitor and historian alike. They apparently did not share their persecutors' preoccupation with cataloguing, anxious as the latter were to attribute to each exactly what was due to him, no more, no less.

This need to identify, classify and label groups so as better to convict and fight against them doubtless, somewhat paradoxically, led the inquisitor into confusion. His need for clarification, so as to find himself on familiar territory, obviously signalled his need for mental security, and meant he risked attributing to one community the ideas of another or reducing an original non-conformist movement to an already identified heresy; in short, bringing unity to what was diverse, and taking for Waldensians dissenters who did not belong to the movement. We too risk falling into the same trap. Amadeo Molnár in the 1960s and, more recently, Grado Merlo drew attention to this point in connection with the Poor of Lyons. In their opinion, the essential concern for the movement at the time was that of identity and continuity. As we saw in previous chapters, divisions had emerged between the Ultramontanes and the Italian Brothers which the meeting in Bergamo in 1218 had only partially settled. The two groups shared the belief that they belonged to the same brotherhood, just as the Italian and Austrian Brothers did, and as their exchange of letters in 1368 demonstrates. Can the same be said of the other splinter groups? Who were those that the Roman Catholics hunted down throughout Europe under the name of Waldensians? What notions did these persecuted groups have of their identity? Before venturing into the community of the Poor of Christ, we should first know exactly who they were, and for this we must be able to recognise them. Defining their identity is essential. It is a matter to which we will now turn.

THE WALDENSIAN IDENTITY

As we have said on more than one occasion, it was not because someone was labelled 'Waldensian' that he necessarily belonged to the movement, particularly since the Poor of Lyons themselves rejected that title. But we know that the two names were in fact equivalent, except that the first originally had pejorative connotations. In any case, in time, the term 'Waldensian' came to have a generic sense, synonymous quite simply with heretic. In practice, the inquisitors, who set great store by identifying each sect, employed a variety of terms when referring to the Poor of Christ. 'These heretics are commonly called Waldensians, the Poor of Lyons or the *ensavatés*', wrote Bernard Gui in his *Practica* at the beginning of the fourteenth century. Fifty years on, Nicolaus Eymericus echoed him in his manual: 'The Waldensians, or Poor of Lyons, or *ensavatés* are named after their founder, a certain Valdes from Lyons.' Both men explain the origins of these titles. There is no need to go back over 'Waldensian' or 'Poor of Lyons' which are both self-explanatory. The term *ensavatés* is more curious. Both men explain it in a more or less identical way. '*Ensavatés* because, in the beginning, the "pure" Waldensians wore a special sign in the shape of a buckle on the instep of their shoes, to distinguish themselves from their followers and from "believers"', explains Bernard Gui. 'They are called *ensavatés* because the purest amongst them wear a sort of badge on their shoes so that they may be recognised', says Nicolaus Eymericus. The matter can be elucidated by comparing the two testimonies. There is little chance that during the inquisition he led or in 1376 when he wrote, Eymericus had come across a single Waldensian wearing a special badge on his shoes so as to be more easily recognised. The Poor of Lyons had long been using their whole art to go unnoticed and so protect their clandestinity. It is preferable to retain Gui's account since, from the beginning of the century, he used the past tense; originally they *wore* a special sign. The name stuck, dating

from the era when, speaking in public, the preachers from Lyons had
invented a sign by which to be recognised so that everyone should
identify the real preachers; the sign chosen, to attest to their voluntary
poverty, was a special sort of sandal called a 'savate', perhaps bearing a
special badge. Whatever the case may have been, the Poor of Lyons
referred to themselves neither as *ensavatés* nor as Waldensians.

How did they refer to themselves? Which names did they deem
positive enough to accept amongst themselves? The inquisitors can
provide us with a first answer. Again, Bernard Gui refers to 'the society
that they call a fraternity' and later on he adds, to be more explicit, 'They
call one another Brothers and go under the name of the Poor of Christ
or the Poor of Lyons.' In another region altogether, towards the middle
of the century, Gallus of Neuhaus refers to Waldensian heresiarchs, that
is to say leaders, 'whom they call Brothers among themselves'. There are
also the names that our 'heretics' apparently used from the earliest days of
their movement, since there is proof of their being in use from the end
of the twelfth century and at the beginning of the thirteenth; names such
as *Pauperes Christi* (Poor of Christ) and *Pauperes Dei* (Poor of God) to
which we can add the expression which was to fall out of use later,
Pauperes spiritu. These are the names the Waldensians appear to have
chosen for themselves. This is at least what several inquisitors would
have us believe, if we can take what they said as true. It is, however,
difficult to imagine why they might have invented or falsified their titles.
On the contrary, they endeavoured to reproduce such concrete information as faithfully as possible so as to identify any Waldensian who might
have thought he could conceal his link with the dissent and so get away
with it. Furthermore, we can refer to the small number of documents
from within the community. From these, we can learn that they adopted
and employed the following titles: Poor of God, Poor of Christ, Poor of
Lyons and, above all, Brothers. This, then, is the first criterion by which
to identify them. When a suspect or defendant being questioned by the
organs of justice accepts that such a name applies to him, or when a
witness uses one of these terms to evoke someone known to him or her,
we are certainly dealing with a member of the Poor of Lyons, called a
Waldensian by his detractors. After all, accepting for oneself and for
others a common name or title amounts to admitting that one belongs to
the same community or spiritual family.

A good many people accused of 'Waldensian heresy', however, fall
outside this definition which is rather over-simplified as it stands. The
conviction that one belongs to a group derives from being conscious of
having a common ancestry. By the fourteenth century, this shared
heritage was based less around the memory of Vaudès than on the legend

that was then growing up giving the merchant from Lyons the Christian name Peter, alleging that he was a priest so as to bring legitimacy to later preachers, and, most of all, by tracing the Poor of Lyons' origins back to the time of pope Sylvester I, or even further back to apostolic times. By so doing, the Poor of Lyons could maintain that they, like Peter and Paul, held their mission from Christ. This belief in a history dating back as far the earliest days of Christianity can be found in testimonies written by leaders of the community, such as the exchange of letters in 1368, for example. While providing a means by which to answer the Roman clerics' argument that Waldensianism was a 'new sect', the belief in their ancestral roots also reassured the Poor of Christ that they were in the right, giving them a prestigious base such as any community needs to ensure its solidarity and without which its survival is compromised.

It is also clear, however, that to exist as a separate group and distinguish themselves from other heretics who were their contemporaries, it was insufficient just to recognise themselves as Poor of Lyons or of Christ, to call themselves Brothers and to claim their ancestry went back as far as the apostles. A study must also be made of their beliefs, since these defined their originality but were also at the origin of their vicissitudes. To what extent are we able to define those opinions which set them apart from other dissents and meant they constituted a homogeneous group? Bearing in mind what has been said above, notwithstanding the various limits we have recognised, it is still possible to isolate certain matters which constitute their particular religious sensibility.

A DIFFERENT RELIGIOUS SENSIBILITY

It is no easy matter to define the specificity of the Poor of Lyons, for a good many variations were apparent from one dissenter to the next, although they still all claimed allegiance to the original movement. Such nuances were exacerbated by geographical distance, the passing of time and the passage from one language to another. Some declarations made by defendants suspected of Waldensian heresy are in stark contradiction to others. By comparing and contrasting them, however, it is still possible, despite more peripheral differences, to identify an essential common ground which constitutes the keystone of the whole dissent. But before analysing these more precise matters, we should consider what had become, two centuries later, of the three founding issues of the Waldensian movement as defined above. Preaching remained essential but had completely changed in practice. Only the leaders of the community were entitled to preach, and the original habit of preaching in public had been replaced by preaching in private, only to the converted, as a result of persecution and clandestinity. Poverty equally remained an essential evangelical value but only the preachers were obliged to respect this rule absolutely. The bible, and more particularly the gospel, remained the ultimate source of reference. Unlike the Roman Church and the later Reformist Churches, the Poor of Lyons deemed the bible was to be read without being interpreted, and its message to be applied literally, a trend known as biblicism or evangelism. This adherence to the letter of evangelical commandments characterises the Waldensian movement as a whole and it was to cause them considerable hardship, for it imposed certain attitudes and procedures which appeared provocative in the society of the time.

Falsehood

Their rejection of falsehood came directly from the holy scriptures. Moralists had accepted that, while falsehood remained a deadly sin, it could be used in exceptional circumstances. The Poor of Lyons quoted the words of Christ which are absolutely clear and unequivocal: 'But let your communication be Yea, yea: Nay, nay: for whatsoever is more than these cometh of evil' (Matthew 5: 37). This would hardly have made their daily life easy. We may guess that they found a certain balance. In any case, the Church could not reasonably reproach them for this moral stand, uncompromising as it may have appeared. A more damaging issue which appeared far more in the trials was their stand on oaths.

Oaths

The Poor Men of Christ utterly refused to swear by oath for the same reason that they had rejected falsehood. Indeed, Jesus himself had said, 'Ye have heard that it hath been said by them of old time, Thou shalt not forswear thyself, but shalt perform unto the Lord thine oaths: But I say unto you, Swear not at all' (Matthew 5: 33–4). This rule would appear to have been respected faithfully. The inquisitors all describe this as characteristic of the Waldensians. Nicolaus Eymericus wrote of them, 'They never swore by oath.' Before him, Bernard Gui had reported that 'they maintain and they teach, with no exception and no explanation, that all oaths, in courts of law or elsewhere, are forbidden by God and are thus illicit and to be condemned for they interpret in an excessive and unreasonable manner the words of the holy scriptures and of the apostle St James condemning oaths'. The rule was therefore binding and absolute. By obeying it, the Poor of Lyons actually denounced themselves before the courts, for the inquisitor was required by law to open proceedings by asking the defendant to swear on the bible. By refusing to do so, the suspect immediately laid himself open to doubt: 'You are deemed a Waldensian heretic who believes all oaths are illicit and worthy of condemnation.' In this declaration, Bernard Gui draws on canon law which he quotes: 'If some of them, acting upon condemnable superstitions, refuse to swear by oath, they shall for this be judged to be heretics.' This made the inquisitors' work considerably easier, while making it much harder for the accused to resort to ruses. Nearly all the Waldensians questioned in court tried to avoid the need to take an oath. Let us take, for instance, the case of Raymond of Costa, interrogated by Jacques Fournier on 9 August 1319. When asked to swear, on the bible open before him, to tell the truth, he answered that he dared not swear in any way at all since once when he had sworn to tell the truth he had fallen ill. The bishop then asked him to promise by his faith to tell the truth which he likewise refused to do.

When asked if he believed that swearing to tell the truth was a deadly sin, he answered that he did. Asked whether he thought he would have to swear to tell the truth to save his life, he answered that he believed he would not have to swear as it would be a sin and if he did, some misfortune would surely befall him.

This is how the unfortunate man's trial began; from the outset he was convicted of Waldensian heresy.

Purgatory

The denial of purgatory, again deriving from the holy scriptures, was another characteristic of the Poor of Lyons. The Roman Church knew full well that there was no trace of purgatory in the bible, having gone to so much trouble founding this belief on a few allusions in the Old Testament. As Jacques Le Goff has shown, the belief in a third place in the hereafter became established amongst lettered clerics precisely in the twelfth century. While being intellectually enriching, abolishing the dualistic universe of paradise and hell, it still represented a theological novelty that took a long time to become accepted. It was only in about 1255 that it became a heresy to deny the existence of purgatory, and the doctrine behind it was only fixed in 1274 by the Second Council of Lyons. In other words, when, in the first years of their existence, the Poor of Lyons denied the existence of purgatory, they were also in keeping with Roman theology. In fact they proved more faithful to the tenets of Catholicism than Rome itself when they continued to deny what the Church came to accept. This is another issue on which all the inquisitors agree. When questioned in Giaveno in Piedmont on 21 January 1335, a witness declared he had heard André Sacherii saying that 'there was no purgatory in the hereafter; those who did evil went straight to Hell, those who did good went to Heaven'. This was a common belief amongst the Poor of Lyons. It was expressed in the south of France, in Austria and in Bohemia throughout their history.

Confession

The rejection of falsehood, oaths and purgatory were constant elements in the Waldensians' faith. There was a fourth issue which, unlike the other three, was less a matter of faith than of practice. Not that the two domains can be artificially separated, for most theoretical choices required concrete expression, and many religious acts implied a stand had been taken, if only implicitly. As we saw in earlier chapters, it would appear that without actually wishing to take the place of the official clergy and to administer the sacrament of penance, the Poor of Lyons were from their early days called upon to hear their followers' secrets; as time went by, faced with the carelessness or inaptitude of clerics, their particularly critical situation and finally with excommunication, they agreed to hear real confessions, convey proper penance and administer absolution. This was, in any case, the way things stood in the fourteenth century. Interrogated in 1319, Raymond of Costa confirmed such practices, as did the suspects in Piedmont tried in 1335 and 1373 and also those interrogated by the inquisitor Gallus of Neuhaus in Prague between 1345 and 1349. A certain Heinrich, for example, was asked how often he had confessed to leaders of his sect. He replied:

I have confessed twice. The first time, I was led by Elisabeth, my brother's widow, and her sister Grelda who had told me what good men these leaders were and how pure their faith ... The second time, the same confessor came to my house last year, around the feast of St Martin, and again I confessed to him, he bade me do penance which I performed in part, believing it would help my salvation and also that he had the right to grant or refuse absolution.

All the inquisitorial documents bear witness to the practice of confession. Bernard Gui, for example, wrote in his *Practica*:

They claim to have received – this is what they believe and what they teach – from God and God alone as the apostles did from Christ, the power to hear the confessions of men and women wishing to confess to them, and also the power to absolve them and impose penance. They thus hear confessions, absolve and impose penance, without ever having been ordained as priests or clerics by a bishop of the Roman Church; they even deny its power, and by doing so hold their authority neither from God nor from his Church, since they were expelled from the Church by the Church itself, outside which there is neither true penance nor salvation.

This is not merely the opinion held by inquisitors who might have deformed the truth. The letters exchanged between the Brothers in 1368 refer to this practice which is admittedly labelled a 'half-sacrament' by those who had just returned to the embrace of the Roman Church.

Donatism

This observance, like that of the eucharist which we shall examine below, since it was less generalised and less constant, represented in practice a double-sided principle which is inherent in the history of the Waldensian movement and to which the inquisitors referred as a 'heretical article'. There was nothing particularly innovatory about the first aspect. It took up a deviation from doctrinal norms which originated in Africa in the fourth century and was condemned by the Church at the Council of Arles in 314 and in Carthage in 411. It was labelled 'donatism' after Donatus, bishop of Carthage. The donatists believed that the sacrament was valid if the minister's life was sufficiently worthy; the Roman hierarchy maintained that as long as the rites and intentions of the Church were respected, the priest's words were effective, irrespective of his personal life. As far as Rome was concerned, even if the sacrament was administered by a cleric living in mortal sin, it remained valid. By the end of the twelfth century, certain Brothers, particularly from the Italian branch, had adopted a donatist position, while their French counterparts remained faithful to the traditional teachings of Rome on this point. This differing of opinion, which surfaced during the meeting in Bergamo in 1218, was described above. It is easy to understand why this donatist position came to predominate within the Waldensian community. It was a widely held belief that a bad cleric could not give a true sacrament nor a notoriously corrupt priest hear confession. This was succinctly voiced by a man accused of heresy by the inquisitor Gallus of Neuhaus in Prague on 26 June 1337: 'What forgiveness can a priest who is himself a sinner grant me?' Once the Church began persecuting them, the preachers tended to hearken more to the appeals of the population wishing to confess to the poor men who appeared far more faithful to the holy scriptures than did the Roman clergy.

The second aspect, which developed from the first, concerned how this attitude was put into theory. Gradually during the thirteenth century, a dual line of thought deriving from the donatist question had emerged amongst the Poor of Christ which was fully integrated by the fourteenth century. Any priest failing to imitate Christ and the apostles in his daily life lost his sacerdotal power; on the other hand, any man living an apostolic life in absolute poverty, even if he was a layman, was granted by God the power to consecrate the sacrament. This amounted to a double justification of the Waldensians' mission. First, from a negative point of view, the priests of the Roman Church led unworthy, if not dissolute, lives and thus no longer had the right to deliver the sacraments. The congregations, however, were in need of the sacraments for their salvation. Second, from a positive point of view this time, the Poor of Lyons, who led apostolic lives as itinerant preachers with no worldly goods or work, could alone claim the right to meet these needs. Holding their mission from God, even if the Church forbore to recognise it, they were both fit and ready to answer to fellow Christians' spiritual needs. The faithful, those at least who belonged to the community and accepted the Brothers as their 'masters', were indeed convinced that priests were inadequate and that the evangelical lifestyle adopted by the Brothers granted them their power. All testimonies are unanimous on this point, as the trials bear witness, even those held in Pomerania on the other side of Europe. Cune Conradi, for instance, a man of forty years of age questioned in Stettin on 22 November 1392, denied the existence of purgatory, refused oaths and falsehood and maintained the practice of confession observed by the 'heresiarchs' and his donatist vision of the clergy. These were indeed the five structuring principles in specifically religious terms on which Waldensian dissent was founded and which, in their eyes, vindicated it.

NUANCES AND VARIATIONS

There were other differences which alienated the Waldensians from the Church of Rome but, although often related to questions of some importance in terms of religious life, they were neither as generalised nor as permanent in the history of the Poor of Lyons as were the five points discussed above. Two matters characterise mostly the beginning of the movement, two others were more widespread towards the end, the fourteenth century representing to some extent a pivotal point in their history.

The death penalty

On the grounds of absolute respect for the holy scriptures, the Poor of Lyons rejected capital punishment in the early days of their movement. They indeed quoted Jesus' words: 'You have heard that it was said by them of old time, Thou shalt not kill; and whosoever shall kill shall be in danger of judgement. But I say unto you, That whosoever is angry with his brother without a cause shall be in danger of the judgement' (Matthew 5: 21–2). They also cited Jesus' words to Peter when he sought to defend him: 'Put up again thy sword into his place: for all they that take the sword shall perish with the sword' (Matthew 26: 52). This was an entirely theoretical position since none of the Poor of Christ was part of the civil magistracy. It was nonetheless recorded as one of their 'errors', for example by Bernard Gui:

> On the same grounds [as refusing to take oaths] the following error is maintained: since all judgement is forbidden by God and is thus a mistake, a judge therefore rises up against God if he condemns a man to chastisement of the flesh or death whatever the situation and the cause may be. This is because they apply without the necessary interpretations the words of the holy scriptures where it is written, 'Judge not and you shall not be judged', 'Thou shalt not kill' and other similar texts. They do not understand these, and can grasp neither their meaning nor their interpretation; while the holy Roman Church has wisely interpreted them and passes their meaning on to the faithful according to the doctrines of the Fathers and doctors and to canon decisions.

In fact, within the community, opinion was not unanimous on this point and it would appear to have become increasingly vague over the years. In 1530, however, leaders within the movement doubted whether God had commanded civil authorities to punish murderers, thieves and delinquents with death.

The eucharist

The Poor of Lyons came to celebrate the eucharist, as they had come to hear confession, as an answer to the extreme situation in the twelfth century, when congregations were abandoning mass on account of the Cathar heresy and also the unseemly lives led by priests. A certain evolution can nevertheless be traced. In the beginning, they observed the 'breaking of the bread' (*fractio panis*) on the model of Christ during the Last Supper. It would appear that this celebration was only held once a year, on Maundy Thursday. This is what Raymond of Costa described at considerable length, when being questioned on 5 January 1320 in Pamiers (Ariège, France); the ceremony included bread, wine and fish. The officiant asked God to bless them, 'Not as a sacrifice, nor as an immolation but simply in remembrance of the Holy Supper of Our Lord Jesus Christ and of his disciples.' When the bishop asked him what virtue he attributed to the bread, wine and fish once they had been duly blessed, Raymond replied: 'No special virtue results from this blessing; it is done only in remembrance of the Lord's Last Supper.' In this era, however, Bernard Gui reports that they did believe in transubstantiation: 'They are firm believers and maintain that the body and blood of our Lord Jesus Christ are present. If anything is left of the sacrament, they keep it until Easter and then finish it entirely. During the year, they give only consecrated bread and wine to the sick.'

It is quite likely that divergences grew up between the Poor of Lyons concerning the symbolical or real value of the Last Supper. Certain differences were expressed at the meeting in Bergamo in 1218 and can be heard again in the letters from 1368. Statements from defendants during the trials were vague, or, when precise, contradictory. Without further details, it is sometimes maintained that Christ is not present in the eucharist, sometimes the contrary. When Christ's presence is affirmed, it is in various ways, now in body, now in spirit. Jacques Ristolassio, condemned by the inquisitor on 8 March 1395, declared that 'the host which has been consecrated and placed in the receptacle does not contain the real Christ since he could not live there'. This practical-mindedness amounted to denying the real presence. On 5 June 1373, Lorenzina attributed the following opinion to another suspect: 'The body of Christ is not found in the host which the priest has consecrated.' In a different region, following Jean Perruza from the Vallouise valley (Hautes-Alpes, France), the Waldensians from Barge believed that 'Whosoever belonged to their sect could consecrate the body of Christ.' Things thus become clearer: once again, as in the case of confession, the donatist trend accounts for these divergences.

In this case, Bernard Gui had well understood their position:

They maintain secretly, but not publicly, that during the sacrament at the altar, the bread and wine do not become the body and the blood of Christ if the priest celebrating or consecrating the office is a sinner; by sinner they mean any man not belonging to their sect. Similarly, they also claim that any good man, even a layman who has not been ordained by a Catholic bishop, can consecrate the body and the blood of Christ, so long as he belongs to their sect; women, too, may do the same according to the same principles. If we are to believe what they say, every saint is a priest.

This was clearly and unequivocally expressed to the inquisitor in Prague in 1337 when a suspect in a church declared to the consecrated host after the Elevation: 'If you are really the body of Christ, I adore you; if you are not, I don't adore you.' To the astonished laymen around him, he explained 'I suspect the officiant of having been with a woman last night and so of not being able to consecrate the sacrament.' On 23 March 1387, while being questioned, Laurent Bandoria from Piedmont living in Osasco in the Cluson valley maintained even more simply and precisely that 'A bad priest can neither make nor consecrate such a good sacrament as a good priest can.' If the donatist trend was to become a permanent feature in Waldensian belief from the thirteenth century onwards, the conception and the practice of the eucharist were to be considerably modified. This can easily be explained, for while some held that good Catholic priests could consecrate the bread and wine, others believed that, in fact, only the Brothers could do so since they alone lived in apostolic poverty.

Ecclesiastical power

The disparaging opinion that the entire community of the Poor of Lyons came gradually to hold of the Roman clergy was to have a series of consequences which threw into question many traditional religious practices. In the beginning, as we saw above, Vaudès and his followers did not dispute ecclesiastical power outside the question of their excommunication which they deemed unjust. Gradually, as their condemnation became more effective, their reprobation was extended to other matters, as was described above during the meeting in Bergamo, and later, as far as some members were concerned, to all the rulings of the Church which were not directly taken from the holy scriptures. As a result, the various measures taken against the 'heretics' such as privation of office, excommunication and anathema, as well as the indulgences granted by Rome, were declared to be worthless. In the early fourteenth century, people like Raymond of Costa did not yet hold such extreme views. Others, however, were already thinking in this way. This enabled Bernard Gui, never a master of understatement, to write: 'The sect accepts neither canonical sanctions, nor the decrees and constitutions of the sovereign pontiffs; they equally refuse rulings concerning fasts, saints' days and the decrees of the Elders. Having strayed from the path of truth, they believed these to have no worth whatsoever, they despise, reject and condemn them.' Nicolaus Eymericus echoes him, more laconically: 'They consider as worthless the decrees and statutes of the sovereign pontiff.' Their positions were really far more nuanced. But in the fourteenth century on this matter too, it was the hardline attitudes which held sway, even if later testimonies show that more pacific attitudes had also persisted.

The saints

The discussions in fact hinged on the power of the keys. This had been conferred by Christ on Peter and the apostles: 'Whatsoever ye shall bind

on earth shall be bound in heaven: and whatsoever ye shall loose on
earth shall be loosed in heaven' (Matthew 18: 18). The question was:
who held that power? The apostles alone? The bishops who claimed to
be their successors? The pope and his delegates? Neither the pope nor his
forebears since they lived wrongfully, or at least had done since the time
of pope Sylvester? If the latter case were true, then only the Poor of
Lyons really held that power since, by imitating the apostles' life of
poverty, they were their true followers. They rejected the edicts of the
pope and the bishops, having refused to recognise that they held the
power of the keys; this also explains why the Poor of Lyons subsequently
rejected purgatory and indulgences. As a logical extension of this, they
called into question the pope's power to canonise saints. This explains
why the Poor of Lyons were reserved in their attitude towards the cult of
saints which, as is well known, engendered a host of practices, all more
or less superstitious, based on relics and pilgrimages which were also
thrown into question:

These heretics refuse to accept the reality of miracles within the Church due to
the merits and prayers of the saints who, they maintain, have never intervened in
any way. In the same way, they insinuate amongst themselves that the saints in
heaven do not listen to prayers and pay no attention to the homages we on earth
pay to them; the saints do not pray for us, it is therefore useless to entreat their
suffrage. Consequently, the Waldensians hold in contempt the solemnities which
we celebrate in honour of the saints, as well as the other signs of veneration and
homage; and on saints' days, if they can do so without too great a risk, they
work.

Statements from the community in Piedmont produced before the
inquisitorial courts in the middle or at the end of the century are clear on
this point: 'We should not pray to saints asking that they intercede for us
with God; our prayers should be addressed to God alone'; 'The apostles
and the other saints have no power and should not be applied to.' In
Prague, this is cited as a heretical article: 'The saints should be neither
invoked nor venerated, nor should the Virgin Mary.' In fact, from
different angles and in different ways, the Poor of Lyons were throwing
into question the very authority of the Church. But was this not merely
a question of opinion limited to these 'poor fellows'? We now have to
ask why such points of view made them dangerous and how they could
trouble, even to some small degree, the all-powerful Church of Rome.

THE DANGERS AND THE STAKES

Nowadays, life in society is completely secular and laicised, in most
countries at least, making it difficult to understand both why clerics set

about tracking dissenters with such dutiful assiduity and also why certain dissenters were so wilfully determined to die for their ideas. It may appear positively outrageous to us, if not pointless. This is because we have not borne in mind the social consequences of the stands described in this chapter, nor the real significance of the debate. A doctrinal opinion does not of course automatically imply a precise, concrete, unequivocal attitude that can immediately be recognised. For example, what practical difference would there be as far as confession is concerned, between a communicant who firmly believes the priest forgives his sins, another who believes the priest is merely advising him and a third who inwardly contests the power of a priest thought to be unworthy, or of the priesthood itself for that matter, but who obeys the ritual to conform to the societal practices of the era? Each thinks differently, but who knows? Indeed, who minds? On the other hand, there are certain theological stands on dogma or morality whose repercussions in everyday life could not fail to be noticed, at least in a religious, clerical society such as that in the middle ages in western Europe. Religion was everywhere; everything had a religious dimension. If civil and ecclesiastical power were distinct, and indeed obeyed separate codes of laws taught at university, one could not exist without the other. The Church and the crown were closely united. The pope, the spiritual head of the Church, was also a temporal sovereign in the Papal States. Consequently, nothing bearing on religious matters could fail to interest both the clergy, whose power was directly implicated, and state rulers whose legitimacy was dependent on their coronation and whose authority was partly dependent on support from the Church. The people in general were also concerned for they tend to distrust non-conformists. In more ways than one, by adopting attitudes they could hardly dissimulate, the Poor of Lyons were flying in the face of the times.

It is easy to imagine how their rejection of falsehood, if this were strictly applied, led to various diplomatic problems in their daily life and more especially at particularly critical moments such as in courts of law. It is also more than likely that their reservations about the eucharist, confession, various ecclesiastical rules, if not the clergy as a whole, and the cult of saints sometimes caused serious difficulties, especially to those who lacked tolerance, an interpretative sense or indeed artfulness. Most of all, however, there are two characteristics of the Poor of Lyons which were maintained steadfastly throughout their history, the absolute nature of which cannot have failed to draw attention to them, by which I mean their rejection of oaths and the existence of purgatory.

Again, the reader today needs some imagination to go beyond our present conceptual scheme, avoid anachronisms and attempt to understand the consequences of such a stand. Nowadays, we accept conscientious objectors and respect the religious convictions of those who refuse to take oaths. As for purgatory, who worries about that? The same did not hold in the middle ages. Feudal society as a whole was founded on the practice of pledging one's good faith. A pledge was required at all occasions: taking possession of land; the annual oath of allegiance to the feudal lord; for marriage; to seal all sorts of promises and contracts; and, as we have seen, in courts of justice. Refusing to take oaths did not amount just to putting oneself outside the law, but also outside society. Could a person who refused to take an oath be trusted? The Church and the state were unanimous in exacting this rite and condemning those who opposed it.

Denying the existence of purgatory had equally dramatic consequences. During the fourteenth century, once this belief had been firmly established in the hearts of people who were distressed about their chances of life everlasting, it gave rise to a whole host of practices to which the clergy were quite partial, since they were expressed in money and represented not inconsiderable incomes. Demonstrations of piety included alms for souls in purgatory (converted into masses), masses for the dead (provided for even by will and testament), various prayers for the deceased (which were known as 'suffrages for the dead'), pilgrimages and the purchase of indulgences – practices to which the people were almost as attached as the clergy themselves but which the Poor of Lyons challenged. Their challenge was expressed in practical terms by refusing to fulfil these devotions or by failing to request such observances. It cannot have taken the parish priest long, knowing his flocks as he did, to work out which parishioners never commissioned masses, absolutions or other prayers for the dead. On a local level, a certain amount of complicity was sometimes possible, for there are recorded cases of comprehensive or even positively indulgent clergymen, particularly in Austria and Bohemia, but generally speaking, the Poor Men's attitude denounced them, if not immediately then in time – for example, when a bishop or inquisitor came to visit. In this way, attitudes which may initially appear quite trivial, being purely theoretical, gave rise to actions or abstentions which were compromising and dangerous. Any member wishing to respect the finer demands of his faith was courting real danger.

If the Church and the state were so united in their determination to track down these dissenters, it was because they believed the affair was important. The question of their number was irrelevant. It had become clear that to dismantle ecclesiastical rules amounted to undermining society itself, founded as it was on religious bases. Refusing to vow by oath was no small matter, as the authorities were well aware. The repressive measures they took against what may appear to have been a simple, dispersed, inoffensive group were not disproportionate. Ideas are what counted; it was the principle that mattered. If discussions were going to touch on the right of officially recognised authorities to promulgate laws they deemed just, if obedience could be conditional and if the conscience of the individual could function as a self-appointed judge of established authorities, then where would it all stop? No organisation within a society could allow this. For this reason, the witch hunt launched against the Poor of Lyons can come as no surprise. Despite their apparent innocence and kindliness, they were, perhaps unwittingly, intriguing against medieval society and the Church which therefore had no option other than to fight and reject them. Believing differently also meant living differently. And living differently implied having to contest and fight, if only peaceably.

BIBLIOGRAPHY

Amati, G., 'Processus contra valdenses in Lombardia superiori, anno 1387'. *Archivio Storico Italiano* 37 (1865), 39 (1865).

Duvernoy, J., *Le registre d'inquisition de Jacques Fournier (1318–1325)*. 3 vols., Toulouse, 1965.

Eymerich, N. and Peña, F., *Le manuel des inquisiteurs*, ed. L. Sala-Molins. Paris and The Hague, 1973.

Gonnet, G., 'I valdesi d'Austria nella seconda metà del secolo XIV', *Bollettino della Società di Studi Valdesi* 111, 1962, pp. 5–41.

Le confessioni di fede valdesi prima della Riforma. Turin, 1967.

Kurze, D., *Quellen zur Ketzergeschichte Brandenburgs und Pommerns*. Berlin, 1975.

Le Goff, J., *La naissance du purgatoire*. Paris, 1981.

Merlo, G. G., *Eretici e inquisitori nella società piemontese del Trecento*. Turin, 1977.

Patschovsky, A., *Quellen zur bömischen Inquisition im 14. Jahrhundert*. Weimar, 1979.

4

THE FIFTEENTH CENTURY: THE RISKS OF LONGEVITY

At the time of Vaudès, the merchant of Lyons, who could have foreseen that his movement would evolve over the centuries as it did? A great number of religious trends which emerge and develop within the Church hardly last beyond two or three decades. The life expectancy of a spiritual family that is reprobated, hunted down and forced underground by political and religious authorities alike would appear likely to be even shorter. And yet, in spite of being persecuted, the Poor of Lyons were still alive and well two centuries later. This fact in itself is quite astonishing, but it was, predictably enough, interpreted differently. In the eyes of some people, this vitality was a clear indication that they were indeed 'a heresy' which, like a noxious plant, takes deeper root and is all the harder to weed out. According to others, that such a fragile minority should survive in so hostile an environment was itself proof that their views were just and that God was according them especial protection. Such is the ambiguity of signs, and such are the contradictions of humanity. But the facts are still there, interpret them as we may. This is all the more remarkable considering how very inauspicious the conditions were; Molnár indeed describes how, 'in fact, historically speaking, the movement was dying by 1400'.

To begin with, clandestinity for the Poor of Lyons represented a grievous constraint. It was a direct contradiction not just of their primary mission, but, more to the point, of the words of the gospels. Hence the strong temptation to link their cause to other heterodox movements whose evangelism was clear and distinct. One such movement might happen to benefit from more favourable circumstances and so grow in strength and come to light. For the Poor of Lyons, the risk of being engulfed by a larger movement had to be offset against the desire and need to swell their numbers. Later, their imposed clandestinity meant that what had initially been an open, if not a rallying, group had to be transformed into a form of secret society open exclusively to initiates, making their movement even more fragile. As a result, over the years, the Poor of Lyons lost the popular image they had enjoyed amongst their contemporaries. While they were appreciated and even sought after at the end of the twelfth century, when they wandered through the towns preaching poverty and repentance, they were progressively alienated and marginalised by the Church hierarchy. Consequently, once they had begun to be hunted down as heretics, that is to say public enemies, they were gradually estranged from the population and, as a result, became strangers. People with something to hide could hardly be desirable company. They soon came to be suspected of harbouring dubious intentions and of practising terrible deeds of all sorts; in other words, they became the new scourge or scapegoat. Ultimately, their dispersion throughout Europe would obviously not help them to communicate on a functional level, nor to co-ordinate on an institutional level. It would also hinder their spiritual unity.

A DIASPORA

It is impossible to evaluate with any accuracy how important the Poor of Lyons were in terms of numbers. There are several reasons for this, the principal one being the complete absence of data in an era so far removed from our statistics-obsessed times. Certainly, they were never more than a tiny minority, even if, on a local level, within a particular village for example, they might have represented the majority if not the whole of the population. However, one of the most striking character-istics of the community of Brothers was how widespread their implanta-tion became, which is at the same time one of the most restricting factors. Few dissenting movements have expanded in such a way. From its origins in Lyons, the Waldensian impetus quickly spread to the south-west of France, an ideal land for preaching, having already been won over by the Cathars. But by the end of the twelfth and the beginning of the thirteenth century, their missionary work extended eastwards towards Provence, Comtat and, on the other side of the Alps, Lombardy; and northwards into Burgundy, Franche-Comté and even further afield to the borders of Lorraine and Alsace. However, as we have seen in previous chapters, it was in the fourteenth century that the major phase of expansion occurred. At this time, communities of Poor Men were reported in Gascony, the Dauphiné, Valentinois, Diois, Provence and

Comtat venaissin; in Piedmont, Calabria and Apulia in the south; finally eastwards in the Rhine valley, and in Thuringia, Saxony, Bavaria, Austria, Brandenburg, Pomerania, Bohemia and Silesia. The dynamism in the fourteenth century deserves comment.

There is little information enabling us to assess the speed with which the Poor Men multiplied, or the means they used and the exact geographical limits they reached. The documentation available to us has been, for the most part, provided by the inquisitorial trials, a good deal of which was most certainly lost, especially if we bear in mind that, according to the practice of the times, if capital punishment was pronounced, judicial records were burnt at the stake with the prisoner. With what remains of the documentary puzzle, incomplete as it may be, we can, however, reconstitute certain elements. We can note, for example, how the French implantation gradually dwindled. As the movement pushed eastwards, it failed to maintain its initial bases – those in Lyonnais, Rouergue, Languedoc and Gascony. In Jacques Fournier's registers and especially from Raymond of Costa's statements, we can, admittedly, trace a few members of the community of Brothers born in these regions but this is clearly a far cry from the numbers recorded one or two centuries before. The efficient persecution in these regions, such as that led by Jacques Fournier and Bernard Gui, doubtless explains this decline.

On the other hand, a new zone opened up in the Alps, on both sides of the present Franco-Italian border: in the Dauphiné, Briançonnais, the valleys of l'Argentière, Vallouise and Freissinières; in Piedmont in the valleys of the Po and its tributaries. In these regions too, however, their numbers were not static. Lombardy had been the stronghold of the Brothers' implantation in Italy in the thirteenth century – this was certainly the case, for example, at the time of the meeting in Bergamo – but the region declined in importance, later to be replaced by Piedmont. Merlo has shown clearly the extent to which religious dissent there was widespread and varied. But even within the Piedmont region, the situation evolved considerably, as a comparison of the beginning and the end of the fifteenth century shows. Towards the end of the previous century, much of the plain was under the influence of various 'heterodox' ideas. The situation narrowed from this point on in two distinct ways: first on a religious level, for until this date the Poor of Lyons had been mixed if not wholly muddled up with various others dissenters, many of whom are difficult to attach to a precise trend, but who were gradually eliminated. They might have been burnt at the stake, been victims of repression, or simply have been lost from sight by dint of dissimulation; or indeed, faced with the pressures of reprobation, they may have begun to conform once more. Alternatively, they may have joined the Waldensians, won over by the attraction of this movement. Whatever the case may have been, the profusion of contesting voices which had flourished in the Po basin died down. The Inquisition had got the better of all but the Poor of Lyons. There is also a second level to be considered, which is geographical, for the extent of their settlement had diminished. Whereas they had previously been found over a wide area across the Po valley, this now shrunk to encompass little beyond the three 'Waldensian valleys', the Chisone, the Germanasca and the Pellice which became from then on the Poor Men's most solid and densely populated bastion. This reduction in terms of space corresponds to changes in the manner in which they settled. While they avoided choosing locations at an altitude which were too easily tracked down, they also withdrew from the largely populated plains into more isolated sites.

The Alpine division, which had formerly been of rather secondary importance, thus became the nucleus of the community of Brothers. Armed with their religious convictions, settlers had already set off from these bases into Calabria towards the middle of the fourteenth century. This was only the beginning. Proper colonies from Piedmont and the Dauphiné settled in southern Italy, in Calabria and Apulia. This migratory stream would seem to coincide with waves of persecution. There is an example of this, remarkable for its rarity, in 1477. On 5 May, three inhabitants from 'the Dauphiné' signed a contract for a sea passage (*naulisamentum*) with a ship owner at a notary's office in Marseilles. Although the exact residence of the Dauphinois men is not stated, they were clearly Waldensians. Indeed, another identical deed was also signed in September of the same year, inscribed by the notary in his register under the title '*naulisamentum pro valdensibus*' (transport by sea for Waldensians). The contract concerns the transport of the signatories 'with all their society'. The second, more detailed deed fixes the number of passengers at 150 at a price of one gold écu per head, other than 'suckling babes'. A migration was evidently being organised. All possible precautions were taken – sufficient drinking water had to be provided, dangerous areas were to be avoided. Their departure was clearly definitive, since the deed even stipulates that the passengers could take household equipment. Where exactly was this circle of Dauphinois Waldensians heading? They intended to split up into two groups, one of which would disembark in Naples, the other in Paola. The first group was plainly heading for Apulia, the second for Calabria; both would then join and so reinforce the communities of Poor Men which had already settled. We know that a ruthless wave of persecution had been organised in the Alps in 1475. Once again, we can note that repression led to emigration, but also to expansion.

Another major wave of migration also set off from the Alps to found a new pole of dissent. In this case, as the migrants looked westwards for a new place of exile, it was as if they sought to express their nostalgia for their original lands in France and to retrieve some of their lost ground, although this is figurative for we could hardly suspect the Poor of Lyons of harbouring strategic visions of conquest. Provence and Comtat-Venaissin offered vast areas lying fallow since the disasters of the fourteenth century. The regions had been devastated and drained by plague, war and roaming soldiery. Entire villages had been abandoned; the few surviving towns had diminished considerably. Deprived of the incomes from their untended estates, landowners calculated the loss of profits and sought to rectify this by attracting new settlers to their lands. Furthermore, in the second half of the fifteenth century, while a real shortage of labourers existed in the lowlands, where the diminished population could not meet labour demands, the Alpine regions were, on the contrary, experiencing great demographic tension. As Comba has demonstrated, this was in part due to the natural development of the area which had been less affected by the turmoil of the previous century; it was more particularly a result of the economic transition taking place in the highlands. Until this time, it had been an agrarian region, despite the haphazard nature of harvests, a consequence both of the poor soil and the rugged terrain as well as the harsh climate, but it gradually turned more to animal husbandry, whose produce was in increasing demand, selling well and far afield.

This move towards a pastoral economy, for which the Alpine regions were better suited, had the great advantage of promising higher incomes. However, it also required a reduced labour force, thus leaving many workers inactive. Many yeomen were forced to sell up. The hardships of former times gave way to widespread poverty. This, and the persecution then being organised against the Poor Men from the Alpine regions, prompted many a poor wretch to set off towards Provence in search of new lands. In this way, numerous towns and villages in the lowlands were repopulated. The Luberon region, in particular, a hilly forested area to the north of Aix-en-Provence, welcomed some 1,400 labourers coming from the dioceses of Embrun and Turin in the mountains. If we count their families too, this influx amounted to more than 5,000 people, three-quarters of whom arrived between 1470 and 1510. A fair majority of this new workforce came from Alpine villages pinpointed since the fourteenth century at least as 'Waldensian'. In this way, a certain number of Poor Men, concealed within a major wave of migration, fled both poverty and the Inquisition; the two were indeed often linked, since suspects found guilty of heresy automatically had their goods confiscated. They then settled in about thirty different localities in the Luberon, making this region one of the strongholds of Waldensian settlement in western Europe, and certainly the foremost site in France along with the Dauphinois area.

As far as the 'conquest of the east' is concerned, we know this was accomplished primarily in the fourteenth century, as a result of prosecution. The community had taken root particularly in Austria, in Styria above all. The letters of 1368 had been exchanged with their Austrian brethren. The inquisitorial trials confirm this pattern. This region then provided a base from which settlers set forth eastwards as far as Bohemia and Moravia, then northwards along the shores of the Baltic Sea and into Brandenburg. The geographical situation in the east would appear not to have changed much in the fifteenth century. The Austrian community altered in size, for its numbers diminished considerably, doubtless due to the particularly efficient inquisitorial skills of a certain Henry of Olomouc in Styria and Moravia. He managed to lead many Poor of Lyons, including a number of key figures, back to the embrace of Rome, as testified by the exchange of letters frequently evoked. Years later, at the beginning of the following century, another inquisitor, Peter Zwicker, the Waldensians' foremost oppressor in central Europe, recalled the 'pious memory' of his predecessor, remarking on the lasting effects of his work. Yet again, the persecuted community tracked eastwards, the original bases weakening as a result. It was as if the Poor of Lyons were being hounded further and further east towards the very edges of Catholicism, if not Christendom.

The form of expansion which the dissent took in the fifteenth century is quite striking. The Poor of Lyons hunted down by the inquisitors in the east, in Pomerania, Brandenburg and Bohemia, nearly all belonged to the German-speaking population. Jan Hus's friend, Jerome of Prague, proclaimed in his *Recommendacio* of 1409 that heretics had been brought from abroad to be burnt alive in the 'holy city' of Prague, whereas no heresy had ever been apparent within the Czech population itself. If he is exaggerating a little, his words are probably not wholly unfounded. The expansion eastwards was related to migrations of the population and to Germanic colonisation in eastern Europe, following a similar pattern to that studied above in relation to the Piedmont-Dauphinois Alps and the Provençal-Comtat lowlands. This is particularly interesting. In the very earliest days of the twelfth century, the movement relied for its dispersion on the persuasive powers of its preachers and the worthiness of their example, by which they could convince and convert new members. The

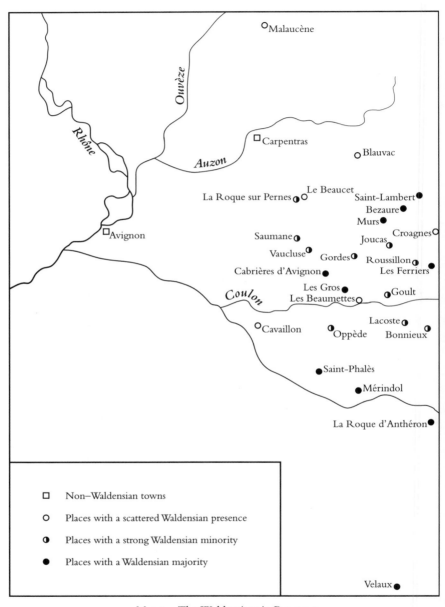

Map 1   The Waldensians in Provence

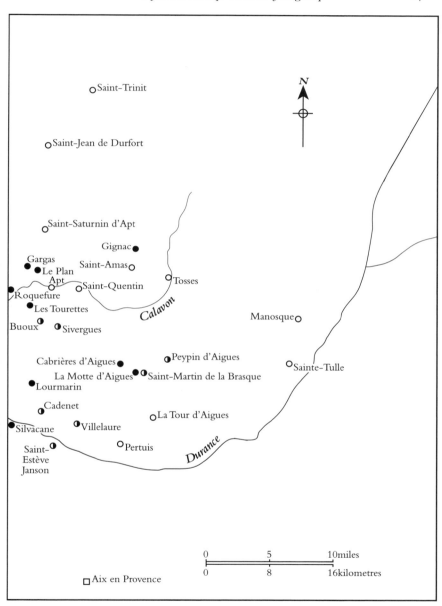

○ Saint-Trinit

○ Saint-Jean de Durfort

N

○ Saint-Saturnin d'Apt

Gignac ●

Gargas
● ● Le Plan   Saint-Amas ○
Apt
● ○ ○ Saint-Quentin   ○ Tosses
Roquefure
● Les Tourettes   *Calavon*

Buoux ◐   ◐ Sivergues   Manosque ○

Cabrières d'Aigues ●   ◐ Peypin d'Aigues   ○ Sainte-Tulle
La Motte d'Aigues ● ◐ Saint-Martin de la Brasque
● Lourmarin

● Cadenet

● Silvacane   ◐ Villelaure

Saint- ◐   ○ Pertuis   *Durance*
Estève
Janson   ○ La Tour d'Aigues

| 0 | 5 | 10miles |
| 0 | 8 | 16kilometres |

□ Aix en Provence

enthusiasm inspired by their preaching and their life of itinerancy and poverty ensured the development of their community. Initially, the protection and then the leniency of the Roman clergy contributed to this development. The persecution resulting from their excommunication was differently beneficial to their cause. It explains the dissemination of their ideas in the thirteenth and fourteenth century. After this, the movement began to lose momentum.

All those accused of Waldensian heresy interrogated in the second half of the fourteenth and in the fifteenth century and questioned as to the origins of their faith, came from families who were already members of the dissent. Margareta, for instance, the wife of the tailor Hertlin, was interrogated in Ceské Budéjovice in Bohemia by the inquisitor Gallus of Neuhaus on 18 March 1338. In her family, two relatives of the older generation had already been burnt at the stake for heresy: Kunla, her mother's sister and Wencla, her father's sister. Another example is forty-year-old Cune Conradi from Gryfenhagen, interrogated in Stettin on 22 November 1392, who declared he had been 'born into the sect'. Interrogated in the same year, in the same town, Peter Gossaw and Jacob or Zdeneke Rudeger declared their fathers and mothers were 'of the Waldensian sect and died in its fold'. Are further examples necessary? It is clear that the happy days of open preaching and converting were a thing of the past; henceforth the torch was passed within the family. New members were recruited amongst relatives. This led to considerable changes. If faith is passed on by blood, if the truth is inherited rather than learnt, a religious community tends to become an ethnic group, and is therefore easily spotted by certain family names, for in such conditions homogamy was bound to become usual. In practical terms, this led to a form of introversion, segregation, or sclerosis even, in stark contrast with the dynamic spontaneity of the original impetus. A certain homogeneity settled over the entire milieu. On a sociological level, from this time onwards, and for the reasons we have studied, the Waldensian population – we might even go so far as to say 'people' – was composed of shepherds and farmers. Would this standardisation, which increased as time went by, be sufficient to offset the pressures of an increasingly far-flung diaspora across Europe? This tendency too was working insidiously and gradually gaining in strength.

ONE COMMUNITY?

Who can be unaware of the difficulty? All those who, for family, professional or humanitarian reasons, have been faced with human migration and the problems of immigration will understand all the better. It is certain that belonging to the same professional body creates strong links. Sharing the same faith undoubtedly reinforces these links. Holding in common a dangerous secret inevitably binds people together all the more firmly and ardently when the risks they run are so great. Besides, differences and disagreements tend to be played down, if not effaced, before a common enemy. These factors predictably contributed to the way the Poor of Lyons forged a community in the true sense of the term. An inevitable obstacle nevertheless became apparent as, and because, the movement expanded – the 'price of glory' to some extent, if we may speak of glory in such circumstances; I am referring to the problem of language. As we have seen, Vaudès and his companions were originally anxious to break with Latin, the only sacred language accepted by the Church to pass on the Word of God. What was the use, they contested, of proclaiming the holy scriptures in a language the population did not understand? This was the reason why Vaudès himself commissioned the translation of some books of the New Testament into Franco-Provençal, the vernacular in Lyons. This pastoral concern was laudable, essential even. However, abandoning Latin so as to be understood by the local people also, paradoxically, amounted to severely limiting their field of action. It meant depriving themselves of the only international language in existence, the only language which could cross national frontiers and whose only limits were those of Christendom itself. The dilemma was enormous. They had to choose between the vast but superficial scope of Latin with which they could be understood everywhere, but by the lettered populations only, and the spoken dialect, with which they could hope to be fully understood but only by those who belonged to the same linguistic group.

The difficulty was slight while their preaching was limited to the city of Lyons and thereabouts. Their missions into the south of France, Gascony and later Provence and the Dauphiné cannot have posed any great problems. There were local differences which the people from region to region recognised but these provinces all belonged, in linguistic terms, to the domain of the *langue d'oc*. Within these bounds, even on the other the side of the Alps, people could understand one another quite easily. As the movement spread into Burgundy, it came into contact with the northern French dialect. Lyons was particularly well situated on this linguistic frontier. The preachers therefore adapted as easily for their missions northwards as they had in the south. They could thus reach all French-speaking regions without needing to learn a new language or commission new translations. The same held for the whole territory of 'Provence' which stretched in places as far as southern Italy where, even in the sixteenth century, the Calabrians called the Poor of

Lyons who lived there, and who were descended from the settlers more than one century before, the *Provenzani*. It was the expansion eastwards that represented a real difficulty.

The Poor of Lyons reached the Germanic margins very rapidly, for their presence is registered from the beginning of the thirteenth century in Metz, Strasbourg, Trier and the Rhineland. We have no record of the linguistic obstacle they must inevitably have had to face as they preached to a population speaking neither French nor the *langue d'oc*. Clearly, they must have had to adapt their words and writings when they adopted the Germanic tongues. As in the southern *langue d'oc* provinces, there was no common language in Germany, and a vast range of linguistic varieties could be found. But in this case too, the linguistic common ground was sufficiently large for people to understand one another despite certain considerable differences in idiomatic expressions, accents and pronunciation. Although the Franco-Germanic frontier had been reached in the early thirteenth century, the expansion eastwards occurred, as we saw above, only in the fourteenth century. We may interpret this latent period as the necessary delay while they adapted to the new linguistic territory. This would imply that it took the Brothers nearly a century to overcome the barrier of language. Such an explanation is of course merely a hypothesis, for no testimony confirms this interpretation. What is known for sure is that an important number of Waldensians had penetrated Germanic regions from the Rhine to the middle of the Danube as far as the Oder and even the Vistula and that these territories represented a real entity, the unity of which was to a considerable extent linguistic, although various divisions could be listed.

The doubtless exceptional but remarkably revealing case of the Waldensian Friedrich Reiser, from Swabia, will be studied at greater length below to illustrate the phenomenon. Reiser travelled throughout the Germanic lands visiting Brothers from Basel and Fribourg in Switzerland to Brandenburg, from Strasbourg to Prague. How would such a mission have been possible without the linguistic unity of this vast territory? Two factors admittedly reduced the difficulty. First, it must be borne in mind that populations were exceptionally mobile. At the time when the eastern lands were being conquered, most peasants, including those dissenters who appeared in court, were not living in their birthplace. This is made strikingly apparent by the interrogations. It is now known that the old rural world was far from being as 'immobile' as it was formerly made out to be. In the Germanic lands, however, numerous large-scale migrations had taken place which were not unrelated to the Inquisition. We may therefore surmise that, for two or three generations, a native language or dialect was maintained within families. Outside definitive migrations, geographical mobility can also be traced for temporary or periodic moves dictated by trade or finance. Whole populations were ever on the move, taking with them from one town to the next not only merchandise and credentials but also ideas, opinions and beliefs.

These two circumstances linked to mobility lead to the second factor reducing the problem of linguistic diversity, that of bilingualism. This may come as a surprise to the contemporary reader living in a time of intercontinental exchange and of European unification where we still doggedly refuse to speak anything but our mother tongue. Our ancestors of the middle ages, even the peasantry, would appear to have been much less restive. To begin with, they all knew a smattering at least of Latin, which they heard every Sunday at compulsory mass. A few decades at this rhythm probably ensured they knew by heart a series of prayers, and therefore of words, phrases and whole passages in Latin, the general meaning of which they came to understand. Moreover, just as they do today, the migrant populations had not only to maintain their mother tongue out of faithfulness and to preserve a certain identity, but they also had to master a new language to adapt to their host country. We should not make too much of these difficulties, real as they were, for there were few migrations from one linguistic zone to another where the tongue would be completely unfamiliar, as for example the move from the *langue d'oc* regions to the Germanic lands. The German-speaking populations in Bohemia are exceptional only in appearance, for in this instance a complete colonisation in the full sense of the term took place, that is to say agricultural, cultural, linguistic and even, in the case of the Waldensian dissenters, religious. The only examples of genuine bi- or trilingualism can be found amongst the leaders of the community, such as Friedrich Reiser who, being also in contact with the Alpine division, must have known their language, unless they communicated in Latin. It is indeed quite striking to see the Poor of Lyons turn back to the language of the Church to communicate with the outside world; this occurred in 1530, for example, with the reformers, and in 1533 with the Bohemian brethren. But there is nothing really astonishing about this, for Latin was after all the language of the sciences and the only means to communicate between nations. As far as the rest of the community was concerned, all those interrogated by the inquisitor spoke in German, whether in Styria or in Pomerania. In the fifteenth century, therefore, the Poor of Lyons found themselves confronted with an evolution in two different directions, which was potentially divisive.

At this point, the result of the preachers' linguistic choice and the consequences of the expansion eastwards link up. In fact, at the end of the fifteenth century, we may wonder whether we are really dealing with the same community in the Cottian Alps as in Brandenburg, for example. Had unity been preserved in spite of this geographical explosion and linguistic diversification? Simple as it may be, the question has rarely been analysed by specialists, who tend for understandable and practical reasons to limit the area of their research. But these limitations are themselves revealing. I do not believe that they reflect the rarity or the nature of the documentary resources. No researcher to this day has yet defined a domain of enquiry situated on the linguistic frontier to include the two major branches which developed from the first impetus in Lyons. It has indeed always been a question of two separate unities.

Immediately after the first period in Vaudès's lifetime, during which only the southern areas were affected, the expansion of the Poor of Lyons meant that they quickly came to span two linguistic zones, one French-speaking, the other the *langue d'oc*. The sufficiently short length of time during which this continued (approximately a century) and the basic proximity of the two Latin-derived languages meant the community could be maintained without any major problems. The emergence of a few groups on the Lorraine and Rhineland boundaries created a peripheral phenomenon. With the expansion in Germany in the fourteenth century, a third zone opened up which, far from being negligible, came to represent the main body in terms of numbers, particularly in Austria. The diaspora, across almost the whole of Europe, therefore counted three bodies: France; Provence and Italy; and Germany. As a result both of the common ground linking French and the *langue d'oc*, and especially of the original bases in France being diminished, the community of Brothers came to be divided essentially into two branches, one western, speaking the *langue d'oc*, the other eastern, speaking different German dialects. The cleft between the two was already distinguishable at the end of the fourteenth century and its effects became more apparent as time went by.

What was initially no more than a language difference gradually developed into a split in sensibility and finally mutual, good-natured ignorance which is doubtless worse than open conflict. This unawareness, even if it was not total, was at least habitual. Only in particularly dramatic moments or exceptional circumstances can any exchange be traced between the Poor of Lyons in the west and their Brothers in the east. Friedrich Reiser, for example, was in contact with the Alpine division and Luc of Prague travelled to Italy in 1495 to visit Rome and also the Brothers from central Italy. Representatives from the Alpine and Czech communities would appear to have met at the beginning of the sixteenth century. While these meetings bear witness to elements the two bodies had in common, they also indicate that these were sufficiently loose to be seen as exceptional. On both sides of the divide members recalled the existence of Brothers in the other region, but did they really believe they belonged to the same community, the same religious family? It would appear most doubtful and, personally, I do not think this was the case; as we shall see when we consider how the brethren were organised, each of the two divisions had its own separate body of preachers.

In this way, as a result of its internal evolution and the dynamism which made the expansion through Europe possible, the Waldensian movement became a diaspora. With the passing of time, the diaspora soon gave way to a double-sided unity, in which each side tended to live independently. The linguistic factor came in time to play a determining role. This is surely the fate of all displaced minorities. Unity became essentially theoretical; it was a community in name only, and members tended no longer to consider it as such. To this development within the movement must be added the way it was perceived by others, particularly by detractors on the outside. There was not only persecution such as that described above, but also more insidious, diffuse attacks by which the image of the Poor of Lyons was degraded and deformed in the minds of the population.

THE CRIME OF *VAUDERIE*

It is difficult to say which is the more damaging, an open attack or perfidious calumny; declared hostilities or preposterous hearsay. We know that the Poor of Lyons rejected the terms 'Waldensian' and '*vaudois*' constantly employed by their persecutors. Reducing a spiritual movement, the base of which was so evangelical, with such vast repercussions, simply to the man who founded it was tantamount to deforming its inspiration and its meaning. Yet the labels became so frequent that in the thirteenth and especially the fourteenth century they replaced the twelfth century 'Cathar' as synonyms quite simply of 'heretic'. At this time a new development occurred in the semantic field of this term.

The phenomenon of witchcraft, which has been relatively well analysed in recent times, is linked to a combination of social, psychological and religious factors too long to be studied here. We should just take note of the obsessional mentality which grew up in this era, from the fifteenth to the sixteenth century, after the wave of disasters during the previous century, leading the population, and the clergy in particular, to consider Christianity as a besieged Jerusalem, assailed by the forces of evil, as Satan and his armies let fly, betokening the end of time. Sorcerers and witches represented the diabolic troops engaged in this dramatic conflict. Witchcraft constituted an omnipresent danger, at work everywhere. Jean Bodin, a French legist of the sixteenth century, defined it as follows: 'A sorcerer is one who employs diabolic means intentionally in an effort to achieve his aims.' In terms of law, it was not the Church's preoccupation, for witchcraft was a civil crime, related to public order, and therefore the concern of the secular authorities. In the papal bull *Super illius specula* of 1326, however, John XXII qualified witchcraft as a heresy. Indeed, the diabolic pact, with its Sabbath rite, amounted to spreading aberrant religious beliefs and practices. This became the Church's official stand. It was not until the end of the fifteenth century, however, that witchcraft was systematically hunted down. In 1484, in the bull *Summis desiderantes affectibus*, Innocent VIII invited the inquisitors to repress witchcraft, particularly in the Germanic countries. Two years later, the corresponding handbook 'The Sorcerers' Hammer' (*Malleus maleficarum*) was circulated, written by the inquisitors Henry Institoris and Jacques Sprenger with, as an exordium, a copy of the papal bull making especial mention of the two Dominicans by name. This document truly marks the beginning of the witch hunt. Moreover, it indicates a new turning point by associating popular magic and witchcraft. Henceforth, common practices deriving from traditional rural folklore which had formerly been deemed harmless or even beneficial could be judged to be diabolic, related to sorcery and therefore heresy, and so the concern of the Inquisition. Even if the most serious modern accounts estimate that approximately 5 per cent of those accused were actually executed, it was still by the thousand that heretics and sorcerers alike met their tragic fate at the stakes that were to burn across Europe for more than a century.

The term 'Waldensian' or '*vaudois*' was used pejoratively from the start, to refer to Vaudès's disciples, in other words his 'sectarians'. Towards the beginning of the fifteenth century, the word *vauderie* or *vaudoiserie* appeared, meaning sorcery, and *vaudois* was used to mean sorcerer. In 1438, the Swiss sorcerers arrested in Fribourg belonged to the 'Voudeis' or 'Voudesie' sect. In 1440, pope Eugenius IV wrote to Amadeus VIII, duke of Savoy, who had meanwhile been elected by the ecclesiastical council as another pope under the name of Felix V, complaining that he faced a number of sorcerers or 'Waudenses' in his states and that he had even been swayed by them. I doubt whether there were more sorcerers in the Alpine regions than there were elsewhere. I rather suspect that the 'Waldensians' from Savoy, that is to say from Piedmont, had already been bracketed with sorcerers by the papal chancellery. The document entitled *La Vauderie de Lyonnois en brief* dated

1460 makes the confusion complete. It persists in the trials throughout the second half of the century; in 1452 in Provins, in 1453 in Evreux and especially in Artois some years later.

In 1459, the affair known as the '*vauderie* of Arras' erupted. In fact it was to have repercussions throughout the states of Philip 'the Good' right to the end of the century, although the trials themselves only lasted from 1459 to 1461. There is no reason to recount the dismal tale here; it will suffice to recall the essence insofar as it relates to the present study. Fifteen men and women who were accused and found guilty of the crime or sin of *vauderie* perished at the stake. Some people, historians included, believe the prisoners could have been Poor of Lyons, wrongly accused of witchcraft, hence the assimilation that later came to be made between the two concepts. It is in any case now uncontested that the proceedings concerning the *vauderie* of Arras were directed against sorcerers. This becomes clear when one reads reports of the trials, statements from the leaders of the prosecution and accounts and descriptions by contemporary witnesses. The *Traité de vauderie* drawn up by Jean Tinctor in 1460 insists it was dealing with the 'sin' of *vauderie*, which is infinitely more serious than pagan idolatry, Christian heresy or Muslim heathenism, being an 'accursed and unnatural sect' whose danger lies in the fact that it would develop to bring about 'the total desertion and destruction of Christianity and even the end of the world'. So what exactly was *vauderie*? Let us examine how the inquisitor Lebroussart began his sermon to the crowd that had gathered around the stakes set up on 9 May 1460 in Arras, in which he explained the nature of the crime justifying the sentence of death passed on the five 'Waldensian' culprits: 'When they wanted to indulge in *vauderie*, they took an ointment which they made in the following way.' The recipe for the said ointment is then given. He later continues, 'Then, with this ointment they coated a small wooden rod, their palms and their hands, then put this rod between their legs: immediately they vanished, or so they thought.' There follows a description of the Sabbath: the banquet, the profanation of the crucifix, devil worship and sexual orgy. All the chroniclers took up the details. As early as 1440, Lefranc, in his *Champion des Dames*, described their diabolic assemblies as follows:

> It is true, I have heard it said, and believe
> That old women, not two or three
> Or twenty but more than three thousand
> Go together some in threes
> To see their diabolic families ...
> I tell you I saw in Chartres
> How, from the time when she

> Was sixteen years old, or thereabouts,
> On certain nights from the Valpute
> On a pole went off
> To visit the whorish synagogue
> Ten thousand old women in a waste
> There were commonly.

A manuscript of this work in the Bibliothèque Nationale in Paris has a caricature in the margin depicting two witches astride broomsticks, and the caption: 'Vaudoises passe-martin' (Waldensian women on broomsticks). There is no need to say more; the case is quite clear: the *vauderie* of Arras is a story of witchcraft, nothing more. Vaudès's disciples, the Poor of Lyons, had nothing whatsoever to do with it as the documents relating to the trials clearly show.

A TENACIOUS CONFUSION

The term *vaudois* had thus acquired a new meaning. It signified both heretic and sorcerer, although it is difficult to say quite how this came about, or to trace back the obscure connotational paths which led all kinds of villains to be called *vaudois* and made the term itself an insult. This was in any case what happened, as we can see in Fribourg in Switzerland in 1408 where the noun *voudeise* was taken as approximately synonymous with *putain, ribaude, murtrisser, laronese* (whore, harlot, murderer, thief). Another semantic shift then occurred, in circumstances we know little about, but where the general meaning is clear. According to Hansen, a German historian at the beginning of the twentieth century, the label *vaudois* was apparently used for the first time to refer to sorcerers in the French-speaking regions of Switzerland and in Savoy. In these parts, *vauderie* meant lust, and sodomy in particular. A man accused of this in France was called *bougre* (Bulgarian, or bugger), in Savoy *vodeis*. Since *bougrerie* or *vauderie* was believed, wrongly, to be an act of heresy, heretics tended to be accused of *bougrerie* or *vauderie*. In these regions, during the great wave of persecutions at the beginning of the fifteenth century, people commonly called sorcerers *vodeis* or *vaudois*. Meanwhile, the notion spread that the satanic Sabbath was a practice common to Cathars and the Waldensians. A theologian, for example, entitled his treatise against sorcerers written in 1450, *Errores gazariorum seu illorum, qui probam vel baculum equitare probantur* ('Errors of Cathars or those who ride on brooms or rods'). Jurists and theologians, finding the term *vaudois* applied to sects of sorcerers, equally used the expression without further consideration. In this way, the double confusion grew up, between *vaudois* meaning *bougres* (sorcerers) on the one hand and *vaudois* meaning heretics (Waldensians) on the other. Huizinga, for example, wrote that 'the common term for magic in France in the fifteenth century was *vauderie*, which had lost its original meaning denoting the heresy of the Vaudois, or Waldensians'. Duverger, writing in 1885, states that 'From the fifteenth century onwards in the Netherlands, the label "vaudois" was used almost exclusively to refer to sorcerers.' The confusion may have been absurd; but it is well known that the most commonly held ideas are not necessarily the most rational or reasonable. It was also to die hard.

The association was so simple, yet so deeply rooted, that centuries later it re-emerged in reference to the French Protestants, the link being quite plain in the end. In his *Mémoires*, Claude Haton (1553–82) wrote of the year 1567:

Following the aforementioned Huguenots there was a host of *vaudois* and sorcerers, a great many of them in any case were from this profession, as experience has shown them being in these regions of Provins, for in several houses, using their spells and magic, they found goods which had been hidden and stored in various places ... Others had hidden their money in the linen and swaddling of babes in arms; the said *vaudois* were seen to divest mothers of their said children; this occurred in all the places where the said *vaudois* were living.

Further on in the text, in the year 1572, following the Massacre of St Bartholomew and the 'miracle' of the hawthorn which had flowered out of season in the Saints-Innocents cemetery in Paris, we read:

This shrub was visited and touched by everyone on the bark, branches, leaves and flowers to see whether it were not a trick worked by magic art or enchantment by enchanters, sorcerers or *vaudois* and it was found that it was not, it was the virtue of God that was working there.

Almost one century later, Gabriel Martin, abbot of Clausone in the Dauphiné wrote a pamphlet in all seriousness, published in Paris in 1641 entitled *The religion taught by the Devils to the Vaudois sorcerers of whom those of the so-called Reformed religion claim to be the descendants*. He most logically concluded: 'Why should we not say and shout abroad that the doctrine of the Religion claiming to be Reformed is the doctrine of the Devils?' The confusion was therefore maintained for a long time, doubtless because it was a simplistic, popular and therefore effective weapon with which to discredit the *vaudois*, that is to say the Waldensians, in the minds of their contemporaries. This was most certainly a considerable handicap which the Brothers had to overcome in their mission. Their public image became loathsome. While they did everything in their power to lead an evangelical life, they found themselves accused of heinous crimes against God, the Church and humanity. We can thus better understand why, exposed to widespread reprobation, they may have felt the need to draw nearer to other dissents with convictions similar to their own for which they had likewise been condemned by Rome. From the outset, this was the case with the Poor from northern Italy although it was quite a limited endeavour in the end. The most far-reaching movement of protest in religious, political, economic and social terms that Europe had ever known was to develop in the fifteenth century, however, in lands where the Waldensians were already present, taking root in Bohemia.

THE HUSSITES

Although there are various testimonies attesting the presence of 'heretics' in Bohemia from the beginning of the fourteenth century, we have little detail concerning their specific identity. In 1315, for example, fourteen heretics were burnt at the stake in Prague. Historians have put forward a wide range of theories: it has been said that they were Cathars, Waldensians, Beghards or Brothers of the Free Spirit, among others. We cannot discount the possibility that the same sort of syncretism had spread through the country as it had in Piedmont, which makes all attempts at identification rather speculative. For a long time it was believed that there was no evidence of Waldensians being present in the country until about 1360, when the Inquisition led by Henry of Olomouc was particularly severe in Styria. Research by Patschovsky, however, to which we have already referred, has established that as early as 1335, the inquisitor Gallus of Neuhaus had located Waldensian settlements particularly in the south on the Moravian border, in the Neuhaus area. Peter of Pillichdorf, a Viennese university professor and canon writing in 1395, maintained that the Inquisition had led a thousand 'Waldensians' to be converted in Thuringia, Brandenburg, Bohemia and Moravia. There is, of course, no way we can verify such allegations. Certain signs, however, enable us to trace what would appear to be an upsurge of Germanic Poor of Lyons in Bohemia at the very end of the fourteenth century. In other words, a solid presence had long been established when the Hussite revolution came to a head.

We have not the space here to retrace the astonishing story of this movement which stirred up an entire country, against which whole armies were pitted, which for years managed to defy princes and emperor, inquisitor, councils and the pope; in other words all the representatives of Church and state authority. We cannot consider here their religious beliefs based on the bible, the movement of anti-establish-ment protest rallying the poorest populations, the national character which marked the Bohemian people so strongly as they asserted their anti-German identity, the cultural revolution centred on the Czech language, the oratory powers of the impassioned popular preachers, the attempt to establish a new economy, the development of new fighting tactics on the battle field, the special role accorded to songs and finally the various trends which troubled, divided and eventually destroyed the movement and the bloody repression which followed. The reader wishing to study this would be well advised to turn to the works of Macek and Molnár which have the advantage of being scientifically thorough.

We shall consider only the elements of direct interest to us here, that is, those linked to the evolution of the Poor of Lyons. The Czech heretics were similarly named after their founder, Jan Hus, born in Bohemia in 1369. A priest, dean and then rector of Prague University, he was influenced by the teachings of another theologian and reformer, John Wyclif, the 'evangelical doctor' of Oxford. Hus voiced his beliefs in Latin and Czech in his virulent sermons and incisive writings directed against the Church. Excommunicated in 1411 and again in 1412, he was summoned to the Council of Constance in 1414. Accepting the safe-conduct issued by the emperor Sigismund of Luxembourg, he decided to attend. The Council condemned him and he was burnt at the stake, but his disciples saw him as a martyr and a patriot. His execution provoked the Hussite uprising which developed into a fully fledged insurrection when in 1419 the emperor succeeded his brother Wenceslas as king of Bohemia. The fathers of the Council of Constance reacted impassively to the situation, urging the sovereigns to launch a crusade to weed out the Bohemian heresy like that which had been led against Catharism in Languedoc. The emperor directed the offensive against the patriot–heretics and was only to be recognised as king of Bohemia in 1439 after the Iglau agreements. To what extent were the Poor of Lyons involved in this upheaval? To answer this question we must consider briefly how the Bohemian situation had evolved.

A number of studies which set out to establish the nature of relations between the Waldensians and the Hussites drew on the writings of the former to trace the increasingly important influence of the latter. The ensuing debate as to whether the Poor of Lyons had modified Hussite thought, or vice versa, is somewhat outmoded now. The question could not be settled once and for all, quite simply because the Poor of Lyons' writings, to which we shall return later, present the considerable drawback of not being dated; nor can a date easily be ascribed to them. No-one can, in any seriousness, maintain how influences were working without being in a position to determine the order in which documents being considered were written. In any case, from our present point of view, the debate is a relatively secondary one. It would appear that Hus had only a theoretical knowledge of the Waldensians' ideas. Being convinced of his orthodoxy, he refused to be equated with the 'Waldensian heresy'. His position was, however, relatively close to that of the Poor of Lyons, particularly as far as poverty and reading the bible were concerned, but he may not have known this. Besides, it is highly likely that, as a university master, he had little respect for preachers and writings lacking in scholastic method. From 1412, however, his attitude would appear to have altered. Fleeing the city of Prague, where an interdict was in force because of him, he lived as a preacher, doubtless visiting areas in the south of the country where the Poor of Lyons were present. Although nothing has been ascertained definitively as far as contacts between Hus and the Waldensians are concerned, there is no doubting that the reformer had modified his point of view. At this time, the theologian and university rector wrote, 'I have just understood that simple, poor preachers, poor laymen and even women are capable of defending the truth with more courage than the Doctors of the holy scriptures usually do.' There is no reason not to suppose that his meetings with the Poor of Lyons contributed to this evolution. On the other hand, nothing else can be asserted as far as Jan Hus himself is concerned.

We may thus wonder at what point the Hussites' original misgivings concerning the Poor of Lyons gave way to a more kindly disposition, if not more. Let us read Molnár on this question:

The spirited opposition to the trafficking of indulgences set within the events of 1412 reveals how much Matthew of Janov's, rather than Wyclif's, ecclesiology corresponded to the real situation. The minority Church of the saints, faithful to the simple tenets of the gospel but persecuted in the name of so-called Christianity which was a Christless travesty, was engaged in a spiritual combat for which it was unarmed in material terms. Deprived of all support from the public authorities, humble and ready to endure suffering, it believed solely in the Word as it had been preached, which came to be tangible in the communion of the eucharist. With such a vision of things, this Church was doubtless ready to recognise the affinities it shared in outlook with the Waldensians as soon as they came into contact. On a popular level, this meeting was soon to come about in southern Bohemia. On an intellectual level, it was facilitated in Prague thanks to theologians who encountered Waldensians from the Germanic countries.

Before the military operations were launched, the Hussite movement had found the symbol of union in the form of the chalice which was offered during the sacrament of the Last Supper to each lay person; it was an innovation whose roots went back to the primitive Church, whereas Rome would not accept communion with both species.

It was one of Hus's colleagues, Jacobellus of Stribro, another striking theologian who died in 1429, who first showed an interest in the history and testimonies of the 'Waldensians'. He recalled how, for the sake of the gospel, they had been victims of persecution for two centuries. That such an opinion should be expounded in Prague constituted a turning point. Succeeding Hus to the chair of the Bethlehem chapel at the University of Prague, which had become the only remaining moral and spiritual authority in Bohemia after the Council of Constance's prestige collapsed, Jacobellus of Stribro dared officially to defend the Waldensians who had until then been viewed with distrust, declaring that they were persecuted 'not for erring but because of the Lord's gospel'. The years 1415–16 marked a very clear evolution in relations between the two spiritual families, the Poor of Lyons and the Hussites. They also moved closer together in terms of religious options, as can be seen at the famous college 'At the Black Rose', the university house of the Bohemian nation at Prague University where prestigious teachers such as Friedrich Epinge and Peter and Nicholas of Dresden taught. Within a few years, the college became far more favourably disposed towards the Poor of Lyons. The Englishman Peter Payne, Wyclif's interpreter and a friend of Nicholas of Dresden, who settled in Bohemia at the end of 1414, was the first to have frequent contact with Vaudès's disciples in Germany. In their refusal of oaths and the death penalty he saw tenets common to his own evangelism and became convinced that the two causes should draw together. The radical Hussites thus appear to have been close to the Poor of Lyons. As in all movements, divergences and later a schism rapidly occurred between 'moderates' ready to adopt a compromise and 'radicals' who stuck fast to their principles. The latter included scholars from the college 'At the Black Rose' who considered reforming the Church by uniting the radical Hussites from Bohemia and the Poor of Lyons scattered throughout the Germanic lands.

In the spring of 1419, uprisings broke out. Public gatherings took place; the Utraquist mass (with communion in both elements) was celebrated by exhilarated peasants in the Bohemian hills. The radical rebels, whom the inspired clergy had roused with their biblical reminiscences and apocalyptic images as they spoke the Word of God saying they were climbing Mount Tabor (the mountain in Lower Galilee where Christ's transfiguration is traditionally believed to have taken place), decided in 1420 to found a town in southern Bohemia which they called 'Tabor', hence their name Taborites. When the news of the Taborites' peaceful uprising reached Prague, revolution broke out. The capital dreamt of founding a new state, as the model of universal reform, particularly since the king had just died. The Hussites refused to recognise the new sovereign, the emperor Sigismund. A compromise was drawn up by the moderates (the Four Articles), while the pope and the emperor prepared for war and Jan Zizka went to Tabor to recruit a popular army. This army had a resounding victory when it went to defend the besieged city of Prague and successfully drove back the crusaders of Sigismund and the papal nuncio Fernando. At this point, Jacobellus of Stribro began to distance himself, realising that the Waldensian positions had been incorporated into the Taborites' radical thinking. Some attacks were even directed against the Poor of Lyons. It is, however, clear that the Taborite movement went beyond the traditional pacifism of Vaudès's disciples. What indeed was their attitude?

Although we have no explicit testimony from the Poor of Lyons, we may be justified in supposing that the Bohemian brethren had evolved as far as adhering to the positions defended by the Hussites' radical wing. But we should not forget that they represented just a tiny minority from the European diaspora which, being used to living in clandestinity, tended to be very chary of calls to open reform. Payne tried to goad the German network of Waldensians into joining a sustained evangelical mission across Bohemia, but by 1425 it seemed that failure was inevitable. Meanwhile, a second crusade was defeated in October 1421 by Zatec's troops. The Hussites were proving to be invincible on their own territory but unable to spread further afield. While they were the victors in their own country, they were also limited within it. From 1428, the Taborite leaders began justifying a war of expansion; in March they left Bohemia, crossed Moravia and Slovakia and reached Silesia; in June they reached Nussdorf, near Vienna. The fate of the Hussite revolution, however, depended on the increasingly fragile union between the Taborites and Prague.

The Poor of Lyons followed the events in Bohemia with keen interest. A striking example of this is Friedrich Reiser, already mentioned above. He was an itinerant minister of the German brethren who travelled to Tabor. He had a clearly defined project: to unite with the Hussites to bring new life to a diaspora that was being stifled from the inside and weakened by perpetual persecutions from the outside. Reiser arrived just as theologians and Taborite leaders were trying to break down their isolated positions. He met up with Payne again and set about copying the New Testament, probably into German. Meanwhile, the offensive led by the Taborite leader Procope was still gaining ground. In February 1430, his forces crossed Saxony, Thuringia and Franconia and stopped outside Nuremberg. A conference between Catholic and Hussite theologians was even planned, but the pope's formal opposition prevented its taking place. In 1431, a group of Hussites met in Cracow with theologians from the university; the delegates included Procope, Payne and Reiser. In August 1431, a third crusading force succumbed to the Hussites, overawed by the Taborites' wagons and songs.

A curious event took place in September 1431. The Taborite bishop Nicholas of Pelhrimov came to Prague and ordained Friedrich Reiser, at his request. Reiser then stayed to serve the Taborites, without forgetting his brethren. It was probably he who acted as an intermediary, keeping the Alpine Brothers informed of the situation in central Europe. Also in 1431, the Dauphiné brotherhood undertook to raise funds to send to the Czechs, much to the consternation of French clergy who met in Bourges in February 1432. The proposed union between the Poor of Lyons and the Hussites thus had staunch supporters on both sides, Procope and Payne on one side and Reiser on the other. The three men met again in 1432 in Basel for discussions with the Council that had just opened there. While discussions were to focus on the Four Articles, the fathers of the Council only really intended to discuss the chalice, in the hope of possibly reaching a compromise. In this way, they skilfully attracted the Czech nobility and declared the Taborite position to be heretical, thus provoking a division between the radical Taborites and the Prague Utraquists. From this point on, the fate of the Hussites was decided. The Taborites were defeated in battle in Lipany in May 1434, during which Procope died. When a peace agreement was signed in 1436, the moderate Hussite Church was finally recognised. The political cause was lost. The grand project of universal reform had run its course; all that remained was the Taborite spirit which the popular preachers sustained tacitly or openly.

On a religious level, defeat signalled a return to pre-1420 positions and to non-violent means of defending reform. The positions maintained by the Poor of Lyons were thus reasserted. Reiser, who apparently assumed the title 'by the grace of God bishop of the faithful who deride Constantine's donation to the Roman Church', led a mission conforming to the Waldensian model which nevertheless clearly bore the Taborite stamp without the political connotation. In 1450, Reiser and his friends met again in Tabor where an itinerant mission into Germany was planned, led by four bishops. The leaders agreed to assemble every three years; meetings were held in Engelsdorf in 1453 and in Zatec in 1456. They should have met in Strasbourg in 1459, a mission that Hussites who remained faithful to the spirit of Tabor had decided to finance. When Reiser was arrested in early 1458 by the Inquisition of Strasbourg, thus causing the planned meeting to be cancelled, he was found to be carrying two hundred florins. Having recounted his life during the trial, he was tortured; he denounced several Brothers and recanted before being handed over to the secular arm and burnt at the stake on 6 March 1458.

In about 1457, the Unity of Czech Brethren was founded as a result of the meeting of the last radical Hussites with Taborite sympathies but who deliberately renounced all uses of violence. The movement broke from the moderate Utraquists over the question of apostolic succession. From 1467, the Unity began electing and training its own ministers, while the Utraquists continued to commend ordination by Catholic bishops. Another attempt to make common cause with the Poor of Lyons was encouraged by Stephen of Basel, called a 'Waldensian priest', but he was eventually burnt at the stake in Vienna. Relations were, however, maintained further afield, with the Poor of Brandenburg for example, or with the Italian brethren at the end of the century when Luc of Prague visited them.

All things considered, what can we conclude concerning relations between the Hussites and the Poor of Lyons? The two communities were certainly close in terms of their religious sensibility, particularly concerning the holy scriptures. They also drew together when attacked by the same inquisitorial procedures. The Poor of Bohemia were clearly very attracted by the Taborite movement which they in turn influenced; eager to be able to express their dissent openly, they adhered to its positions and in the end merged completely. Later, they formed parishes of the Unity of Czech Brethren. In this rather paradoxical and certainly revealing way, the Poor of Lyons who sympathised most with the Hussite reform were eventually engulfed by it. We are now certain that the entire Waldensian diaspora in Europe was in contact more or less regularly with the Unity, and that its ideas were influenced by Taborite positions. Can we, from here, conclude, as Molnár does, that an international Valdo-Hussite movement existed? Personally, I do not believe so for two reasons. The first is that it was more a project than a reality; the second is that, according to the testimonies in existence, the project was shared only by a small number of members.

By choosing to last, to survive, this was the risk the Poor of Lyons ran. If the fifteenth century appears a somewhat dark era in their history, it is not because documents are few and far between but rather because the community as a whole had been impaired. Their original unity had hardly lasted at all, not so much because of the internal dissension which various factions may have brought about, but because of their dispersion, for expansion in geographical terms was always achieved at the expense of communication, without which there is little or no common ground. The Brothers' popular image had also been defiled in the eyes of their contemporaries. The century-long work of the Inquisition was gradually bearing fruit. The most warped rumours were widely accepted by a population rendered excessively credulous by an environment which troubled them because they could not understand it. Not only were sorcerers called *vaudois* but Vaudès's followers were suspected of witchcraft. In the end, as their enemies attacked them on all sides, as trials seemed to become increasingly frequent (Alberto Cattaneo's crusade in the Dauphinois Alps in 1488–9, for example), the Poor of Lyons were tempted to ally themselves with other dissents, particularly when, as was the case with the Hussites, the dissents held sway over an entire country for some years and looked set to ensure the triumph of the Word of God. When alliances of this sort occurred, however, such as when the Bohemian communities merged with the Unity of Czech Brethren, it was at the cost of their own originality, as a result of being so cut off from their Brothers in the west with whom links were clearly becoming strained. After tentatively surviving for three centuries, this was the situation of the Poor of Lyons at the beginning of what are known as modern times.

We shall now, however, interrupt the chronological sequence that has been followed so far. Indeed, before continuing with what will be the final stage of the adventure, a pause is necessary to consider certain structural elements of the original movement in Lyons. There were important aspects which were not merely a result of the conditions and the times, even if minor differences of time and place can be identified. The dissent cannot be properly understood if we fail to examine three of these characteristics, which may have been innate or acquired but were, in any case, essential components that will structure the next three stages of our study: clandestinity, which came to be a lifestyle; organisation, the essential prop for survival; and literature, a second culture in itself.

BIBLIOGRAPHY

Audisio G., *Une grande migration alpine en Provence* (1460–1560). Turin, 1989.
  'Un exode vaudois organisé: Marseille–Naples (1477)'. In *Histoire et société.*
  Mélanges G. Dubuy. 4 vols., Aix-en-Provence, 1992, vol. I, pp. 198–208.
Cegna, R., *Fede ed etica valdese nel quattrocento.* Turin, 1982.
Comba, R., *La popolazione in Piemonte sul finire del Medio Evo. Ricerche di demografia storica.* Turin, 1977.
Duverger, A., *La vauderie dans les états de Philippe le Bon.* Arras, 1885.
Gonnet, G., La 'vauderie d'Arras'. In *I valdesi e l'Europa.* Torre Pellice, 1982, pp. 99–113.
Macek, J., *Jean Hus et les traditions hussites.* Paris, 1973.
Marx, J., *L'inquisition en Dauphiné.* Paris, 1914; reprinted Marseilles, 1978.

Molnár, A., 'Les vaudois en Bohême avant la révolution hussite'. *Bollettino della Società di Studi Valdesi* 116, 1964, pp. 3–17.

'Les vaudois et les hussites'. *Ibid.* 136, 1974, pp. 27–35.

Jean Hus, Paris and Lausanne, 1978.

Tapié, V.-L., *Une église tchèque au XVe siècle: l'Unité des Frères*. Paris, 1934.

Vinay, V., 'Friedrich Reiser e la diaspora valdese di lingua tedesca nel XV° secolo'. *Bollettino della Società di Studi Valdesi* 109, 1961, pp. 35–56.

$$5$$

THE CONSTRAINTS OF A LIFE IN HIDING

The original inspiration of Valdès was based on spreading the Word of God and encouraging men and women to be converted, and this shaped the lives led by his friends and disciples who became the movement's preachers. Their preaching obviously had to be open and public, and continued to be so as long as the decrees concerning their exclusion were not put into practice. During the thirteenth century, however, the Poor of Lyons were forced into hiding, as all surviving records confirm. Although their clandestinity was not an intrinsic part of the movement, it was to last as long as the movement itself, inevitably marking it so profoundly that it came to constitute an essential, even congenital feature. It is impossible to understand what these people's lives must have been like if, even momentarily, we lose sight of the fact that while there may have been periods of relative calm, persecution could start again at any moment. The truth of the matter is that if reprisals eased off from time to time, they never really came to an end. How can we possibly apprehend the complexity of the situation and the ambivalent attitudes which sometimes appeared, or evaluate how difficult relations were, making their survival over the centuries into a real exploit, if we fail to take into account one of the most deeply rooted aspects of the community's state of mind, that is, their awareness of being hunted down? Members had to be forever vigilant, measuring the importance of their words and deeds. Can anyone who has not experienced such a situation really imagine what it was like? However habitual it was, it was nonetheless dramatic. Convinced that they had access to an essential truth which was vital for their own salvation and that of their fellows, they felt the impelling need to spread the word, or at least to preserve it and pass it on whilst being officially forbidden to do so and prevented in various practical ways; they were forcibly obliged not only to hide their convictions but to allay suspicion by paying lip-service to opinions they reproved. The situation lasted years, even a whole lifetime, for centuries on end. How can an individual or a society forced to live in this way not fall prey to a sort of schizophrenia which for survival's sake they wittingly had to maintain?

Both Church people and dissenters were unanimous in recording that the Poor of Lyons went into hiding. The two sides equally agreed that it was a sign of weakness, if not a fault or a blemish on their identity. The only real difference was that, as far as the Brothers were concerned, it was a stopgap measure. This can be seen in the answer given by the young preacher Pierre Griot, questioned by the inquisitor in Provence in 1532 as to 'whether it is not wrong to teach and preach a particular doctrine secretly; he answers that it is wrong to hide the truth'. The two sides, however, did not attribute their secrecy to the same cause. When witnesses or those accused of Waldensian heresy spoke, they all maintained that they had behaved in this way by force. This is illustrated by the dialogue between Pierre Griot and the Dominican Jean of Roma:

So why they are ashamed to preach their doctrine in public,
– he answers that he believes it is out of fear.
Questioned as to whether their doctrine is good or bad,
– he says that they believe it is good.
Questioned, since they think it is good, why they do not preach in public
– says in reply that it is from fear.

The same reason was put forward by the preachers Morel and Masson when, in 1530, speaking openly and freely this time, they presented their community to Oecolampadius, the reformer of Basel. It was the reprisals that were responsible for both the diaspora and clandestinity: 'As a result of being frequently persecuted, our people have been dispersed across many lands ... We certainly do not dare to show ourselves publicly in any place.' The tone of their statements suggests a two-sided avowal that is not without contradictions: dissimulation was necessary and so justifiable; at the same time it was a sign of fear, and so a source of guilt.

If persecutors and persecuted alike were unanimous both in identifying their clandestinity and in considering it to be wrong, opinions differed over its significance. Interpretations drew in part on the question of age. As we saw in previous chapters, the movement's 'novelty' was often used in the courts as an argument with which to prove Waldensians guilty of propounding erroneous doctrines. On the same grounds, the Poor of Lyons claimed their genealogy went back to pope Sylvester or even the apostles. Their ideas clashed in a similar fashion when interpreting their clandestinity. As far as the inquisitors were concerned, proclaiming the Word of God was a sign of the truth; dealing in secrets amounted to abetting error. This is illustrated by Jean of Roma's hand-written treatise *Declaratio infelicis secte valdensium* against the Waldensian sect completed in 1533. Having established that the sect was new because it could only be traced back to 'Peter Valdo' of Lyons in about 1230 (*sic*), he writes, 'Despite its being condemned, the said sect still persevered and, like the snake which slithers secretly and the fox which lurks in its den, it has lasted.' We should note in passing that, from the traditional arsenal of zoological similes which every inquisitor kept at hand, Jean of Roma selected those animals which above all connoted craftiness, duplicity and wiliness. Is there any need to add that the Poor of Lyons did not see things in the same light? Whilst admitting that their clandestinity was a sign of weakness, they blamed the Church for persecuting them and so forcing them into hiding. It was as simple as that. This amounted to saying that, as far as they were concerned, preaching in opportune or stricken times was less important than keeping alight the flame of truth and passing it on to the next generation, even if this meant hiding it under a bushel if needs be. As we will see in the next chapter, the nature of the preachers' mission had radically changed.

We should, however, be careful not to misinterpret the situation. At no time did the Poor of Lyons justify their attitude. On the contrary they were ashamed of it and wished things were otherwise. It was therefore a far cry from what Calvin, in 1540, called 'Nicodemism' – religious behaviour which he stigmatised, for it combined, in a deliberate and calculated manner, adhering tacitly to the Reformation, whilst continuing to maintain Catholic appearances, without being in the slightest troubled by this duplicity. The Waldensian Brothers were truly perturbed by their situation and found the perpetual tension difficult to accept, particularly since one may wonder if they really managed to live in disguise. Generally speaking, is it really possible to hide the truth of one's identity over a long period of time? How is it possible to ensure one never lets slip a word, a gesture or a reaction which would instantly be picked up and interpreted by a suspicious neighbour, offering a glimpse of the person's intimate convictions? Can self-repression, on both an individual and a collective level, be total and lasting? My own answer, which constitutes one of the presuppositions on which my approach to history is based, is that in time it will either break down or the dissimulated identity will be lost altogether. Moreover, if this is true in general, how much more fitting is it in the case of the Poor of Lyons.

As we have seen, the conditions in which they lived were particularly exacting and some of their precepts were impossible to dissemble. Rather than passing unnoticed, such rigorous laws revealed to people round about the beliefs of the men and women who respected them. We might say that 'practising Waldensianism' amounted to declaring oneself to be different, putting one's life in danger and denouncing oneself. Was this possible? Was it not in contradiction with the duty of passing on the truth? Was it not impossible to resolve such a dilemma? It was essential that a solution be found, if not on a theoretical level by doctors of theology, at least on an empirical level in their daily life, without which the Brothers would all have been effectively and quite rapidly wiped out. We know this not to have been the case, so how did the Poor of Lyons manage to maintain their identity based on stringent evangelical principles and to preserve themselves from extinction which would have been the inevitable result of applying these strict principles? We have reached a point in our study which is fascinating from the point of view of human behaviour.

WORDS AND ACTIONS

To appreciate the conclusions reached by the analyses presented below, the reader should bear in mind the characteristics specific to the Poor of Lyons, on which their difference and hence their dissent was based, that we examined earlier. To have an overview of the diaspora in spatial terms and the movement as a whole in chronological terms, we have to leave aside individual opinions and trends, such as isolated factors present only at a certain time or in one particular community of Brothers. Details and even nuances must be temporarily disregarded to enable us to draw up generalisations. Here, we shall restrict ourselves to the founding tenets, those recognised as such by inquisitors and the Poor of Lyons alike, recurring in all the various settlements across Europe throughout their history, which can be vouched for by testimonies in one form or another. On the other hand, to assess the significance of a religious dissent, our enquiry cannot limit itself merely to these founding traits. Certain aspects, essential as they may have been on a theological level, may have proved inconsequential in practical terms; conversely, others of little doctrinal significance may have proved of such importance in the manner in which the community practised their religion on a daily basis that they developed into behavioural patterns, if not clear signs of identity, easy to pinpoint everywhere.

Let us take two relatively recent examples to illustrate these rather abstract reflections. In the late 1960s, debates which were sometimes extremely heated broke out within religious communities in France, to the point of stirring up lasting resentment. What was so important at the heart of the matter that it created unyielding divisions? For Catholics, the debate concerned the use of Latin for the mass and the need for clerics to wear cassocks; for Protestants, the discussions were centred on robes worn by pastors and the singing of psalms. In theological terms, the stakes were non-existent; on a practical level, the answers to each of the questions revealed particular concepts of religion, which became 'signs', rallying points and the proof of a certain identity. From a doctrinal point of view, the matter was of little importance, but in affective terms it was loaded. On the other hand, essential questions concerning dogma were often not developed into concrete issues; as a result, members of the Church performing the same rites could well interpret them in a diverging or even contradictory manner. Baptising one's child, for instance, can be an act of faith, of social convention, of superstition or indeed a mixture of the three. When a person goes to confession, who can say whether it is because they believe in the sacrament, because they feel individual or collective pressure to do so or because it is a form of therapeutic counselling? Who would dare judge merely from watching the ceremony whether a communicant participating in mass or the Lord's Supper interprets the rite in the manner of a Catholic (transubstantiation), Lutheran (consubstantiation), Calvinist (spiritual presence), or Zwinglian (presence through the community)? And this is still presuming the communicant has a clearly analysed opinion which he or she would be capable of expressing.

As far as the Poor of Lyons are concerned, we need to retain from the fundamental issues distinguishing them from Roman Catholics only those which were expressed in real terms by a concrete unequivocal attitude, which are easy to interpret and whose meaning is clear. As has already been seen, there is only one surviving testimony from the community itself that was not extracted under threat and torture. It is the report drawn up by Morel and Masson in 1530 to which reference has already been made and to which we shall return. The greater part of our knowledge of the community comes from its enemies. Consequently, we should leave aside theological matters bearing on dogma or essential moral doctrine which detractors too easily deformed. The question we must ask is the following: in what ways did the Poor of Lyons differ from their contemporaries in the religious lives they led? How did they distinguish themselves from the Roman Catholic context, to the extent that the Roman Church could no longer tolerate their existence? Bearing in mind the reflections above, we shall concentrate on the directives the Waldensians imposed on themselves which defined their

religious originality and found clear, concrete expression in their daily
life. How can these be recognised? One approach is by way of the
declarations made by those accused of Waldensian heresy in courts of
justice. These should then be set against declarations at the end of the
period under examination. Were the Poor of Lyons still faithful to
Vaudès's original inspiration in the sixteenth century, or had time got the
better of its rigour, toning down or even deforming its initial evangelical
character? It is, moreover, essential to consider the ideas the Waldensians
voiced openly rather than under duress. Last of all, it is not enough
merely to examine intentions and theoretical positions, sincere as they
may have been, without examining how these were applied and even
altered in real life. In other words, did the Poor of Lyons really adhere to
the rules of evangelical life to which they claimed to be devoted?

Surviving documents enable us to answer these three levels of enquiry
as far as the late fifteenth and early sixteenth century are concerned. First,
we have a series of trials from the era, particularly those held in
Piedmont, Provence and the Dauphiné. These fit into the long series of
judicial proceedings against heresy which we have evoked time and time
again. We have, however, established that, in terms of beliefs, these must
not immediately be taken at face value. Secondly, an exceptional
document has survived from the Poor of Lyons, which is a rare and
unexpected resource, in the form of the report by Georges Morel and
Pierre Masson. In 1530, these two preachers had been delegated by their
fellows to present the community of the Poor of Lyons to the reformers
Oecolampadius in Basel and Bucer in Strasbourg and to seek their advice
on a series of problems faced by the community concerning the
Reformation, hence the document's name *peticions*. The document is a
report dealing with each point in three parts: the Brothers' beliefs and
practices, the question addressed to the reformers and their answers given
individually. We therefore have a real account of the community drawn
up by the leaders who, for once, were speaking of their own accord. The
testimony is, however, limited, invaluable as it may be. It asserts
principles and positions which, although they are not only theoretical,
for practical preoccupations abound, are nevertheless expounded by the
community's leaders, and so from a certain distance. How did these
principles fare in the daily, clandestine lives of the faithful? Thirdly,
drawing on the fine series of notaries' registers in Provence, I have
managed to answer this question as far as the Poor of Lyons settled in the
Luberon were concerned at the end of our period, that is between 1460
and 1560. In this way, for the first and only time in their history, we
have the advantage of bringing together three sources of light concerning
the Waldensians: judicial evidence, inside testimonies and notarial deeds.

CHANGE AND CONTINUITY

The founding principles differentiating the Poor of Lyons from Roman Catholics were examined in chapter 3. There is no point recalling what they had in common, for it is their 'dissension' which interests us here. In fact, the nine distinguishing criteria defined above (falsehood, oaths, purgatory, confession, donatism, capital punishment, the eucharist, ecclesiastical power and saints), of a varied nature and of variable importance, were all derived from stands taken over two issues, evangelism and donatism; in other words two principles in the mathematical sense of the term, or two axioms which represented the matrix of the whole dissent. As a result of respecting the gospel to the letter, the community rejected a series of compromises or beliefs; because they believed sacraments administered by unworthy clergymen were invalid, they challenged the rights of the priesthood and assigned the priests' duties to their own preachers. How had the Waldensian dissent developed by the sixteenth century?

The nine 'distinctions' did not necessarily find expression in clear, unequivocal, concrete attitudes; this was the case for falsehood and capital punishment, for example. Their stand against the death penalty could only be theoretical since there was no town or region in which Waldensians had influence over the civil magistrature. The second question put to the Reformers, however, concerned this issue: 'Has God commanded authorities or magistrates to punish murderers, thieves and delinquents by death or by other sentences?' They refer to Ezekiel 33 : 11 where it is stated that God does not seek the death of the sinner but desires that he should be converted and live. It was a crucial matter since they were faced with the case of the 'treacherous false followers' who, in return for payments, denounced the 'Waldensian doctors'. Could such traitors be killed? Valdès's beliefs were thus still being debated in the Renaissance era, although such ideas could never be applied in their daily lives since the Waldensians were always on the receiving end where justice was concerned; they never defined or applied the law.

On a different level, it is equally impossible to check whether, as far as falsehood was concerned, their adamant rejection of all lies was effectively applied in their day-to-day existence. No-one can say whether they were really more sincere than those around them. When, during trials, the inquisitor asked suspects what their preachers had taught them, the question of falsehood sometimes arose. In 1392, Herman Gossaw, on trial in Stettin, declared he had been born into the Waldensian sect to which his parents belonged; asked to summarise the beliefs they had taught him, he listed the following: 'do not swear, do not lie, do not malign others, do not lose your temper, do not bear false witness, and they forbade him to do other reprehensible deeds'. This was, however, at the end of the fourteenth century. Certain bearings were lost after this time. The thirty-two errors of the Bohemian Poor listed in 1420 made no mention of this point. And while falsehood does figure among the sixty-three errors ascribed in 1511 to the Waldensians in Paesana in Piedmont, the general tone of the document is so harsh and the positions held so radical that one wonders whether it was really a trial of genuine Poor of Lyons. Claude Seyssel, archbishop of Turin, who wrote a treatise against the Waldensians after visiting 'heretical' parishes in his diocese in 1517, did, however, underline the traditional stand taken by the Waldensian community. Then again, he may well have been doing no more than recounting what had once applied but had since ceased to be so. Whatever the case may be, this original, evangelical precept did not figure in the report by Morel and Masson, enabling us to surmise that four centuries on, the question of falsehood had lost ground and was no longer a basic rule for the Poor of Lyons. This may have been because they had given up defending a tenet that never really developed beyond a theoretical level.

As far as the sacraments were concerned, the Poor of Lyons recognised the seven accepted by the Roman Church, particularly honouring the Lord's Supper and confession. Their holy communion was distinguished by being celebrated only once a year, on Maundy Thursday, and by having three species. As well as bread and wine, they blessed and shared fish, in remembrance of Christ's feeding of the five thousand. This practice would seem to have faded. Morel and Masson make no mention of it other than stating clearly that the Poor of Lyons acknowledge the seven traditional sacraments and, concerning the eucharist, believe in transubstantiation as does the Roman Church. During the trials, there is no reference to the issue; had the inquisitors come across such a 'heretical' practice, they would certainly have referred to it. Confession, on the other hand, was staunchly maintained, revealing the devotees' need for the rite and the support it offered them. From Pomerania to Piedmont, from the Dauphiné and Austria to Provence, all the trials bring up the question of confessing to the preachers. It is acknowledged in the 1530 *peticions*; the two envoys declare that they hear the secret, individual confessions of their people. The rite is beyond doubt; we shall be returning to it in the next chapter, which deals with the preachers.

Ecclesiastical power was challenged by Waldensians everywhere. This should have had formidable consequences, for it implied that they should refuse to respect all decisions made by the authorities, whose very legitimacy they threw into question. This was obviously not the way things worked out. Had the Poor of Lyons refused to obey the pope, bishops and priests, it would have amounted to open revolt, a real trial of strength. They would have been physically eliminated without pity, the secular arm backing up the Church authorities. But the Poor of Lyons survived well into the sixteenth century, proof that they could not put into practice their theoretical stand against ecclesiastical power. We can indeed note that they observed Church rulings as much as anyone else did. They probably avoided buying indulgences, fasting and abstinence on certain days, but we have no real proof. This suggests they were in any case discreet about it, in all likelihood keeping provocative beliefs within the family in some cases. The matter was not taken up, for if there had been open conflict, documents would have survived informing us about it.

It is doubtful whether these five issues would have brought the dissenters to the suspicious attention of the authorities. Two of the five, the absolute refusal of lies and the annual communion in three species, had more or less fallen out of use. No opportunity arose enabling them to put into practice their rejection of the death penalty. As for confession to their preachers, it was of course a compromising act but, if kept secret, it could pass unnoticed. Last of all, the doubts expressed over clerical power remained theoretical. In other words, these beliefs were rarely given expression by clear acts that could identify people as members of the Waldensian movement and so betray those who upheld them. Had nothing else characterised the Poor of Lyons, they would have survived even though their identity would have been vague. Indeed, they would have been assimilated into the Roman Church, becoming 'Poor Catholics'. But their story does not end like this. We should therefore try to examine the four other distinguishing characteristics to see which would have marked them outwardly, even if such external expression may sometimes have been ambivalent, to say the least. For the Poor of Lyons certainly lived a double life. On the one hand, they behaved to all appearances like Catholics to safeguard their relative tranquillity; on the other, they observed a certain number of rites and habits among themselves which ensured that the community continued to exist.

THE CORROSIVE EFFECTS OF TIME

The primary result of their double life was to attenuate those principles which were too binding to pass unnoticed. The five characteristics we have just considered tended to become either confidential or purely theoretical. What about the four others? The power of saints and the Virgin Mary was thrown into question everywhere. The second error of the 'Waldensian heretics' in Bohemia was maintaining that 'the blessed Virgin and the saints in general should be neither adored or invoked'. When interrogated in 1451, Philip Regis from the San Martino valley in Piedmont declared, 'No saint has the power to realise actions or miracles or bestow grace, which God alone can do.' Pierre Crespin from the diocese of Embrun in the Dauphiné recanted in 1489, believing, among other errors, that 'God alone should be adored and invoked in prayer, not the saints.' Monet Rey, from Saint-Mamans near Valence, confirmed in 1494, 'Prayers should not be addressed to the saints; they cannot help us; God alone can.' Claude Seyssel denounced as the ninth error of the Waldensians the fact that 'they refuse to honour the saints'. This denial of the power of saints could not be clearer or more widespread. In concrete terms, it meant working on saints' days, which the Church had declared public holidays, not revering statues and various images of saints, abjuring the cult of relics and avoiding pilgrimages. Was it realistic or even possible to do so? Besides fifty-two Sundays, the liturgical year set aside almost the same number of feast-days generally dedicated to the Virgin and the saints. It is highly unlikely that the Poor of Lyons or indeed anyone managed to get round the obligation to go to mass at least on those days. We have documentary evidence of this, as will be seen below. In certain statements during the trials, moreover, a more moderate declaration often followed a categorical denial. Monet Rey, for example, after voicing the intransigent attitude quoted above, then added, 'Sundays must be more solemn than any other feast-days; other feast-days were invented by the Church, they do not have to be celebrated; people can even work on these days other than on those honouring the apostles and other similarly important days.' This can be interpreted in diverse ways. But what else could they have done? At the most, they managed to refrain from excessive zeal, but they could hardly avoid all general practices and traditions, although they could think what they liked about them. Denying the cult of saints therefore did not necessarily mean assuming clear-cut, deliberately provocative attitudes.

SAILING UNDER FALSE COLOURS

It is not because a minority plays down its differences that it will be allowed to survive – this would be too low a price paid to the mainstream. A positive tribute also has to be paid to the majority; actions have to be performed according to the prevailing customs. This can be borne out by the last three characteristics of the Poor of Lyons listed above. Donatism undeniably constituted one of the founding principles of their dissent. A whole series of unorthodox stands resulted from their attitude over the worthiness of a minister and the validity of the sacrament. To a certain extent, the opinion had little effect in practice, as we saw above. One easily verified case in point concerned payment of tithes. The *dîme*, a proportional tithe, was levied on harvests and payable to the clergy who justified it on the grounds that they had spiritual and charitable responsibilities to carry out in the interests of society. The state supported their view.

The position maintained by the Poor of Lyons, deriving from their donatist tendencies, proved both original and subversive. They maintained that this tax should be paid only to good priests, feeling free to withhold it from others. This was the situation the young preacher Pierre Griot described to the inquisitor Jean of Roma who interrogated him in 1532 in Apt, in Provence: 'The aforementioned Waldensians state that the laity must pay tithes to the said people of the Church, so long as these people are good and fulfil their roles as they should; otherwise, there is no sin in withholding their tithes when the priests do not behave as they should.' This position, which was already potentially awkward, could sometimes develop into a clear-cut refusal to pay at all, as a shepherd from the Luberon explained somewhat carelessly to a canon from Apt with whom he was travelling on 3 May 1532: 'When I make my will, I shall forbid my children ever to pay tithes.' When the cleric enquired, 'Why is that? Are you mad?', the shepherd retorted, 'God never commanded us to pay tithes for if He had done so, it would be the same for everyone but some pay 20 per cent, others 15, others 10.' This stolid common sense threw into question the very manner in which society had functioned until then. This does not, however, mean that the Poor of Lyons categorically refused to pay taxes to the Church. There are no records clearly signalling this. On the contrary, I even came across a labourer, Colet Monastier, from Lourmarin in the Luberon who collected tithes on lands belonging to the bishop of Senez in Provence in three villages largely populated by Waldensians. Not only did the Poor of Lyons pay their tithes, to absentee prelates at that, but some of them even acted as their tithe-proctors. Hence it can again be seen that the Poor of Lyons' donatist attitude regarding the payment of tithes was no more likely to draw attention to their community than was their behaviour concerning the cult of saints. We are thus left with the last two distinctions, which can be traced back to the movement's beginnings: the stand over taking oaths and the existence of purgatory.

From their earliest days the Poor of Lyons gave great importance to the question of refusing to take oaths and to swear in any form, as a result of interpreting exhortations in the gospel to the letter. We have seen the sort of ruses and verbal contortions they employed to evade a practice around which medieval society was organised. Was the initial injunction, binding and absolute as it was, still applied four centuries later? Morel and Masson's report suggests that it was, stating, 'Our people are totally forbidden to take oaths.' Such intransigence was evidently problematic, as a question the two envoys asked Oecolampadius shows: 'Are all oaths forbidden for fear of committing a mortal sin?' For centuries, the Poor of Lyons had unanimously held this to be the case; it would now appear that they had begun to have doubts about their reading of the bible. In other words, their rigid position was no longer tenable in practice. From as early as the fourteenth century, in fact, inquisitors had observed that Waldensians would accept certain exceptions to the rule, such as swearing on oath when on trial so as not to give themselves away.

By the fifteenth and sixteenth century, such behaviour was no longer exceptional. By this time, the Poor of Lyons took oaths as often as other members of the local society, to seal contracts between lords and communities, to complete deeds concerning property and to renew pledges of homage paid to feudal superiors. In 1504, the newly arrived inhabitants of Mérindol in Provence, for example, swore before their temporal lord 'on the holy gospel of God, with their right hand on the holy scriptures'. Similarly, the new settlers arriving in 1495 in Cabrières-d'Aigues, in the same province, individually promised 'and swore to and on the holy gospel of God, laying their hand on the sacrosanct Scriptures'. These were essentially rare occurrences for a local community. But there are also examples of betrothed couples, who, like the settlers above, were undoubtedly Poor of Lyons, promising to get married 'on the holy gospel of God which they touched physically' when the wedding contract was being drawn up by the notary, a perfectly common undertaking at the time in the south of France. Nearly a thousand future brides and grooms living in a 'Waldensian' village in the Luberon drew up marriage contracts in this way between 1460 and 1560; in 89 per cent of cases specific reference is made to an oath being taken. For legal reasons, perhaps, the Poor of Lyons had indeed given up too rigid a tenet that had proved impossible to apply, despite its deriving from one of their original principles based directly on the holy scriptures.

Denying the existence of purgatory was equally a specific characteristic of original Waldensianism. In the last century of their existence, the Poor of Lyons were still upholding their position. All sources are unanimous on this point, from the trials to the polemical treatises and the 1530 *peticions*. The third 'error' of the Bohemian brethren in 1420 stated, 'There is no purgatory, only heaven and hell.' The maxim recurs like a leitmotif during the great crusade against the Waldensians of the Dauphiné in 1488–9: 'In the hereafter, there are but two ways: paradise and hell.' In his *Adversus errores valdensium* of 1520, the archbishop of Turin underlined the same error. The Dominican Jean of Roma was not being calumnious when he accepted as the foremost indictment against the defendant in 1532 that 'the aforementioned Griot began by maintaining that purgatory did not exist in the next world'. The opinion was corroborated by Morel and Masson's report of the same era: 'We categorically deny the existence of purgatory, an invention of the Antichrist.' As far as proclamations of theory are concerned, it is clear that their refutation is complete and unmitigated. If one denies the existence of this transitory place of suffering in the hereafter, however, one should logically also reject 'suffrages' for the dead in the form of gifts, prayers, absolutions, masses and novenas. All such shows of piety were easy to detect in the village communities, particularly since the local clergy counted on such 'casual offerings' to swell their incomes and were therefore vigilant to ensure due payments were made. Could the Poor of Lyons have managed to evade these customs, imperative as they were? Until a few years ago, we might have assumed this to be the case, imagining priests to have been party to it in some way, or at least to have turned a blind eye. An inquisitor from the Dauphiné indeed wrote in 1507 that, according to the Waldensians, 'no gifts should be made, and no prayers said for the dead', but he added: 'In their testaments and *causa mortis* donations, to expiate and redeem their souls, and those of their predecessors and the sins they committed, they order and request that offerings be made at the doors of their parish churches or elsewhere and also that masses and other suffrages be said, requesting novenas with the usual offerings.' This isolated testimony, however, was previously discounted by historians who attributed it to a malevolent or misinformed cleric.

My research based on Provence, particularly that drawing on wills, enabled me, however, to substantiate the inquisitor's declaration. We must first recall that it was then common practice for the rural populations in the south of France to make out their wills in the presence of a notary. Moreover, notaries' registers in the region are amongst the richest and most complete of those preserved in Europe. Lastly, we should bear in mind that wills in the past comprised a first part, often more important than the second, stipulating spiritual measures to be taken, detailing the various gifts and pious legacies left to ensure that the testator's soul, and the souls of his deceased family, should rest in peace. The testator's last wishes concerning bequests came after these spiritual considerations. In Provence, it was customary for the testator, having

commended his soul to God, the Virgin and the saints, at least to order
for the 'salvation of his soul' and 'to redeem his sins' full mass (mass that
was sung, called a *cantar*) for the day of the funeral, a novena (nine
masses), a cantar to be held at the end of the novena and, a year later, on
the anniversary of his death, an 'end of year' cantar. I was able to trace
200 wills drawn up by Waldensians from the Luberon. About 80 per cent
of these request such ceremonies. Can one still believe priests were
conniving and that these clauses in the will remained a dead letter? It is
highly improbable, considering the financial gains the priests stood to
make and also the superstitious mentality which prevailed at the time,
when no-one would have dared to disregard the last wishes of a dead
person. Furthermore, there is formal proof bearing out these practices.
The priest in Roussillon, a village with a large Waldensian population,
kept an account book. All burials which took place between 1536 and
1559 are recorded there, along with the sum of money paid for each one.
Funerals for members of the Poor of Lyons frequently figure in his
accounts. Let us therefore accept as fact that, although they staunchly
denied the existence of purgatory, the Poor of Lyons in fact behaved like
their Roman Catholic neighbours, ordering masses and suffrages so that
the souls of their dead might rest in peace. Judging by appearances, the
nine precepts at the origins of the Waldensian movement, which had so
inspired their initial momentum, would seem to have succumbed to the
pressures of time, being pared down from century to century by the
combined pressure of persecution, dispersion and their instinct for
survival.

Doubts can be traced as far back as the late fourteenth century during
Peter Zwicker's interrogations in Stettin. Two defendants, Sybe Hut-
vilter and Mathias Joris, questioned in 1392 and 1393, declared, 'that
there are only two ways after death' but each added that he 'believed' or
'hoped' in purgatory. A third defendant, Cune Gyrswalde testified that
'he believed there were only two ways after this life, and there was no
purgatory but he prayed for the dead so that God might have pity on
them'. Yet another suspect, Gyrdrud, wife of Tyde Cremer, made the
same declaration. Herman Rudeger 'had heard that God alone should be
adored and invoked and he believed this; however, when in need, he
invoked the blessed Virgin Mary'. Ghertrud, wife of Claus Walther,
admitted that she invoked the Virgin Mary but not the saints. There is
the case of Katherina, wife of Tyde Sachze, who believed in relics as
long as you repented. These confessions enable us to appreciate the gap
that could exist between principles and their application in daily life, and
also between preachers' words and devotees' understanding. All in all,
the Poor of· Lyons behaved outwardly like their Roman Catholic

counterparts. We know this to have been the case throughout the diaspora, leading to charges of duplicity by the inquisitors. As far as Provence is concerned, my research permits me to maintain that the Poor of Lyons attended compulsory mass on Sundays and on feast-days, and went to confession and communion once a year, as every Christian had been required to do since the Fourth Lateran Council in 1215; they had their children baptised by the parish priest and paid offerings to the local clergy as frequently as other parishioners. Morel and Masson confirm this: 'It is the members of the Antichrist, not we, who administer the signs of the sacrament to our people ... For we are forced to go to see and hear the abominations of the Antichrist.' Did these liturgical ceremonies which the Poor of Lyons attended regularly throughout the year really appear as 'abominations'? There is no proof allowing us to be at all certain. But it was these varied, somewhat troubling concessions that had ensured the Poor of Lyons if not the right to survive, at least the possibility of doing so.

There is no escaping the fact that the situation is perplexing. As time went by, certain basic tenets were 'overlooked' and others were played down; we are led to wonder how these Christians continued to differ from others, considering, first, the divergence, that some might call a contradiction, between principles in theory and their application from day to day; second, the systematic, organised camouflage of their beliefs; and lastly, their participation in the life of the parish. As a result of their clandestinity and the outward shows they had to maintain, had they not ended up resembling Catholics to the point of being assimilated again, perhaps with just a touch of originality which was more a matter of reasonable, individual sensitivity than of reprobate and dangerous heretical dissent? At best, was persecution not maintained against heretics in the name of their predecessors' beliefs which had since been lost or forgotten? The truth is that if the Poor of Lyons in the sixteenth century continued to use their name, embrace their past, form a community that was consciously different and accept the pressures of their dissent, suffering vexation and persecution in its name, then they had, despite all appearances to the contrary, maintained a vital and enduring hub of beliefs and practices which fed their strength, nurturing their inspiration, their soul and their identity.

AN IDENTITY

There is clear proof that there were fluctuations and hesitations over traditional beliefs within the Waldensian diaspora. In fact, the most distant successors sometimes bore little resemblance to Valdès's preachers

from Lyons. Their dispersion across Europe had considerable consequences on the different religious sensibilities of the Latin and Germanic
communities, making at best distant relatives of the brethren. A sense of
belonging to the same community still persisted, however. Persecution
doubtless played an important part in reinforcing links which might
otherwise have died away. But the sense of unity which inspired the
Poor of Lyons cannot be explained by the Church's militant hostility
alone, even if it was enacted by zealous inquisitors backed up by the
secular arm. But this would not explain why the community never fused
with other dissenters to the point of disappearing in the course of the
fourteenth and fifteenth centuries. If this did not happen, it was because,
notwithstanding the ways in which the movement evolved, they still
conserved certain characteristics. They held out and, in the Renaissance
period, were still clearly aware that they formed a clear religious entity
that was distinct from both the Roman Church and other dissenting
trends. Their society was very structured, as Morel and Masson's 1530
report makes clear by the frequent repetitions of the terms 'our ministers'
and 'our people'. Despite doubts and hesitations, theirs was a community
in the full sense of the term, resolving matters of integration and
excommunication, administration and social organisation. The survival
of the Poor of Lyons was not only individual but collective. To account
for this fact, simple as it may appear, we must accept a two-sided reality.
On the one hand, they abandoned certain original tenets that were so
uncompromising that members would have been identified instantly.
This ensured their survival. On the other hand, despite these concessions,
they preserved an essential hub of religious convictions. These ensured
that the movement continued to live.

   In the analysis presented above, we sought traits specific to the Poor of
Lyons at the end of the period and came up with very little; this was
because the frame of reference was inadequate. If we failed to account
for a real and indisputable fact, that is to say the endurance of the Poor of
Lyons, and if we seemed to conclude that nothing differentiated them in
the end from their fellow Christians, it was because we did not look
deep enough to read the signs. This is probably because the set ideas we
have concerning the dissent are false and our perception of reality is too
confined and manichaean. The conflict between the Roman Church
and the Poor of Lyons did not pit scoundrels against sterling characters,
or vice versa. The dissenters who managed more or less successfully to
survive from century to century whilst preserving their identity were still
victims, not heroes. They had to find compromises over the basic tenets
of their faith, to negotiate the price of their survival and to admit that
while it may not have been right, it was at least possible to make

'arrangements with the heavens' (Molière). Who could be surprised by this? They may have saved what was essential, but who could say whether the price was too high? With the exception of a few individuals, they were not intransigent militants. They had to be ingenious in innumerable ways to reconcile their cultural identity and their survival instinct. This should only disappoint us if our vision of humanity is too idealistic. We cannot expect more from the Poor of Lyons than we ourselves would be capable of. Everyone has values and principles which are essential structuring elements in their personality and identity. But in our daily lives, these are undercut by compromises and concessions, hesitations and faint-heartedness, adaptations and betrayals. Whether we like it or not, admit it or not or even realise it to be true, this is how we are. To account for the survival of the Poor of Lyons, we need to seek more subtle signs of their dissent which serve as identifying marks. What were these identifying and unifying factors which resisted space and time, which got the better of the Church and the State, and which ensured the community neither dwindled away nor fragmented?

POVERTY

How had the two primary bases, which determined Waldensian inspiration and precipitated its expansion, fared through the centuries? Preaching, as we have seen, had hardly survived at all, undermined at least in its original form by clandestinity, although, as we shall see in the next chapter, preachers continued to proclaim the Word of God in secret. The other remaining issue was poverty. We have seen how the re-emergence of this evangelical virtue in the eleventh and twelfth century was linked to a very particular context: the accelerated development of a merchant and banking class, the growing wealth of the higher clergy, and the Catholic Church's determined commitment to a hierarchical structure inspired by lay models. Moreover, in the same era as the Waldensian movement, mendicant orders emerged, reacting against the same trends. Four centuries on, how had the situation changed? The evolution had been considerable. This is not to imply that banks and mercantilism were less prosperous or that the Church was less rich and less temporal a power. The difference lay in the fact that poverty had ceased to be seen as a value in itself. Faced with the adversity of the fourteenth century, when famished crowds from the countryside flocked to the towns and when alms no longer sufficed to alleviate poverty, people began to distinguish between the deserving and the undeserving poor. Only the former were entitled to private and public charity; the rest were to be condemned. In the age of humanism, poverty was considered as a state of moral dissolution which degraded the human being. In such conditions, could the Poor of Lyons still preserve their faith in an evangelical value which had become outmoded, and in an environment which could no longer understand them? Could their message, which had lost much of its attraction, still find attentive listeners?

The call to absolute, voluntary poverty was more or less the bedrock of the Waldensian mission. The preachers had recruited devotees thanks to the exemplary, apostolic lives they led. But with the diaspora, opinions differed over the real meaning of a life in poverty. In about 1460, for instance, a Brother wrote that the Poor in Austria had abandoned the principle of poverty since they saved collection money and accepted legacies. The transmission of family goods was problematic, even if it was perfectly legitimate from a judicial and moral point of view. It increased differences between families, or even members of the same family, and encouraged the accumulation of wealth, a far cry from Valdès's example. Yet there was never mention of turning down inheritances; on the contrary, the 1530 Morel and Masson report clearly accepts them. And in practice, all the wills I studied in Provence made mention of bequests to heirs. So had poverty also been discarded?

The answer to this question is both yes and no. First, as we shall see, the preachers were still committed to a life of evangelical poverty, which earned them respect and authority. For everyone else, links to poverty were more tenuous. In the Dauphinois trials in 1487–8, the value of alms-giving constantly recurs in the defendants' statements. This is the testimony of Peyronette, from Beauregard near Valence, given in 1494: 'It is better and more worthy to give alms to some poor invalid or leper than to make offerings to the church priests who have an abundance of goods.' This good common sense must have met with the peasantry's approval, appealing as it does to stock anti-clericalism. Marriages and wills of the Poor of Lyons from Provence confirm their attitude to poverty. Dowers and dowries in marriage contracts are a first, clear proof of this. The two practices are well known. In the society of the time, much more than today, marriage was an alliance between two families, on an economic level as much as any other. It resembled, in fact, the founding of a business partnership. No young maiden, beautiful as she may have been, was married for her looks alone. Her father had to pay a certain sum, the dowry, to her intended. The sum was in part decided by local customs but was in the main settled by the two parties. It is worth noting that, in the Luberon, dowries arranged by the Poor of Lyons were always substantially lower than those agreed by Catholics from the same region; 87 per cent of the former, against 34 per cent of the latter

were set at less than fifty florins. In return, the future husband promised
his wife a certain sum, always inferior to the dowry, which became hers
in case of widowhood; this was the dower. Of these 71 per cent were
less than 20 florins for the Poor of Lyons, as opposed to 39 per cent for
Catholics. I naturally made sure that this difference was not dictated by
the different levels of wealth within the two communities. Even very
wealthy families from the Poor of Lyons made more modest settlements.
The simplest explanation for this is that they deliberately chose to
maintain lower levels as a symbolical demonstration of their traditional
attachment to poverty.

Wills are also eloquent on this point. As we have seen, charitable and
pious legacies represented an often considerable part of the will. Again,
this points to the particular attraction of poverty. In Catholic communities, such legacies often took the form of gifts to mendicant orders. For
the Poor of Lyons, practices were different. In 1546, for example,
Catherine Blanc from Cabrières-d'Aigues bequeathed blouses to three
girls from her village as well as a pair of shoes, a hat and a pinafore 'to the
woman who will lay her out and dress her after her death'. She also left
one gold écu and four *émines* of wheat to the paupers of the locality.
Gifts to paupers most often took the form of bread handed out at the
door of the deceased testator's house or at the entrance to the church. It
is worth noting that more Poor of Lyons (36 per cent) than Catholics (20
per cent) made provisions of this sort in their wills. It therefore becomes
clear that the Poor of Lyons were still responsive to the question of
poverty, even if they had a different approach from that at the beginning
of the movement. They had not forgotten the evangelical virtue that had
sparked off Vaudès's crusade, but their approach, less material and less
radical, had developed on a symbolical level.

PLAYING DOWN DIFFERENCE

We have seen how, on a theoretical level, the Poor of Lyons maintained
that God alone must be worshipped and invoked. If there is no proof of
Waldensians openly and provocatively refusing the cult of the Virgin
Mary and the saints, there are many signs suggesting that they tempered
their beliefs. For example, when interrogated during trials, they were all
capable of reciting the Lord's Prayer perfectly, obviously because it is
taken directly from the gospel. They were capable of reciting the prayer
dozens if not hundreds of times in a row, particularly as an act of
penance. Conversely, they were often incapable of reciting the *Ave
Maria*, the invocation to the Virgin Mary, only the opening words of
which are taken from the New Testament. When asked by the inquisitor

to recite the angelic salutation, they did their best to comply so as to avoid suspicion, but this could have astounding results. In December 1392, Jacob appeared before the court of Stettin: 'Asked whether he knew the *Ave Maria*, he answered yes and said, '*Ave Maria, gracia blena, dominus decus, benedictatus a mulieribus fructus frentus tuus, genode uns der heymelisch frowe.*' In the same month, during the same trial, Zdeneke Rudeger also declared that he knew the prayer, reciting, '*Ave Maria, gracia plena, benedicta tu in mulieribus, vruchtus fentenus tui, genede got unnd dy hymmeliche vrowe.*' If we recall the correct words, *Ave Maria, gratia plena, dominus tecum, benedicta tu et benedictus fructus ventris tui*, and bear in mind also that this is only the opening verse, we have a fair idea of how deformed the salutation had become; not only had the Latin been germanised but the formula itself was not known. The full significance of this becomes clear when one reads Clauss Walther's testimony concerning preachers and prayers, given in February 1393: 'He believes *Pater Noster* to be the only prayer, but the heresiarchs told him to learn *Ave Maria* because of their enemies.' It is thus plain that the Poor of Lyons recognised one prayer, the *Pater Noster*, but learnt a few lines from the *Ave Maria* to conform outwardly.

It follows logically and plausibly, although there is again no concrete proof, that if they were reticent about invoking the Virgin Mary, they were even more evasive over the saints. Provençal wills would seem to confirm this. Those drawn up by Poor of Lyons and Catholics alike comprised an opening formula commending the soul of the departed to God, the Virgin Mary and the saints. Further down, however, in the section concerning pious legacies, there was often mention of a gift for candles, a common practice at the time. Paul Donadieu, for example, from Cucuron in the Luberon drew up a will in 1546 which included the offering of ten candles in his parish church, eight of which were to be placed at the altars of St Anthony, St Peter, St John, St Sebastian, St Tulle, St Blaise, St Catherine and St Christol. The testator was Roman Catholic. No wills left by the Poor of Lyons make such provisions, whereas those of their Catholic contemporaries often evoke such bequests. In this case, it is their silence that is telling.

Similar reticence can be found in other parts of the wills. We saw above how the Poor of Lyons adopted local practices concerning masses for the dead. Like anyone else in the village, they ordered burial mass, a novena, a cantar at the end of the novena and a cantar on the anniversary of the death. But funeral ceremonies did not stop at this. Most Provençal wills provided for thirty other masses, called the trental (*trentain* or *trentenier*); those who could afford it – for we must not overlook the fact that such ceremonies were expensive – also requested perpetual mass.

This meant leaving a certain sum of money, usually sixty florins, so that weekly mass could be said, celebrated on the anniversary of the death of the testator, until the said sum had been used up. In other words the mass was perpetual only in name. As far as the two practices were concerned, it is revealing to compare the Poor of Lyons and Catholics: 8 per cent of Waldensians ordered a trental, as against 71 per cent of Catholics; 0.5 per cent made provisions for perpetual mass, as against 24 per cent. Furthermore, the processionary cross, holy water and special candles (*brandons*) were far less frequently requested for the burial of Waldensians than for Catholics: 36 per cent against 53 per cent, 10 per cent against 34 per cent, and 9 per cent against 45 per cent respectively. This relative sobriety concerning what has been described as 'baroque piety', which flourished particularly in funeral ceremonies, signals both the reticence felt by the Poor of Lyons towards what must have seemed to them superstitious excesses and also the moderation with which they tempered their opposition. They had found a balance between conforming sufficiently to prevailing customs so as not to be too easily picked out or at least not to be wholly rejected, whilst at the same time limiting their participation in these customs to preserve their own identity and avoid being completely assimilated. This was the judicious compromise which the Poor of Lyons found; they neither adhered completely nor did they contest vehemently: their social integration was based on moderate compliance.

THE TRANSMISSION OF FAITH

Like any protest movement, the Waldensian community could only emerge and develop by convincing its devotees and converting new members. No-one was born a dissenter; this was an epoch when it was believed nothing was innate, everything acquired. The inspired dynamism of the members was a result of their personal commitment which in turn gave momentum to the desire to expand. Later, they were forced by the pressures of clandestinity to limit their preaching, proclaiming the Word of God only from the safety of their own homes. From the fourteenth century onwards, Waldensianism spread essentially within the family, rather than by converting others. This was at least how outsiders understood the 'sect'. Louis of Pérussis, writing in Provence in the mid-sixteenth century, compared them to the Jews: 'The law and the custom of the Waldensians is to marry only amongst themselves ... like the Hebrews.' We do not know, however, how knowledgeable he really was about the community. A more serious report is that addressed to Francis I at his request by the commissioners of the Parlement of

Provence, acting upon the advice of the inquisitor Jean of Roma: 'They keep many things secret amongst themselves, one of which is that they only marry their daughters to members of their sect.' Similarly, a Dauphinois report sent to the archbishop of Embrun in 1502 stated at the end: 'They do not make marriage alliances with papists.' This might have appeared merely as further calumny attacking the clandestine minority, were it not for confessions made by defendants when on trial for heresy confirming the facts. In 1494, for example, Monet Rey from Saint-Mamans in the Valentinois, described the preachers as follows: 'They admonished all those present, telling them that, whenever possible, they should endeavour to marry their sons and daughters to those they knew belonged to the same sect.' It is, of course, possible that these avowals had been deformed or extorted under duress.

Marriages in Provence can again help us to substantiate hearsay concerning the practice of endogamy. Analysing nearly 800 contracts drawn up in the Luberon gives irrefutable proof. The Poor of Lyons married amongst themselves in 89 per cent of cases, and as far as the remaining 11 per cent are concerned, they may have followed the same rule but I could not identify them with absolute certainty. Similarly, 90 per cent of inhabitants in Cucuron, predominantly Catholic, married amongst themselves; again the remaining 10 per cent may have been Catholics living as a minority in a primarily 'Waldensian' locality. Such figures speak for themselves: marriages in both communities were mutually exclusive. This is all the more remarkable considering that Cucuron is situated in the middle of a Waldensian region, just a few kilometres from several surrounding 'heretical' villages. In other words, the inhabitants of Cucuron, like those from Lourmarin or from the Aigues valley, must have played a sort of matrimonial leap-frog to find partners from families of the same religion. As a result of this religious homogamy, a perfectly clear panorama in terms of onomastics opens up, revealing 'Waldensian' and Catholic surnames. This was doubtless invaluable for the inquisitors. In any case, it enables the historian today to identify, with little risk of error, families belonging to the Poor of Lyons dispersed in Catholic neighbourhoods.

The situation was transparent even at the time. Thomas Guiot, from Pragelato in the Dauphiné, told the inquisitor in 1495: 'The Villot family have always belonged to the sect.' In his anti-Waldensian treatise of 1533, the Dominican Jean of Roma wrote: 'Expelled from the Dauphiné and from Piedmont, they always persisted in their errors, getting worse and worse, from father to son, as if by hereditary law.' This family solidarity in the dissent accounts for the movement's longevity. Despite hardships, fines, exile and the stake, nothing could break the link which had, across decades and even centuries, united the Poor of Lyons with their predecessors. Their forefathers had bequeathed them evangelical truth. They in turn had the duty of passing it on to their descendants. This long chain of fidelity could become their fate; they were not free to choose. The trials in the Dauphiné from 1488 to 1489 repeatedly describe how parents, and mothers in particular, had introduced the witnesses into the 'sect'. On the other side of Europe, in Stettin in 1393, Hans Rudaw explained that he did not belong to the sect, but his wife was a member. He had not forbidden her to confess and receive preachers because he saw no wrong in it. He added, to justify his complacency: 'he had not wanted to forbid his wife but let her maintain paternal rites'. His wife's faith came from her parents. Why, and indeed how, should he go against filial duty?

It is clear, then, that after a considerable period of expansion in the thirteenth century, the movement of the Poor of Lyons shrank. It still extended geographically, because unstable populations were moving, particularly eastwards, in search of land. Such migratory waves were not, however, conquests; rather, they signalled a withdrawal. From this point on, the Poor of Lyons hardly converted any new recruits. They transmitted their evangelical light in darkness, they gathered by night around the hearths of family members. They drew together to gain strength, to remind themselves that they belonged to the long history of Waldensian faithfulness since Vaudès's first call, and that theirs was a movement which had been incessantly betrayed but never forgotten. Within their own homes, they ignored the tremendous risk of being denounced when they harboured their preachers and 'masters' who continued to embody the Truth and to live apostolic lives, proclaiming the Word of God. Could this not be seen as their most clear-cut characteristic, one which more than any other confirmed their identity and remained steadfast throughout their history? The Poor of Lyons were those who welcomed the Waldensian Brothers.

BIBLIOGRAPHY

Audisio, G., *Le barbe et l'inquisiteur. Procès du barbe vaudois Pierre Griot par l'inquisiteur Jean de Roma (Apt, 1532).* Aix-en-Provence, 1979.
   Les vaudois du Luberon. Une minorité en Provence (1460–1560). Mérindol, 1984.
Merlo, G. G., *Valdesi e valdismi medievali.* Turin, 1984.
Molnár, A., *Storia dei valdesi*, vol. i: *Dalle origini all'adesione alla Riforma.* Turin, 1974.
Vinay, V., *Le confessioni di fede dei valdesi riformati.* Turin, 1975.

6

THE NEED TO ORGANISE

The Poor of Lyons were faced with a crucial decision: should they maintain the intensity of their movement or aim to survive? In other words, live their dissent to the full or live long? Every social unit, from the individual or the family to a micro-society, is faced with such a dilemma at some time or another, whether they are aware of it or not. Should they burst forth and spread, irrespective of those social institutions which might fetter or hamper their spontaneity, or organise and structure their energies so as to last longer, albeit with minor adjustments or compromises? Should they maintain the movement's original, somewhat disorganised impetus and so risk disappearing or ensure their survival by drawing up guiding rules and electing leaders? Vaudès's initial spark kindled the crowds and conquered disciples. The first preachers' words and example encouraged people in their masses to turn back to the gospel and to embrace voluntary poverty. However, once the first burst of enthusiasm had died down and the novelty of the movement had worn off, and in the wake of ecclesiastical reprobation, what came next? When certain brethren returned to the fold of the Roman Church, the choice was, in fact, quite limited. Waldensians could either follow their example, recognising the 'error' they had made, or persist in the direction they had chosen, refusing all organisation. In either case, it meant that sooner or later, the movement would disappear. Alternatively, they could adapt to the difficult situation, renouncing certain particularly rigid tenets and accepting a clandestine structure to ensure their essential tenets were preserved and passed on. We know the Poor of Lyons lasted for four centuries. This was possible because they chose survival, the third solution. In this way, Vaudès's opposition movement developed into an organised dissent.

THE PIONEERS

The first groups of preachers, in Vaudès's generation, had to make their mark on the crowds and the towns in which they spoke. They had to attract attention to themselves since theirs was an odd society, to say the least. From the outset, the Poor of Lyons were characterised by three traits which they upheld across the centuries: they were poor, itinerant preachers from the beginning to the end. In the early days, their preaching was open; they proclaimed the gospel in public, often in the parish churches. They were prophets spreading the Word of God in a vivid, bold manner using the idiomatic language of their listeners; the holy scriptures they offered were accessible to all, heard and understood by all. It was quite a change from the readings in Latin and the wordy formulas usually heard in church. In addition, the preachers' sincerity doubtless made their words particularly forceful and attractive. Nor must we overlook the fact that they did not get caught up in tortuous notions justifying traditional attitudes, including those which contradicted the bible. The Poor of Lyons rejected subtle subterfuges, oratory ruses and other stratagems to talk their way round some interpretation or other of the bible. Their approach was primitive and unrefined; the Word of God was not to be interpreted or adapted but followed to the letter. This approach, scoffed at by clerics, sages and academics who deemed it boorish, must have delighted the masses who understood what it was about. The preachers were men and women like them; they did not belong to an ecclesiastical coterie. Another consequence, which was not immediately apparent in concrete terms, was that they reflected badly on the clergy whose lives did not adhere so closely to the holy scriptures. This anti-clericalism, even if was mostly tempered, delighted the population who saw in it one of the traditional veins of their literature and culture. The Waldensians' preaching was all the more effective as they preached first by example.

Poverty was one of the favourite themes of their evangelical mission and had indeed inspired their name: they were 'Christ's Poor Men'. In return, they believed it was the apostolic lives they led that entitled them to preach, a belief contested by the Roman hierarchy. As Durand of Huesca wrote, 'God gave us the grace to preach', and elsewhere, 'Only those holy preachers who have given up their goods for the Lord bear the name of The Poor.' Not only did they preach poverty, reinforcing their words with frequent extracts from the Old and New Testaments, but they also lived in accordance with biblical exhortations. Most members of the clergy saw an ecclesiastical life as a means to an honourable career at least, if not a way to gain social importance. By choosing not to hold church office, the Poor of Lyons refused even to envisage such social benefits as came with all ecclesiastical responsibilities. As beggars, they contrasted starkly with the traditional, secular clergy made up of priests who were all too frequently in search of personal comfort and material gain. Vaudès and his companions did not refuse to work out of laziness, but so as to devote themselves entirely to their mission. Even if, years later, their position was to evolve, they were always to maintain the life of poverty as an ideal.

Itinerancy, which was another specific trait, was not a vocation in itself as far as Vaudès and his companions or successors were concerned. It was the logical result of preaching and poverty, the two other basic principles. Preaching to spread the Word of God and serve the crusade against the Cathars meant they had to travel around incessantly where and when they were needed. Poverty, and a consequent life of begging, required that they move from one place to another seeking alms. Persecution changed nothing in this respect. On the contrary, while changing place too frequently could appear suspicious and so attract the attention of the authorities who were always disdainful towards nomads, timely changes of residence enabled them to escape from a particularly scrupulous Inquisition or from a neighbourhood which had suddenly grown suspicious. Besides, once their movement had become dispersed, the preachers' travels kept them in touch with other members, thus preserving a certain essential unity across the diaspora. These three characteristics – preaching, poverty and itinerancy – remained a constant base throughout the history of the Poor of Lyons.

Other features present in the early days of the movement were later to disappear. The first community, for instance, was mixed. Contemporary observers were astonished by the presence of women, as anyone aware of the status of women in medieval society can understand. Bernard Gui, echoing Stephen of Bourbon a century before, described the origins of the sect in the following terms: 'The man called Valdès or Valdo encouraged a number of accomplices of both sexes in this presumption, sending them out to preach as disciples. Although they were ignorant and unlettered, these people, both men and women, went from village to village ... leaving behind them a host of misunderstandings and mistakes.' It gave the rather misogynist clerics a fine opportunity to scoff at the Poor of Lyons, seeing their promotion of women as yet another example of their folly. This sexual equality, contrasting vividly with the male monopoly in the clergy and the respective status of the sexes in society as a whole, was, however, short-lived. Even by the time Bernard Gui was writing at the beginning of the fourteenth century, the situation had changed. Raymond of Costa, interrogated by the bishop of Pamiers, Jacques Fournier, on 8 January 1320, declared, 'Women may not preach the Word of God, nor may they take holy orders.' The promotion of laymen and more particularly laywomen as preachers had the makings of a socially subversive issue, as did their evangelical literalism. But whether they were finally won over by traditional positions on this point, or whether its unacceptable originality made it too difficult to uphold, the sexual equality was abandoned. It was in fact anachronistic and thus destined to failure.

Another equally contentious idea which was upheld by the first community concerned the absence of hierarchy. We can appreciate quite how remarkable this was if we recall the vision of the world that then held sway, and to which everyone subscribed. The order created and willed by God was by definition hierarchical; any notion of equality was therefore synonymous with disorder and so threatened to unbalance the whole system. There was an uncontested head in the family, the local community, the town and the province; the Church and the state, trades and society as a whole were seen as, and functioned as, hierarchical bodies. Those on earth, in heaven and in hell were variously subordinate to one another. Even God himself, although unique, was also made up of three parts, the Father, the Son and the Holy Spirit, which, even if they were equal, were still ranked in terms of dignity if not power. Any notion of egalitarianism was, in this context, simply revolutionary. Concerning the first 'Waldensian society', Vaudès himself insisted that there be no leader. This was one of the points over which the Poor of Lyons and the Lombardy Poor disagreed and which they debated during the meeting in Bergamo in 1218. It was a position which threatened the survival of the entire group, for without structures it was impossible to pass the faith on.

The changes which came about in the thirteenth century constituted answers to questions that had arisen. If the movement wanted to survive beyond the first sparks of inspiration, to guarantee the unity of a community that had become a diaspora and to meet the challenge of forced clandestinity, it had to accept becoming organised. The Poor of Lyons lost certain remarkably subversive traits by opting to ensure their future. Their evangelism had troubled the Christian authorities by showing them how they could be challenged by the Word of God, claim as they might to apply it, demanding obedience in its name. Over the centuries, the Poor of Lyons upheld poverty, itinerancy and their preaching mission by making inevitable concessions. On the other hand, they had to renounce the noble but unmanageable principle of equality both between men and women and amongst members of the community. In the beginning, brethren, preachers, Poor of Lyons, Poor of Christ, devotees and believers were all the same: synonymous terms all denoting the members of the dissenting community. In the century following the birth of the Waldensian movement, profound changes took place, the most noteworthy being their adoption of a clear hierarchy.

MASTERS AND BELIEVERS

The first modification within the community, allowing a hierarchy to be installed, concerned the distinction made between preachers and other followers. No documents have survived explaining exactly how and why this binary organisation was adopted. Whatever the case, it changed the movement's structure altogether. We can, however, make hypotheses to suggest what happened. In my opinion, the first cause was doubtless that the original missionary spirit was lost, or at least toned down. By the time of the second or third generation, the Poor of Lyons were confronted with an unexpected situation. Banished from society and from the Church, they observed that new followers were no longer being converted but that faithfulness was passed on from father to son. Whole families had grown up, all followers of the Poor of Christ. By necessity, they lived by their daily work. Both the growth of their numbers and the permanent threat of persecution meant they could no longer all live as beggars and preachers. Clandestinity imposes obligations. In this way, one part of the movement, indeed the greater part, settled down, giving up itinerancy, poverty and preaching. This did not mean the community as a whole turned its back on what had formed its very identity. A transfer occurred from the members as a community to individuals within their ranks. In this way, these individuals would maintain the original tenets which the others had been obliged to renounce, functioning as a nostalgic reminder of the movement's first happier days. They would be the group's living memory, showing that their faith was enduring. Symbolically, they would represent the ideal life to which the followers aspired, even if it was impossible to attain.

Besides such difficulties in practical terms, which alone could explain this move towards installing a specialised body within the community, the Poor of Lyons probably also sought to align themselves with prevailing practices. Indeed, as we saw above, total equality was found nowhere other than among the Poor of Lyons. Both the Roman Church and other dissenting groups adhered to a hierarchical model, not to mention lay society as a whole. It is difficult to tell whether the Poor of Lyons were influenced more by Rome or by other 'heretics'. Whatever the case, inquisitors such as Bernard Gui used Cathar terminology when referring to them, calling the group's members 'believers' and its preachers '*perfecti*'. In fact, nothing allows us to suppose the Poor of Lyons themselves used such denominations. The terminology tended to be rather inconsistent. The inquisitor Peter Zwicker referred to the preachers during investigations he was leading in Pomerania in 1392−3 as follows: 'They say that the heresiarchs refer to one another as "Brothers", that during confession they are called "lords" [*dominos*], that they are the true successors of the disciples of Christ.' During this series of trials in Stettin, the defendants referred to their preachers as 'lords', 'preachers' and 'confessors'. The word 'masters' (*magistri*) was also cited frequently during the trials in Piedmont in the fourteenth century. Whatever the terms used, the same distinction or even opposition is established between the flocks as a whole (the faithful, believers) and the leaders (lords, masters, *perfecti*).

Certain terms were, notwithstanding, ambiguous and could be misleading. 'Brothers' for instance sometimes denoted all the members of the dissent, at other times just the preachers. From the fourteenth century on, however, the term was reserved for the latter. The designation '*perfecti*', borrowed from the Cathars is, in any case, incorrect particularly since, at the beginning of the fourteenth century when Gui was writing, such a bipartite division no longer really corresponded with reality and was even on the way to becoming totally obsolete. Reduced by Gui to a dichotomous vision, the division in fact constituted a transitory phase between the initial egalitarianism of the beginning and a new organisation. The movement's internal structure appears to have changed quite rapidly; in any case, within the hundred years after Vaudès, the pastoral body of dedicated preachers, which, while not identical to the Roman clergy bore striking resemblances to it in terms of form, was divided into a series of ranks.

HIERARCHY

From the fourteenth century at least, the Poor of Lyons adopted a tripartite structure which, in keeping with their biblical literalism, could be justified by referring, if not to the gospels themselves, at least to the New Testament in which it is stated that the first Christian community was divided into ranks to fulfil certain responsibilities. In around 1320, Bernard Gui wrote: 'First of all, it must be known that the Waldensians have and establish above them a superior called the "majoral" whom they have to obey, as Catholics obey the pope.' He continues further on, 'The oldest member settles all matters concerning the priests and deacons.' This tripartite conception is not really in contradiction with the binary division into '*perfecti*' and 'believers' which the inquisitor describes. Just as the clerical body, as against the lay members, in the Roman Church is divided into orders at different levels, so the *perfecti* in the Poor of Lyons were not all equal. One might have been tempted to think that the inquisitor, who was writing up his memoirs at the end of his life, was distorting the statements he had heard, attributing an organisation on the Catholic model to 'heretics' as a whole, were it not for a statement made by a 'Waldensian deacon' confirming his words.

During twenty-four sessions from 9 August 1319 to 30 April 1320, Jacques Fournier, then bishop of Pamiers, interrogated a prime suspect. The statement is entitled 'The Confession of Raymond of Costa, Waldensian heretic and Deacon in the sect'. The prisoner indeed confirmed that he was a deacon and gradually revealed the manner in which the community as a whole was organised. They had a superior whom they called not 'bishop' but 'majoral' who, during a ceremony whose rites are listed in detail, ordained priests and deacons. It reproduced the model of the early Church which appointed an episcopacy, elders and deacons, in other words the three orders also maintained by the Roman Church: the episcopacy, the priesthood and the deaconry. It is striking that the Poor of Lyons should also have adopted this three-tier hierarchy, out of faithfulness to the holy scriptures of course, but doubtless also imitating Rome. In this way they offered a sort of ecclesiastical counter-type. It is difficult to know how long this model lasted. During inquisitorial proceedings in Piedmont, the inquisitor Antony of Settimo discovered that in Barge they referred to a 'sovereign pontiff' (*summus pontifex*) living in Apulia in southern Italy who sent preachers out on missions. And in 1451, Philip Regis from Piedmont spoke during his trial of the 'master' (*magister*) who lived in Apulia. But at this time there was no longer any mention made of priests and deacons. During the fifteenth century, previous structures either fell from use or were simplified, and both the eastern and western branches of the Poor of Lyons returned to a binary organisation. There were Masters or Brothers on one side and the faithful or believers on the other.

Leaders, however, continued to be troubled by the model of hierarchical ranks since, in 1530, in the name of their fellow preachers, Georges Morel and Pierre Masson asked the reformers about it. The first *peticion* in fact, was to ask 'whether, between ministers of the Word of God, they were to establish ranks of dignity such as episcopacy, presbyterate and deaconry'. They continued, however, by making clear that 'Amongst ourselves, we nonetheless do not use such ranks.' This testimony, given as I have said of their own free will, proves both that the Brothers had abandoned the tripartite organisation and that they remained in doubt as to whether they had been right to do so, particularly since, as devoted readers of the holy scriptures which they respected to the letter, they were aware that the book of Matthew and also Paul's letters to the Galatians, to Titus and to Timothy contained quotations pleading in favour of the three orders. Whatever the reason, the Poor of Lyons had abandoned them willingly or reluctantly by the fifteenth century. The most simple organisation remained – that of a single body of preachers.

THE ORDER OF BROTHERS

From the fourteenth century, there were two groups within the Poor of Lyons, as we saw above: the Latin or Romance community and the Germanic community. They shared many common points, particularly the pastoral body of preachers. Here, I wish to consider those character-istics shared by both sides, before turning to their differences. Their first common feature, on which all the others depended, leaving its inexor-able mark on the preachers' lives, was clandestinity. It was, admittedly, shared by the whole community but the Brothers' special responsibilities and their particular mission meant that they ran far greater risks. Visiting the faithful posed a very real problem: how were they to be recognised amongst themselves whilst avoiding the eyes of the authorities? They had to invent some kind of code of behaviour or signs that the initiates alone would know. What means of recognition did they have which were clear enough not to be doubted, but also discreet enough not to be dangerous? The preacher Martin, who was arrested and interrogated in Oulx in Piedmont in 1492, stated that during his pastoral rounds with his companion he met three followers near Aix-en-Provence who recog-nised them 'by their clothes, that is to say by their coats'. Some historians believe they might have had a special greeting by laying their hands on one another in a particular way, but this idea would appear to be groundless.

The safest way to be identified was of course by addressing families already known to the movement. This was easy for experienced preachers who had already travelled back and forth across the diaspora. The preacher Jean Gérault, returning from Piedmont with his young companion in November 1532, knocked at the door of an isolated farmhouse near Lourmarin in Provence knowing 'that some of his good friends lived in the house whom he had known a long time and that they would be warmly welcomed'. Indeed, the court statement continues: 'they were welcomed heartily and given food and drink'. For the new preacher, however, unknown to those devotees he had to approach, it was a different matter. In 1451, in reply to the inquisitor who had asked him how he knew that the people he had denounced were Waldensians, Philip Regis explained that he had read their names in the preachers' book. This testimony, unique of its kind, does not mean that such an injudicious practice was typical. Two more common solutions existed to avoid it. The first was that the preacher could learn by heart certain place and family names. On reaching these villages, he could then easily draw up subsequent stops. The second solution was for the Brothers to travel always in pairs, one of whom was acquainted with the underground network, the other being taught the exact geography of their settlements. This practice was especially frequent with the western Brothers.

They were lay preachers, no longer properly ordained as they had been in Raymond of Costa's time, although, as we shall see further on, a special ceremony integrated them into the brotherhood. They constituted a separate group, as clearly marked off from the clergy as they were from their followers. The followers, at least, were highly aware of this difference. Not only did they never take their preachers for Roman clerics, but they also knew they had not been ordained as priests. When questioned by the inquisitor Gallus of Neuhaus at an uncertain date between 1345 and 1349, Heinrich stated that his nephew Cunczlin had confessed 'to a lay confessor'. At the end of the fourteenth century, most Waldensians in Stettin acknowledged that their 'masters' were laymen. Herman Polan did not consider them to be priests; Tylss, wife of Hans Steckelyn, held them to be lords (*dominis*) teaching them what was good, not priests. Peter Lavburch had never considered them to be priests; Marguerite, wife of Heyne Eckard, thought they were Brothers, not priests, because they had not been ordained. There are examples by the dozen, but there is surely no need to cite more. Clearly, the Brothers were laymen; they did not attempt to pass themselves off for anything other, and their devotees were perfectly aware of this. Friedrich Reiser's request to be ordained by a Czech bishop thus appears all the more surprising. It is doubtless an exceptional case illustrating the Hussites' influence on the Poor of Lyons in fifteenth-century Bohemia. Nonetheless, despite the priest's prestige and sacred, semi-magical character, and despite the Brothers' laicity which was clearly proclaimed and understood as such, devotees continued to have faith and confidence in their masters. The esteem and veneration the latter inspired were the result of the harsh lives they chose to lead.

Without repeating what has already been said about those characteristics common to the Brothers across the centuries, we should still emphasise the three vows made by the preacher embarking on his mission. This is stated most clearly by Pierre Griot, the young preacher who had hardly completed his training when he was taken by the inquisitor and interrogated in Apt in Provence in autumn 1532. One of the many details he gave of the Brothers was that 'They promise God poverty, chastity and obedience.' The concisely worded formula is so striking that one is tempted to wonder whether the inquisitor was not deforming the defendant's words to make him confess that Waldensian preachers were living wrongfully as clerics. But this is not the case, for Morel's 1530 report confirms Griot's testimony: 'None of us gets married ... Our food and clothing are provided thanks to the alms given by the people we preach to ... We ministers hold all our worldly goods in common and receive them from the people's alms alone; they are more than enough for our needs.' As for obedience, Morel and Masson refer only to that due from the younger to the older preacher during their missionary travels. But this obedience appears to be almost absolute; describing the younger ministers, they write: 'Without their superior's permission, they dare do nothing at all, not even drink water or shake hands.'

Raymond of Costa, writing in 1320, emphasised the need to obey the 'majoral'; this was also confirmed during the judicial proceedings led by Gallus of Neuhaus in the middle of the century and Peter Zwicker from 1392 to 1394. On 8 January 1337, the bookseller Henri maintained that his brother Rudlin was 'a master amongst the heretics' adding, 'He's a virgin, which is how he came to be admitted to the masterate, for you can never be a master if you are not a virgin.' Candidates were not merely expected to be unmarried and celibate but virginal as well, even if we know dispensations were sometimes granted. In any case, any sexual misconduct led to the Brothers being automatically dismissed from the pastoral body, as Morel's report makes clear. The ministers' poverty is constantly emphasised by references to the Brothers' 'apostolic lives'.

Poverty, chastity and obedience are also the three vows taken by the regular clergy in the Roman Church. Moreover, the ascetic life chosen by the preachers is in many ways reminiscent of the lives led by the most devoted monks. The Brothers thus give the impression of being a genuine mendicant order, particularly since Morel refers to an order of 'Sisters' probably living in retirement in the Cottian Alps. The candidates had to take a vow of perpetual virginity. Those applying to be preachers retreated for a certain time, probably a probationary period, to stay with the sisters. There is also a record in Strasbourg in about 1400 of girls (*dohter*) taking the three monastic vows and becoming 'sisters' (*swester*) who lived from alms. Hence, there existed, as a distant, incomplete reminder of the sexual equality at the time of Vaudès and his companions, a female version of the order of Brothers, that of the Sisters, within the community of the Poor of Lyons.

In many ways the ideal the lay brethren aspired to in their daily lives closely resembled the asceticism commended by the monastic constitutions of the mendicant orders. The pious texts they wrote, which we shall discuss in the next chapter, reiterate the themes of *lo despreczi del mont* (contempt of the world), *castita* and *paureta*. Even the vocabulary is monotonously revealing, with the same considerations endlessly repeated: *mortificant lo carn* (mortifying the flesh); *castigue ben lo cors e lo retorne a servetu* (chastise the body well and return it to servitude); *la via de desciplina* (the way of discipline). Above all, the Brothers were required to be ascetic. They were set apart, renouncing women, the family, possessions and stability. The path they chose was rough indeed, earning them unanimous praise from their devotees during interrogations. All followers everywhere spoke most highly of their masters. They imitated the life of the apostles. They were men who 'fasted often and chastised themselves', as Hans Spigilman said in Stettin in 1394. From Pomerania to Strasbourg or the Dauphiné, they are called 'good men', 'honest men' and are seen quite simply as saints. Essential as their asceticism was, however, it was only one aspect of their status in the community. The order of Brothers, if it was an order, was not a contemplative one. It did not form the object of its own existence. It existed for its people, for the faithful, and its vocation was to turn to them. The preachers had to embrace their servitude rigorously in order to serve the mission with which they had been invested and fulfil it amongst the believers.

BEARERS OF THE WORD

Preaching was the Brothers' foremost duty. Their initially public preaching became secret; they left the churches and public squares to speak within the families of the faithful. The Brothers were also called 'preachers' (*prediger*) in the Germanic lands. Their mission was essentially to proclaim the Word of God and therefore to read the bible. This entailed several conditions. The preachers had to learn to read. This may appear banal to us, but we must bear in mind that in the fifteenth and sixteenth centuries, about 80 per cent of society, both urban and rural populations, was totally illiterate. The Poor of Lyons at this time had an entirely rural population, and even fewer people could read in the country than in the towns. This gives us a clearer idea of the Brothers' exceptional status. During their training, they learnt to read and write; as a result of their studies, they knew by heart entire chapters of the New Testament, particularly the gospels of Matthew and John and certain apostolic epistles. The choice underlines their particular sensibility which we shall return to when we consider the relations between the Poor of Lyons and the reformers. The Brothers did not only rely on their memory, but carried small books with them from which they could read out passages to their listeners. The reading was followed by a sermon, both in the language spoken in the country: a Romance tongue in the west, Germanic in the east. From the earliest days, preaching in the vernacular was a characteristic feature of the Poor of Lyons.

When the first part of the meeting was over, the Brothers met the devotees individually to hear their confessions. This activity is often overlooked, forgotten, or, more to the point in my opinion, disregarded, although innumerable testimonies bear witness to it from Piedmont to Pomerania, from Provence to Bohemia. As we saw above, followers interrogated by Gallus of Neuhaus freely acknowledged confessing to laymen. They sometimes even referred to the Brothers as 'confessors' (*Beichtiger*). In this respect, the Dauphinois trials are astonishing considering the number of converging statements. In that region, the tradition dated back a long way; one man had been confessing to the preachers for twenty-seven years, another for thirty-six years, two more for forty years, one for forty-seven years. Almost every defendant acknowledged having turned to a preacher to confess, at an average of once every two years. The devotees from Stettin declared in 1392–4 that they confessed their faults once or twice a year. The accused did not own up to confessing to laymen as a result of being vigorously cross-examined by courts seeking to exaggerate their offences. Morel and Masson's 1530 report confirms the practice: 'Once a year we visit our people who are dispersed and live in different villages, and we listen to them in secret in individual confession.' They justify this as follows: 'We believe it is useful to listen to the confession of sins, without observing any special time, with the sole intention of offering consolation and help to the infirm, the ignorant and to those seeking guidance, as it is said in the holy scriptures.' The facts are clear; we should now consider their significance.

It is possible that confession represented no more than advice offered to one's fellow. This appears to be suggested in Morel and Masson's report. In reality, things were quite different. The followers believed they were confessing and being absolved. In the middle of the fourteenth century, a Bohemian defendant gave the following statement:

Asked whether he had received penance,
– he answered yes.
Asked whether he had observed the penance which had been imposed on him
and if he believed it would help his salvation,
– he answered yes.

In 1487 many defendants from the Dauphiné maintained that
preachers 'had the power to pardon or to withhold absolution'. In 1495,
Thomas Guiot from Pragelato in Piedmont acknowledged having confessed to the Brothers, saying that they had assured him they had the
power to absolve him and he had believed them. The rite they followed
was indeed much the same as that of absolution in the sacrament of
penance. In 1494, Monet Rey from Saint-Mamans in the Valentinois
described the rite of penance in detail: 'After the sermon, the preacher
retired into a room bidding him to come to him to confess ... which he
did, and he confessed to him on his knees. Then, when his confession
was over, he absolved him in the manner priests do, by laying his hand
on his head.' As penance he was enjoined to say the Lord's Prayer many
times, as many as he could, and to give alms according to his means. In
the same year, Peyronette from Beauregard, also in the Valentinois,
admitted that:

Every time these preachers came to the house of her now deceased husband she
confessed her sins to one of them, on bended knee, as if she had been before her
own priest and, having confessed, he absolved her by laying his hand on her head
as priests do. Asked about the penance which had been imposed on her by the
said preachers or masters for the sins she had confessed to, she said in reply that
she had to say *Pater Noster* many times, as many as she could, then fast for a few
Fridays and give alms according to her means.

Defendants from Stettin refer repeatedly to the Lord's Prayer as the
penance imposed upon them. Aleyd, the wife of Thyde Takken, testified
about the preachers who had heard her confession as follows:

They ordered as penance that she eat but bread and water for four or five feast-
days and also for the four feasts of the *Estive Quadragesime* and fifty *Pater Noster* on
the feast-days and a hundred on Sundays, not *Ave Maria*; they required, however,
that she know *Ave Maria* because of the priests who might question her about it.

Peter Ostyrricher was required to fast on bread and water, and to
recite *Pater Noster* twenty times each day and as many times as possible
on Sundays. 'He undertook his penance and thought he was absolved
and that this penance would help his salvation.' Peter Lavbruch also
respected the penance imposed on him, convinced that he was thus
pardoned and that it would aid his salvation: *Pater Noster* a hundred times
on Sunday and fifty times on feast-days, not *Ave Maria*, and for ten days,

to abstain from beer and fast on bread. This again attests the Poor of Lyons' predilection for the Lord's Prayer and their reserve, to say the least, concerning the angelic salutation.

There can be no doubting that the followers were confessing and seeking absolution. One prayer from 1404 used by preachers to absolve sins goes as follows:

> May our Lord who forgave Zacheus, Mary Magdalene and Paul, who freed Peter from the chains and Martha and other penitents, forgive you your sins. May the Lord bless you and keep you; may the Lord show himself to you and have pity on you; may the Lord look on you and grant you peace. And may the peace of God, which passes all understanding, keep your heart and your spirit in Jesus Christ. The Father, the Son and the Holy Spirit bless you. Amen.

If they were really forgiving sins, we should still note the different wording from that used in the Roman Church. The priest says '*Ego te absolvo*' (I absolve you); the Brother just said, 'God forgives you.' The nuance is greater than it may appear. In the eyes of the followers, however, less attentive as they were to subtleties, the preachers had the power to forgive sins.

Confession, however, was certainly not of secondary importance for the Poor of Lyons. It was, on the contrary, at the heart of the Brothers' mission and the followers knew this, even if we do not know whether they were very attached to it. It would indeed appear that, in the west at least, a person's first confession to a preacher constituted a rite of passage of sorts, signalling his or her entry into the community of believers. Let us take two witnesses from the dozens of suspects interrogated by Alberto Cattaneo in the late fifteenth century. Pierre Lantelme 'confessed eight years ago when he entered the sect of the Waldensians'; Pierre Passet 'wanted to marry the daughter of Jacques Villot but could only do so if he became a Waldensian. Then a *barbe* [preacher] came to his house asking him if he would confess to him and he heard his confession and received him into the Waldensian sect.' The fact is attested innumerable times. Yet each such testimony is from a member of a family of believers. This was obviously not enough. Believers had to adhere in person, often at puberty, between twelve and fifteen years of age. This first confession did not, however, prevent believers from admitting their faults to the parish priest once a year or taking communion at the church, as often, or as rarely, as any average Catholic did. Many suspects in Stettin, such as Peter Ostyrricher, declared that 'he had confessed to priests and received the body of Christ in communion without saying he belonged to the sect'. Whatever the case, the trials make it clear that confessing to a Brother or receiving the preachers into one's house was considered proof that the person belonged to the community. The inquisitor always asked the double question, 'Have you received them? Have you confessed to them?' A positive answer identified the suspect as a member of the Waldensian heresy. In truth, these are the two surest criteria in concrete terms: a member was someone who received the preachers as visitors and/or confessed to them.

During their mission of preaching and hearing confessions, the Brothers collected the offerings given by the believers. Thomas Griot told the inquisitor who asked him if he had given the preacher anything after confession that he had given 'one quarter' (*quart*). Monet Rey explained that this was the tradition: 'He paid the confessor two or three *gros*, as was customary.' We know this sum was used in part for the upkeep of the pastoral body, in part to help the poor, as far as the western Brothers were concerned at least. Considerable sums were gathered and brought back to the Brothers in this way each year. Interrogated in Pinerolo in 1451, Philip Regis declared that he and one of his colleagues gathered a tithe each year which was then transported to Apulia; 300 ducats were thus transported in March 1449. In 1533, the inquisitor Jean of Roma wrote that these preachers 'are believed to have gathered 600 gold écus in one year in the dioceses of Apt, Cavaillon and Carpentras'. As we saw above, Morel confirmed the practice of alms-giving in his community, underlining the generosity believers showed to the preachers. He adds, 'From the living and often from those on their death-beds, we receive abundant gifts of money and other items.' In this way, the community supported a pastoral body so that it might serve it exclusively. It represented a concrete, financial expression of gratitude that reveals how useful the believers saw their preachers to be.

At this time, however, the Brothers no longer constituted a single body as they had in the beginning. A division had developed within the community which reflected the way in which the community of the Poor of Lyons had evolved. This was not because of a religious conflict as had been the case in the thirteenth century, but the result of their dispersion which had finally created two poles: the Romance populations in the west and the Germanic populations in the east. It is understandable that the preachers should have been in their turn affected by the division, seek as they might to be close to their people and to speak their language. In the fifteenth century in any case, this was the situation: there were in fact two bodies of preachers, one for each linguistic group. There was surely no other choice. Contact between the two geographical divisions diminished as time went by, becoming rare occurrences in the fifteenth and sixteenth century. Admittedly, everyone was aware of the existence of the Poor of Lyons' other pole, but there were no longer any activities in common and even their organisation was independent. In fact, from this point on, there were two communities. It would appear that the eastern Brothers also developed a network of missionary rounds, training for their preachers and houses to receive them and organised annual meetings but the sources are limited and we are far from being certain. In fact we know nothing other than what we learn from the trials instituted against them. There are no records directly concerning the preachers, as there are for their western counterparts, with the exception of a unique document concerning Friedrich Reiser's trial in the middle of the fifteenth century. But quite apart from the fact that the original document and the sixteenth-century copy were destroyed during the fire in Strasbourg library in 1870, Reiser's personality and his Hussite influences make this case quite exceptional; we cannot reasonably draw from it any conclusions concerning the German brotherhood as a whole. We are, on the other hand, much better informed about the preachers from the west.

THE BARBES

Concerning the community in the west, the documents at our disposal are first of all those from the many judicial proceedings in the Dauphiné from 1487 to 1495, during which the believers spoke at length about their preachers. The cross-examination of Philip Regis in 1451 is more unusual because he was a sort of lieutenant or deputy for the Brothers. Jean of Roma's anti-Waldensian treatise written in 1533 is particularly comprehensive because the inquisitor had officiated against the Provençal communities and had himself interrogated two preachers; he therefore had direct experience of the cases he was investigating. He has indeed provided us with detailed accounts of the eight sessions during which he interrogated Pierre Griot. This document is not the only surviving account of a preacher's trial; there are two others, detailing the proceedings against Francesco of Girundino and Pietro of Jacopo held in 1492 in Oulx (Dauphinois Alps); and against the Provençal master Jean Serre from Murs whose final confession was in 1539. The most precious testimony is again Morel and Masson's report, for here the two preachers speak freely of the pastoral body to which they belong. Our knowledge of the Brothers from the west is determined by these documents, some of which are hand-written and hitherto unpublished.

First, there is the question of their name. Unlike their counterparts in central or eastern Europe, the Waldensians from the Romance lands did not call their preachers 'Brothers', 'masters' or 'lords', but *'barbes'*. The term requires an explanation. It is of Romance origin. In his dictionary,

Frédéric Mistral defines it as follows: 'A respectful title given to an elder in a community or to an uncle in the Piedmont Alps and in the county of Nice.' In fact, even now, 'uncle' in the Piedmont dialect is *barba*. In 1530, Pierre Griot referred to a preacher with whom he had travelled as 'Uncle Georges'. When, by night, preachers arrived in Tourettes, a hamlet near Apt, a messenger went to inform Jean Tasquier that 'the uncles had arrived'. The term in fact has a broader meaning than this. Even today in Provence, an elder in a village is frequently called 'ouncle', a name which is both respectful and affectionate. The word was therefore not unfamiliar to the cultural environment at the time; it was just transposed into the religious field. In this way, a believer could announce the uncles' arrival, as did the messenger from Tourettes, without necessarily arousing people's suspicions. One of the characteristics of the Poor of Lyons is that they adopted this term for their leaders and were alone to do so.

The term used in this sense only appeared in their community in the fifteenth century. To my knowledge, it occurs for the first time during Philip Regis' trial in Pinerolo in 1451. It then became popular, later documents referring to preachers in this way during the last century of the Poor of Lyons' existence. This term, and this term alone, occurs in trials, Jean of Roma's treatise, the 1533 Warning (*avertissement*) issued by the Parlement of Provence and in Jacques Aubéry's defence speech in 1551. Pietro of Jacopo and Francesco of Girundino arrested in 1492, Georges Morel and Pierre Masson sent as envoys to the reformers, Jean Serre from Murs and Jean Gérault from Embrun, Pierre Griot and innumerable others quoted in the various documents are all referred to, and refer to themselves as *barbes*. If the term does mean 'uncle', the meaning which persisted was neither the French 'oncle' nor the provençal 'ouncle' but the sense denoted in the Piedmont vernacular. This demonstrates clearly how important Piedmont had become in the western diaspora, for a vocabulary is always more revealing than one might think. Piedmont had pre-empted the Dauphiné, Provence, Calabria and Apulia as the Poor of Lyons' principal bastion.

Barbes were recruited from among the faithful. This gave the college of preachers a particular nature, considering the predominantly rural character of the Poor of Lyons. In social terms, they were clearly distinguishable both from the Catholic clergy and from what was to become the reformed pastoral body. Morel and Masson write, 'In truth, our men who are to be received as preachers are almost always herdsmen or farm labourers of twenty-five years of age and thirty at the most and all are completely uneducated.' This emphasis on their ignorance is doubtless an implicit reference to the writings in the bible, for yet again, in the book of Matthew, Jesus declared, 'I thank thee, O Father, Lord of heaven and earth, because thou hast hid these things from the wise and prudent, and hast revealed them unto babes' (Matthew 11: 25). The *barbes'* geographical origins and their social status reflect the situation of the diaspora. Various sources inform us about the origins of 79 of the 107 *barbes* who are recorded in the fifteenth and sixteenth century: forty-seven were from Piedmont, thirteen from Umbria, eight from the Dauphiné and six from Provence; each of the last five comes from a different region. The Piedmont domination is unquestionable.

It was essential to train the young peasants for their pastoral mission. The letter from the two *barbes* in 1530 describes the training imposed on candidates. Candidates volunteered by addressing themselves to the college of *barbes* during a meeting. Those with a good reputation were selected and enrolled for training which took place during the winter months only over a three- or four-year period. They then learnt to read, write and to recite by heart books of the New Testament, particularly Matthew and John. When the winter training was over, their practical apprenticeship began. An older *barbe* took a younger man with him on his pastoral rounds to train him as a preacher. This official initiation as a speaker, even if only in clandestinity within the Waldensian community, represented a form of social and religious promotion. In this way, formal training in winter alternated with practical training in summer. At the end of this period, there followed a retreat with the Sisters living in virginity somewhere in Piedmont where, for a year or two, they concerned themselves with 'worldly activities'.

Finally, when the full training period was completed, the disciples were admitted to what Morel refers to as the 'ministry of the presbyterate and of preaching' during a rite including the laying on of hands and the eucharist – a rare trace, at this time, of the celebration which was apparently only practised on this occasion. Then followed a special rite: the change of name. Naming was of considerable importance. Discussions were lengthy, and unanimously considered essential, as names were chosen for those who had been born again. This implies that the stakes, symbolical as they were, were nonetheless crucial. Giving a name is an act of appropriation. When, at the beginning of the world, God intended making man the king of his creation, he gave him the right to name all the animals: 'And out of the ground the Lord God formed every beast of the field, and every fowl of the air; and brought them unto Adam to see what he would call them: and whatsoever Adam called every living creature, that was the name thereof. And Adam gave names to all the cattle, and to the fowl of the air, and to every beast of the field' (Genesis 2: 19–20).

If choosing a name is of such moment, how much more so is changing it. This is what masters in ancient times did with their slaves as a mark of their proprietorial rights; the practice lasted for centuries. When the monastic orders established that a novice beginning his religious life should change his name, it was as a sign that the new monk had been reborn and belonged absolutely to God, to whom he devoted himself by taking the vows of chastity, poverty and obedience. The same held for the *barbes*. One of the two *barbes* arrested and interrogated in 1492, Francesco of Girundino, explained this, saying 'that when their grand master, whom they call *committe* makes them *barbes* and gives them power, he changes their names; and that before being made a *barbe* he was called Francesco and, when he had been made a *barbe*, he was given the name Martin'. His companion Pietro of Jacopo had become the *barbe* John. The example of the gospels again fully justified this tradition. When John took his brother to Jesus, 'Jesus beheld him, [and] he said, Thou art Simon the son of Jona: thou shalt be called Cephas, which is by interpretation a stone' (John 1: 42). This practice, the religious significance of which is obvious, was also a measure of prudence, for it would embroil police enquiries. It makes our work more difficult too, for often *barbes* are only referred to by their Christian names. In any case, it is a feature which reminds us that the *barbes* and their Brothers in the east really constituted a form of religious order.

It is quite astonishing to learn how seriously the training followed by the *barbes* was taken. It was admittedly limited, but that it existed at all was a merit, particularly considering the indigence suffered by the Catholic clergy in these times. From this point of view the college of *barbes* was without contest superior. Highly traditional as it was, particularly concerning the importance given to learning by rote (but let us not forget that people immersed in an oral culture were capable of what appear to us as prodigious feats of memory), their apprenticeship was based on the holy scriptures, not on commentaries as was the case with university training at the time, nor on pious works. It was, moreover, perfectly adapted to the needs and aims of the community: the *barbes* learned the books of the bible in the vernacular, thus eliminating all language barriers, an exercise which also gave them practical training for speaking in private.

A SECRET ORGANISATION

When their training was completed, the real mission began. 'Thus prepared and formed', states the Morel report, 'they are sent out to evangelise two by two.' The Dauphinois testimonies from 1487 confirm that they always travelled in this way. In Oulx in 1492, the two *barbes* travelling together were arrested at the same time. Two preachers, Georges Morel and Pierre Masson were sent to consult the reformers in 1530. Pierre Griot travelled with Jean Gérault from Piedmont to Provence in autumn 1532. This pairing was again due to their desire to follow the example of the gospels. When Jesus first called his twelve disciples, he 'began to send them forth by two and two' (Mark 6: 7). Likewise, 'the Lord appointed other seventy also and sent them two and two before his face' (Luke 10: 1). It was also quite simply common sense to work in this way, as Pierre Griot both clearly and naïvely explained:

When the preachers set out in twos, one is the principal, the other simply his companion who is sent with him for several reasons. The first is to learn the New Testament, the second is gradually to practise preaching, the third to report to the congregation if his said master had spoken befittingly and if he had taught people well about the sect or if, on the contrary, he had defended the Roman Church.

Pairing thus had a triple function: teaching, training and control.

This micro-society in the simplest degree, limited as it was to two individuals, still respected a hierarchy, for the elder of the two men was the master. The power he exercised was justified by his greater knowledge. This structure is confirmed both by the Morel–Masson report and Pierre Griot's confession. Those who would like to see the Poor of Lyons as an egalitarian society compared to the hierarchical structure of the Catholic Church are projecting on to them an *a priori* notion that is belied by the testimonies. There is nothing surprising about this hierarchy, for the Poor of Lyons grew from and belonged to a society that was thoroughly and structurally hierarchical. We saw above that their original inspiration was egalitarian and therefore revolutionary, which is why it did not survive the test of time. The master's power, however, was not absolute; the testimony the younger of the two men had to provide about his master during the annual synod established a certain reciprocity.

The letter to the reformers in 1530 describes how, 'Once a year, we ministers all meet to discuss our affairs in a general council.' This was confirmed by Pierre Griot, cross-examined two years later:

All the *barbes* and preachers of the said sect meet once a year between the mountains and the region of Piedmont. In this way, this last year they met in Piedmont in the Luserna valley in a place named Le Serre in which place there are but ten or twelve houses. And they always meet towards the end of the month of August. And he has heard it said they always meet in this country.

The young man, whose experience was limited, made several mistakes.

The meetings were not always held in Piedmont since, in 1530 for example, they apparently met in Mérindol in Provence. Piedmont was probably the most frequent choice, offering as it did a safer refuge at the bottom of the valleys which were only just accessible. The meetings could bring together many men, even if only the *barbes*, that is to say the Brothers from the west, were present. In his *Historia breve* written at the end of the sixteenth century, Gerolamo Miolo asserted that 'once 140 of them met at a synod held in the vale of Laux in the Chisone valley'. The inquisitor Jean of Roma alone identified 40–42 preachers. It is impossible to give a precise figure for it certainly varied.

Once all the Brothers from the various regions across the western diaspora were present, the meeting could begin. Here, too, we should not imagine an egalitarian assembly. The hierarchy's rights prevailed. The direction of the synod was collegiate, as was the organisation of the body of *barbes* and, issuing from this, the entire community of believers. Although, as we saw above, the 1477–88 trials and the *barbes* cross-examined in 1492 evoke a 'grand master', I have found no trace of this from the beginning of the sixteenth century. The term may, however, have referred to one of the leaders. Pierre Griot is accurate on this issue: 'In their synodal congregation, there are four governors of their synod, by whose advice all the others are governed. And the four who preside at present are called Louis, the oldest, the other Stephen, the other Daniel and the fourth Luke.' It is difficult to identify these people, for there are no further details. This annual gathering was essential to exchange information and co-ordinate the Poor of Lyons' religious life. News from every corner of the diaspora was recounted. At the synod in Le Serre, for example, 'was Antoine Guérin, a hatter from Avignon who told the said company how there was an inquisitor in Provence called master Jean of Roma, who took people from their sect'. The entire community could thus harmonise and listen to the vicissitudes in the different regions, even finding solutions or at least organising help.

The *barbes* also brought back the alms they had collected. As we saw, Philip Regis in 1451 declared he had received 300 ducats two years before. This is attested by Jean of Roma as well as by Morel and Masson. It is again Pierre Griot who informs us about how the money was used. He explains that the governors 'give them as much money as is needed for their journey and, when they return the following year, if they have money which has been given them as they preach during their travels they all put it in common before the entire congregation. And the said money is distributed for the needs of the poor of their sect.' The inquisitor only paid attention to the provisions made for travelling, completely overlooking their concern for poverty which so characterises the Poor of Lyons. The royal commissioners, on the other hand, who were members of the Parlement, only retained the second aspect in a report addressed to Francis I in 1533. They noted that at the annual synod the *barbes* 'bring all the money they have collected and there, they order that it be distributed amongst the poor of their sect'. The role of the synodal congregation was therefore to enable information to be exchanged and gifts of money to be distributed and shared. It was also an opportunity to control the *barbes'* lives, morals and their mission.

Pierre Griot affirmed that if the preacher had not spoken befittingly and if he had not preached well, 'he would be disciplined and reprimanded also if he has taken the money of the poor, if he has not lived a chaste life, if he has scandalised the people, if he has not been diligent and exemplary. For if he has faulted he will be punished or deprived of his preaching mission.' Morel adds, 'Before leaving the above-mentioned council, we all ask each other forgiveness for our faults. When someone commits a sexual sin, he is expelled from our society and he is forbidden to return to the mission of preaching.' Finally, pastoral assignments were defined at the synod. The preachers were organised in twos, one experienced man, one younger, and each pair was designated a missionary zone. As Morel states, 'We are transferred two by two from one place to another. Indeed we do not stay in the same place for more than two or three years, with the possible exception of the old men, who are sometimes authorised to stay in the same place for life.' The peregrinations of the *barbes* and the eastern Brothers are essential, firm characteristics. Pierre Griot states that 'The four governors send out their preachers in twos to different lands and provinces.' This mobility, conforming perfectly with the evangelical model, had spiritual advantages, for example by preventing the *barbes* from getting too attached to one family or person. It was also an efficient way of escaping more easily from investigators and hindering their inquiries. Jean of Roma had understood this: 'The aforementioned preachers never come two years running to the same province so as not to be recognised, but are transferred from province to province. So, when one has left a province, another one comes the following year.' These expeditions were carried out clandestinely, so as to protect the *barbes*. The mission, however, remained perilous, despite their pre-cautions.

LABOUR AND PIETY

There is no need here to go back over what we have seen to constitute the Brothers' mission in the east and the west. Preachers across the diaspora were characterised by their clandestinity, by the fact that they preached and heard confession solely within benevolent households, possibly by signs identifying them to one another, and by alms-collecting. Apart from Friedrich Reiser, an exceptional case with an exceptional destiny, who trekked back and forth across central Europe (his name indeed means 'traveller'), we know little about the Brothers' missionary itineraries. We can, however, learn about the duration of their travels, in the west at least, from two *barbes*, Martin and Jean, interrogated in 1492. One year before, Martin and another companion had come to France via Mont Cenis and visited the provinces of Bourbonnais, Rouergue, Forez, Auvergne, Limousin and Bordelais. The following year he set off with the *barbe* Jean, but he fell ill and had to remain in Italy. Jean went on alone through Genoa, Nice and Provence to visit Vivarais, Auvergne, Velay, Beaujolais, Chambéry in Savoy, Gap and the Dauphiné. Meanwhile, Martin recovered and set off with André d'Anani via Genoa, Nice and Aix-en-Provence; they crossed Vivarais, Auvergne and Beaujolais and finally reached Lyons where the two companions met six other *barbes*.

Martin and Jean set off again as a preaching pair as they had before to Velay, Auvergne, Forez and Beaujolais. They went through Lyons again before travelling to Bresse, Geneva, Annecy, Conflans, the outskirts of Albertville, Aiguebelle, La Chambre, Saint-Jean-de-Maurienne, Valloire in Savoy, Névache, Bardonnèche, Savoulx and finally Oulx where they were arrested. It had not been intended as their final stop. They had planned to go to the valleys of Cluson, Saint Martin and Luserna and return westwards to Freissinières, L'Argentière and Vallouise before going to Lombardy where they had arranged to meet two other *barbes*. This gives us an idea of the hundreds if not thousands of kilometres covered by these religious vagabonds during the course of a season's preaching. The area attributed to the preachers was not always so vast. It must have varied considerably according to the density of believers living in any one place. Whatever the case, the annual meeting, generally in Piedmont, made the length of a missionary circuit even greater. Yet the *barbes* carried out their tedious and gratifying mission faithfully and untiringly, despite the ever-present risks they ran.

The *barbes* claimed to exercise a profession so as to justify their travels more easily to authorities ill disposed to nomads. The rare professions they are recorded as having are thus all characterised by the need to travel. Originally, Vaudès was certainly adamant that the preachers should not work. The apostle should live by his words in order to dedicate himself entirely to his mission. Did the same hold for the *barbes*? In Barge, in the mid-fourteenth century, masters from Apulia stopped at the home of a merchant Antonio Volpi. Being in the habit of receiving visitors, the merchant aroused no suspicions in the town when strangers called on him. The *barbe* from Apulia evoked by Philip Regis in 1451 indeed passed himself off as a merchant. The defendant himself and his companion, both 'lieutenants of the *barbes*' claimed to be haberdashers. Others were needle-makers, to such an extent that presenting a needle-case sometimes became a means of recognising the *barbes*. Jean of Roma wrote to the Parlement in Aix saying, 'The preachers go the whole world over, apparently vile and simple mechanics', by which he means craftsmen.

Nevertheless, there remained the question of paid labour in relation to the *barbes*: was it only a cover for their clandestine activities or was it a real means by which to live, complementing the alms they received? The Protestant historian Gerolamo Miolo, writing at the end of the sixteenth century, said, 'They devoted themselves to medicine, and surgery and some of them also practised mechanical and manual arts such as carving wooden spoons, making purses and needles according to the custom of the country and they tanned skins following the example of, and imitating Saint Paul.' In their report, Morel and Masson affirmed that 'We do various manual crafts to please our people and to avoid idleness.' In other words, certain preachers did work. Medicine appears to have been a favoured occupation. In his *Histoire ecclésiastique* written in 1644, Pierre Gilles noted that: 'Each man ... apart from the knowledge and exercise of his ministry was also learned in an occupation of some sort, and especially medicine and surgery, for which they were much heard and esteemed.'

There are many indications that health was one of the *barbes*' special concerns. In 1487, Odin Crespin from Freissinières in the Dauphiné, recounted during his cross-examination how, some years before, he had had an injured leg. His uncle told him, 'If you will believe me, I shall take you to a man, a great cleric, who will quickly cure you.' This is what happened. Odin's uncle and the *barbe* spoke together, then Odin came into the room alone with the *barbe* who questioned him about the place where he lived and asked him if he habitually swore oaths. He was then examined medically: 'Then he wanted to see his injured tibia and said to him; if you will do as I say you will recover. And he told him that he would apply a herb called miltalha to it.' Morel and Masson confirm this particular concern for sickness: 'When someone is ill, if we are called we visit the patient to bring consolation in the form of exhortations and prayers; and sometimes we visit the infirm, without even being called, being aware of their indigency, to help them spiritually and physically.' Furthermore, in its collection of 'Waldensian documents' the University

Library in Cambridge possesses a short text of three folios dating from the fifteenth century written in vulgar Latin, which constitutes a sort of manual for making medicines, giving the composition, the means to concoct and use them, instructions for use and their efficacy.

The meaning behind the *barbes'* medical training becomes clear if we recall that the Poor of Lyons spurned the cult of saints, their shrines and their relics to which the people of the era normally turned in times of sickness or infirmity. Waldensians did not appeal to the healing saints but preferred to turn to their *barbes*. 'Saints are not to be applied to when in need [*necessitatibus*], for they cannot help us', said Thomas Guiot in 1495. Furthermore, the *barbes* must have been aware that this activity, which was both charitable and productive, was also in keeping with evangelical advice. The holy scriptures themselves urged caring for the sick and the infirm. Moreover, the Brothers doubtless felt that by acting in this way, they were conforming to the apostolic life they sought to live. They were 'healing the sick' as Jesus had ordered his disciples when sending them on their mission (Matthew 10: 8). The Brothers' mendicant order probably doubled in this way as a hospital order.

The final trait to consider which, while not limited to the duration of the *barbes'* mission, was no less an important feature in their daily lives, is the piety of these men. We know their asceticism to have been rigorous. It was reinforced by pious practices the formalism of which may appear astonishing now. Morel and Masson's testimony, the sincerity of which is beyond doubt, attests that:

As is the custom we pray humbly on our knees for a quarter of an hour or thereabouts, every day, morning and evening, before and after dinner, before and after supper, at midday and sometimes at night, when sleep evades us, and after the meeting with the assembled people. But when we want to eat or drink, we nearly always say the Lord's Prayer. In truth, we do not say these prayers out of superstition or in vain belief or in respect for some time or other, but prompted only by the honour of God and the good of the soul.

Whatever the *barbes* may say, this ritualism is strangely reminiscent of the hours of prayer which ordered the monk's day. The reformers in 1530 were astonished by the Waldensians' attachment to pious rites. The *barbes* were accustomed to these ancestral traditions which they shared in common with the regular Roman clergy.

A FUTURE *BARBE*

We shall conclude this study of the *barbes* with a concrete example. Morel and Masson's letter is particularly rich in information about the preachers but it evokes them as a body; no room is given to individuals. Apart from the 1492 trials, the proceedings led against Pierre Griot are the best means by which to apprehend what a *barbe* really was in practice. We have already referred to the accounts of the cross-examination on several occasions and considered the relevance of Griot's words. It is now appropriate to stop to consider the man who, against his will admittedly, provided and presented the information we have analysed. One fine October day, which is nothing uncommon in the splendid Provençal autumn, Pierre Griot was returning from the annual synod which had taken place that year in Le Serre in the Angrogna valley in Piedmont. As was customary, and indeed prudent, the wayfarer was not alone. From Gapençais he had been travelling with his fellow *barbe*, Jean Gérault, who came from Embrun. They had put up at the 'Saint-Marc' in Sisteron and at 'Le Sauvage' in Manosque. The next day, when they had turned off the highway by the river Durance which they had been following, they dined at La Bastidonne before arriving after nightfall in Lourmarin, at last in the Provençal region settled by the Poor of Lyons. They did not enter the village but knocked at the door of one of the big isolated farmhouses called *bastides*. Pierre spent twelve days there before being seized, while his colleague was absent, by the inquisitor Jean of Roma, probably after being denounced. He was transferred to the episcopal prisons in Apt and was subjected to eight cross-examinations in November and December 1532.

From session to session, without torture being used, the prisoner's resistance was felt to waver. Initially he replied laconically, attempting to hedge leading questions and feigning illness or ignorance. Little by little, he began to speak more freely, eventually confessing spontaneously and even anticipating the interrogator's questions. The resulting statement, written essentially in French, contains a multitude of details about the Poor of Lyons, their organisation, the 1532 synod which we shall be returning to later, and also the defendant himself. He was a native of 'the region of Briançonnais, in the diocese of Turin, a place called Pate-mouche', a hamlet which still exists in the upper Cluson valley beneath the Sestrière pass. It thus came under the spiritual authority of the archbishop of Turin and the temporal authority of the king of France for at the time the Cluson valley was in the Dauphiné. The family name Griot is characteristic of Pragelato, the parish to which Patemouche belongs. All the Griots registered came from here. There is nothing extraordinary in the fact that a Griot born in Pragelato should come to Provence and belong to the Poor of Lyons. When he was tried, he was about thirty years of age and affirmed that his father and mother were still living and that none of his family had died a violent death. He could, however, be dissembling, for a positive answer would instantly have confirmed the inquisitor's suspicions. Pierre had heard of Cattaneo's crusade in the Alpine valleys in 1487–8 during which twenty-one Griots from Pragelato were cited for Waldensian heresy.

Pierre was a bachelor and two years before had been a muleteer by trade. Since then, he had become a barber because 'his industry had taught him to know how to heal several wounds'. When the house where he was staying was searched, a barber's pouch had indeed been found which he claimed to own. He had been following the special training intended for future *barbes* for two years. He had learnt to read and write; indeed, on two occasions he signed the statements drawn up after the cross-examination, writing in the *langue d'oc* used in Briançonnais. He already knew several books of the New Testament by heart including Matthew and the catholic epistles in his mother tongue. His teacher during the winter training in theory had been Jean Serre, 'the lame man from Murs', an important, learned *barbe* who was finally captured and who recanted in 1539. In the spring of 1531 and 1532, Pierre had accompanied Louis, 'one of the principal *barbes*', on a preaching tour which had taken them 'to *bastides* and *plans*' (large isolated farmhouses and table-land). They visited families of believers in fifteen or more neighbourhoods in Provence and Comtat venaissin in the northernmost region of the Luberon. On this occasion, he spoke aloud to read from the holy scriptures but did not apparently preach.

This pastoral team confirms what the Morel report says about hierarchy. Pierre Griot was not yet a *barbe*, as he told the inquisitor: 'He had not yet been received as a preacher, for he had only joined the congregation that year, and there, he had been given as companion a certain Johannet, who is from the Embrun region, to come and preach in Provence.' When the *barbe* Louis encouraged him to speak aloud, he protested, 'How can I do that? I'm not a clerk, I can hardly read.' To which the pedagogue replied, 'You will learn, little by little.' He could not, however, speak when or wherever he chose. Jean of Roma had noticed this organisation:

The custom observed among the preachers of his sect is that the first and more knowledgeable man should preach and teach in the *bastides* and more learned houses and his less experienced companion should preach in the poor houses. This is why, being less apt, he has never preached in the home of Michel Serre, but he did go to the house with another man named Louis. And the said Louis preached in the house of the said Michel Serre.

Pierre Griot was in fact always paired with an older, more competent *barbe:* Louis, Georges, Antoine Guérin, Jean Gérault. This demonstrates in concrete terms the inequality which prevailed in the preaching couple, as described by Morel and Masson. It was based above all on learning.

The young man's knowledge at this time certainly appears rudimentary. His ignorance of theology reflects the Waldensian belief that a future *barbe*'s initial training should be mostly bible-oriented. Griot was in a singularly disadvantageous position before the Dominican leading the trial. He was, moreover, untrained in oratorical skills whereas the Black Friar revelled in what could have become a verbal fencing match. We can even sense his disappointment at having an adversary who was beneath him. He seeks debates, even bringing supplementary elements to the defendant's case which he considers so weak. He exploits difficulties, engages in subtle biblical exegesis, quibbling over tiny points of logic to convict the defendant, of course, but also for the pleasure of demonstrating his own verbal dexterity. He quite visibly relishes his own reasonings and his skill at resolving problems in keeping with the strictest rules of academic disputation. He invariably presents and expounds his *lectio* following the traditional scholastic method: authorities, discussion, conclusion. The two men facing each other evidently came from different worlds intellectually, culturally and spiritually speaking.

On a judicial level too, the young man's ignorance was visibly damaging. When the inquisitor asked him whether he knew of any mortal enemies in the land of Provence, he missed his opportunity and answered no. The testimony of a 'mortal enemy', however, was always impugned, otherwise the proceedings were cancelled. Even over the holy scriptures, Pierre Griot was no match for the Dominican 'professor of the holy scriptures'. While Griot could cite seventeen extracts from the bible, the inquisitor could retort with ninety quotations taken from the scriptures, the Church Fathers and even Aristotle. The future *barbe* even proved unversed in the history of his own Waldensian community. He failed to justify their preaching in secret which was in apparent contradiction with the holy scriptures. He was similarly confounded when Jean of Roma questioned him about the origins of his sect. Griot answered that it dated back to apostolic times. The inquisitor then asked 'why the sect was not spoken of before Peter Valdo three hundred years ago, seeing that the apostles were a good twelve hundred years before Peter Valdo'. Griot 'replied that he really did not know what to say on the matter'. The inquisitor then triumphed, giving what was an implacable verdict in those times when age was a certain guarantee of value: 'It is a new sect then.' Griot's only answer was that he had only known about it for two years, since the beginning of his training.

We do not know what happened next to Pierre Griot, as the trial was interrupted. By law, 'heresiarchs', meaning leaders and preachers of heresy, were condemned to the stake without even being offered the chance to recant. But the young *barbe* and many other defendants were apparently spared, doubtless by an order from the king in spring 1533 suspending Jean of Roma's proceedings. Pierre Griot emerges again sixteen years later in the registers of the Parlement of Provence. He is cited as a witness on 4 June 1548 during proceedings for heresy against Poncet Martin from Roussillon. The list of witnesses includes 'Pierre Griot, from Briançonnais, in the diocese of Turin, from the place called Patemouche'. We do not know whether he was present as a free man or a prisoner. He was, in any case, still alive, probably at the price of the inevitable abjuration.

Pierre Griot hardly comes over positively during his trial. But certain mitigating circumstances should be recalled in his favour. First, he was still young and in training, which explains both his lack of experience and certain deficiencies in his learning. Next, such source material as this is hardly in the defendant's favour, always presenting him in an uncomfortable and humiliating situation of inferiority. With the exception of a few great *barbes*, however, he was doubtless typical of the preachers recruited from among the devotees and trained as he went along. The young man is a fair illustration of the pastoral body from the Poor of Lyons. He embodies the characteristic features of the *barbes*: a native of the Alps and a bachelor, he could read and write, he practised a trade, received the initial training for preachers and dedicated himself to itinerant, clandestine preaching. Ultimately, during his trial, a dramatic, moving and often pathetic occasion when his life was in jeopardy, Pierre Griot, the future *barbe* showed himself to be typical rather than rare, more fragile than heroic and is all the more endearing for it.

A SPIRITUAL POWER

What power did the faithful attribute to these *barbes*? It had to be considerable to survive in such a potentially unstable context. In the case of a serious clash of opinions between a *barbe* and a devotee, and it could happen to anyone, there was always the fear that the former might be denounced. A clandestine authority is remarkably vulnerable. Traitors were not unheard of, as Morel's report and Griot's example make clear. On the whole, however, the Poor of Lyons were faithful to their preachers. This meant they protected their clandestinity, recognised their utility and accepted their authority. The image the devotees kept of their leaders, as attested by the court reports, was positive from all points of view. They greatly esteemed the preachers who permanently put their lives in peril to bring help and support to their flocks. The trials unanimously make it clear that the Brothers' apostolic life earned them this consideration. Their power derived positively from the same reasoning that negatively denied the priests of the Roman Church their authority. In other words, the Waldensian believers had perfectly understood the 'donatist' message. Just as the pope, the bishops and the priests no longer had the power to give valid sacraments and had lost their authority because their lives were unworthy, so the preachers, living as true disciples, were as a consequence invested with authority.

This manichaean vision is attested simply and clearly in all the testimonies. In 1487, Jean Juvenal from Mentoulles said of the *barbes*: 'Their sect is the best because they live as apostles and follow the life of Christ and of poverty and they have the full power to accord or withhold absolution.' In the same year, his compatriot Jean Fabre clearly appreciated the causal link between a lifestyle and the power deriving from it: 'The *barbes* have the power to grant or refuse forgiveness because they keep apostolic lives, but not the priests of the Roman Church whose lives are too lax.' Monet Rey from the Valentinois spoke thus of ecclesiastics in 1494: 'Because of their bad lives, they do not have more power to absolve than the preachers or masters of this sect. Laymen as they may be, they have the same power as priests and ecclesiastics.' Further into his trial, he delivered a theoretical explanation of sacerdotal power:

Preachers and priests proceed from the same order. But the priests have swayed towards avarice and the sensualism of the world and they [the preachers] have remained in poverty which they have observed to this day. They were ordained by God to preach the true Catholic faith in the world as the apostles did but, so that evil men may not find them, they have to proceed with caution and prudence.

He of course justifies clandestinity in passing.

This conceptual explanation, which the people understood and accepted perfectly, was summarised in a saying that recurs on every page of the Dauphinois trials: 'One's authority is in keeping with one's goodness' (*Quantum quis habet bonitatem, tantum habet et auctoritatis*). This opinion, which was widely shared by the Poor of Lyons, corresponded to the teaching of the preachers. In 1495, Thomas Guiot reported that the *barbes* 'told how the ecclesiastics led lives which were too lax while they, the *barbes*, kept good, holy lives ... They said that in their holy lives they took after Saint Peter and that they had the power to absolve sins.' Even Claude Seyssel, archbishop of Turin, admitted in his treatise

of 1520 that one reason for the expansion of the Waldensian heresy was
the unworthiness of the clergy.

The homage to the *barbes* echoed also from the east. When the
inquisitor Gallus of Neuhaus, leading investigations in Bohemia in about
1345, asked a suspect how they named their preachers in the sect, the
man answered that they called them 'important [*noti*] and good men'.
The followers from Stettin at the end of the fourteenth century speak of
'good men', and 'holy men'. Let us take the example of Sophia who
appeared in court on 9 February 1394. Questioned about what she
thought of the Brothers, she replied, 'that they are good men sent on
their mission on earth by God, that, like the apostles, they have the
authority to preach, to hear confessions, to forgive sins, to impose
penance, better than priests, and she thinks they are priests but not
consecrated by ritual by the bishop of Kammin nor sent by the bishop'.
This double affirmation, according power to the Brothers and refusing it
to priests, and recognising the preachers as laymen, recurs like a leitmotif
in the proceedings. The same opinion was prevalent in Bohemia in the
mid-fourteenth century, as we saw above. There is no doubting that the
followers held their preachers in the highest esteem.

The believers from Pomerania interrogated in Stettin attribute a
curious particularity to the Brothers. A good number of the peasants
called to give testimonies maintained that the preachers' message and
their pastoral action was guaranteed by the journey they allegedly made
'before' or 'in' paradise where they listened to God's word in order to
receive authority and wisdom from God or an interceding angel. The
frequency of such voyages varies from one declaration to the next:
yearly, according to some; or the overriding opinion, where the
symbolism of the number is clear, 'seven in seven years'. The Poor of
Lyons' belief in their Brothers' journey to paradise is attested in Austria
and Bavaria in the first half of the fourteenth century. The myth was
enriched with two further details from two declarations. The first
specifies that their return is realised 'in diverse tribulations, by the fields,
in the thorns'. The journey would thus be a kind of ritual initiation to
conquer good by refusing evil, acquiring a spiritual prize which they
would then pass on to their believers.

The theme is taken up in a richer deposition by Aleyd, the wife of
Thyde Takken, from Baumgarten near Könisberg:

Two of these apostolic Brothers and heresiarchs came before hell and heard the
wretched clamour and saw the devils bearing souls to hell and saying: 'this one
committed adultery, this one was a usurer, this one was an innkeeper', and
likewise other sorts of vices of the souls. Then they went before paradise and

heard the voice of the Lord God giving them wisdom and doctrine, which they should transmit to the men who were entrusted to them on earth.

Aleyd had learned these beliefs from another woman, in the oral tradition. The inquisitor considered her a simple-hearted woman (*simplicem*). The anecdote reveals the folklore with which these populations were imbued. It shows us how cultural folklore and religion mutually inspired each other. Was this belief 'heretical'? On a doctrinal level, it was doubly heretical: neither Roman clerics nor Brothers would have recognised themselves in these strange travellers seeking truth. On a psychological level, it justified the clandestine preaching that was officially prohibited. It confronts us with one of the great, profound realities of cultural folklore in the rural populations of pre-industrial Europe. It evokes the ritual progression of shamanic initiation in traditional stages: a traumatising experience that the shaman manages to overcome, followed by the revelation of his supernatural powers. It comes as no surprise that certain peasants transposed the myth into the religious domain and that the Poor of Lyons applied it to the Brothers.

The preachers come over as the most solid structuring element of their community. They enjoyed real prestige amidst their followers, as the inquisitorial proceedings we have examined make perfectly clear, for which there is a straightforward explanation. These shepherds dedicated their lives to their flocks, giving up family and goods for them; they were preachers who underwent a suitable training period and then announced the Word untiringly despite the perils they faced at all times; they were tireless wayfarers trekking across Europe to rekindle the faith of the believers; permanent messengers, embodying the links that held the diaspora together, exchanging news, maintaining the fragile unity of this community which survived despite its dispersion; they were confessors listening to an anguished population in search of counsel, comfort and forgiveness; imitators of the apostles whose harsh, poor lives guaranteed their authenticity; finally, they were healers, taking care as much of the people's spiritual health as of their bodily well-being.

How could these men have not enjoyed a particular status within their community? In my opinion, three elements account for it. These men had originated from the flocks they tended and could understand them; at the same time they were different, better than them, living in extreme exigency which invested them with an uncontested spiritual power; they were readers and writers, 'clerks' of a sort, which ensured them a privileged position in an illiterate society. Some people from the Dauphiné said they resembled ecclesiastics because they had books; believers from Stettin considered them as priests whilst differentiating them from the Roman clergy. In fact the Brothers and *barbes* represented the quintessence of the Poor of Lyons. Whereas originally all the Poor of Lyons were preachers, little by little the people had to accept that they could constitute but a pale reflection of the ideal life that the Brothers, meanwhile, embodied. They ensured the movement's continuity, they justified the existence of the dissent and reassured the faithful.

It was at this point that, when the inquisitor asked Pierre Griot 'Who are the Poor of Lyons?', the future preacher replied, 'they are the *barbes* who preach the Waldensian sect'. The term *barbe* alone denoted the dissent. During the same trial, Jean of Roma evoked 'the sect of the *barbes*'. The preachers were of such importance that the authorities accorded them a special place. They pursued the *barbes* before the others, they sought to eliminate them first. In 1551, the king's advocate Jacques Aubéry reckoned that the heresy spread because of them; he recommended that the 'dogmatisers and false preachers called *barbes*' be seized. Already in 1533, in the wake of Jean of Roma, the Parlement of Provence had expressed its opinion to Francis I: 'If these *barbes* are caught, may they be punished and executed as heretics without remission, for all the evil comes from them.' In other words, the Poor of Lyons and their enemies all concurred in this respect: the preachers were the foremost members of the movement. They were all the greater because, men of the spoken word and the Word as they were, they were also men of letters and of the holy scriptures.

BIBLIOGRAPHY

Biller, P., '*Curate infirmos*: The Medieval Waldensian Practice of Medicine'. *Studies in Church History* 19, 1982, Oxford, pp. 55–77.
'*Multum jejunantes et se castigantes*: Medieval Waldensian Asceticism'. *Studies in Church History* 22, 1985, Oxford, pp. 215–18.
Chevalier, J., *Mémoire historique sur les hérésies en Dauphiné avant le XVIe siècle.* Valence, 1890.
Fournier P.-F., 'Les vaudois en Auvergne vers la fin du XVe siècle d'après les interrogatoires de deux barbes'. *Bulletin historique et scientifique de l'Auvergne,* 1942, pp. 49–63.
Merlo G. G., 'Sul valdismo "colto" tra il XIIIe il XIV secolo'. In *I valdesi e l'Europa.* Torre Pellice, 1982, pp. 67–98.
Weitzecker, G., 'Processo di un valdese nell'anno 1451'. *Rivsta Cristiana,* 1881, pp. 363–7.

7

A CULTURE OF THEIR OWN: THE WRITTEN AND THE SPOKEN WORD

Dissenters as they were, the Poor of Lyons belonged nevertheless to their time. This did not mean they were completely identical to their contemporaries. In economic terms, they resembled those around them once the main body of believers had given up the original tenet of absolute poverty. Poor and richer fellows lived together in the same religious community. In social terms, they formed an ensemble which was strikingly homogeneous, for apart from a few, rare exceptions, they all worked the land. While it was truly original for a dissenting group to come essentially from the peasantry, they did not contrast in any way with the population in Europe which was predominantly rural from the fourteenth to the sixteenth century. In linguistic terms too, they fitted perfectly into the various regions where they had settled. After the necessary period of adaptation for those of them who were immigrants, which was often the case, they quickly adopted the language used locally in their adoptive country. They indeed adapted so well, so conclusively, that the diaspora was split into two linguistic unities, the Germanic populations and the Romance populations. While links between the two did exist, they nevertheless proved tenuous. Beyond these shared features, the Poor of Lyons were, however, very distinct from their contemporaries. If they were not assimilated over the centuries, it was of course due to their religious dissent in itself, but also more generally to the culture they developed of their own. This was a result of the special role preaching had in their community, of the place the master and the book occupied amongst them, and the favourite themes which the Brothers expounded.

THE STRENGTH OF THE SPOKEN WORD

How difficult it is to picture a cultural environment that is utterly unlike our own. We are assailed by images and sounds; some would say by noise. We are constantly besieged, and the battlefield starts at home with the radio, records and television; it even starts before that, it comes from within. We are created by the image and sound, invaded to such an extent that the previous cultural era, marked by the phenomenal conquest of reading and writing made possible by printing, appears to be outdated, even nearing extinction. In the modern world, the completely illiterate or even analphabetic no longer exist, thanks to considerable efforts to bring a minimum of literacy within everyone's reach. There are of course a growing number of people who learn to read and write but then forget when they no longer use their skills. To understand the distant times of the Poor of Lyons, however, we must go back not only to pre-audio-visual times but to an era predating the printed word.

As far as the majority of the population was concerned, it was also an era before the written word was accessible to all. A manuscript fetched a price well beyond the means of the common people, even when parchment was replaced by paper. Some historians have shown not only how, in pre-industrial societies, writing remained a skill reserved to clerks, who were usually clergymen, but also to what extent rural and urban populations barely came into contact with paper. Peasants in the fourteenth or fifteenth century could feasibly spend their entire lives without so much as touching a sheet of paper. If an opportunity arose to do so, it was in any case quite exceptional. If our ancestors did not own texts themselves, they only set eyes on them at church or in the manor house. In the latter case, it was generally because the lord of the manor had summoned them to pledge allegiance or to pay dues of some sort which the steward would painstakingly record in his register. In church, cumbersome liturgical books would be opened before them, which were all the more impressive, dating as they did from distant, mysterious times; they were written in Latin and proclaimed God's Word. Furthermore, from the fifteenth century, official orders from religious and lay authorities were sometimes pinned to the doors of the parish church.

Such a description must of course be adapted to bear in mind differences in social class, changes across the centuries and also customs from one region to another. A citizen from Florence, for instance, was more familiar by far with the written word than was a contemporary living in the country around Stettin in Pomerania. Similarly, the south of France was a land of written law where a strong tradition of drawing up documents was maintained; these were considered the only irrefutable proof in courts in certain cases. This was at least the way the situation had evolved by the sixteenth century. In any case, in the south, people from the countryside had been used to turning to a notary to settle various deeds and agreements since the fourteenth century. Anyone with possessions wishes to pass them on, which implies inscribing such wishes in a will; a totally illiterate population would therefore need to appeal to a notary, who was an inevitable cultural go-between. In the Provençal countryside, for example, almost every parish had one if not two notaries, which implies they were not short of clients. Who, after all, did not possess a small plot of land, a house or a cave carved into the limestone? The peasants in these regions were for the most part small landowners, although this did not imply they were independent. But even those who truly owned nothing at all could still not avoid the written word at the notary's office, either when signing for a purchase, a sale, a marriage or a will; or perhaps for a loan; or again as a witness to a deed of some sort or another. It would thus appear certain that the peasants from the south came into frequent if not daily contact with the written word.

The people from the south, city-dwellers and the more affluent may well have owned papers, particularly deeds justifying the purchase of goods or property, or the repayment of debts, but this did not necessarily mean they could read them. In the lower classes, it was extremely rare to own a book before the time when printing was truly widespread. In fact, despite the cultural difference described above, the late medieval world was overwhelmingly oral. This had social and mental consequences: the memory was particularly well developed, simple mnemonics were used, groups of story-tellers were elected; there were times set aside for listening to tales, during the evenings for example; readers and writers formed a class of their own. In other words, this oral world was also structured and hierarchical. The truth is that rural society in the middle ages, which has generally been presented as an oral world, and our introduction above is no exception, was essentially silent. The peasantry left few written traces; they also seldom spoke. There is something both worrying and fascinating about the muteness of the rural world, even when faced with urgent needs or cruel adversity. A multitude of defendants found nothing to say when they came before the judge, even though their lives were in jeopardy. It comes as no surprise, in such a context, to learn of the impact a gifted speaker, even with limited experience, might have on such a population. Without mentioning the local priest whom the parishioners accepted all too easily, the frugal preachers could cause a stir. Their appearance, their accents and their elocution were discussed from house to house, and within the family. A sermon could turn into a uprising, even a revolution, as was the case for the Dominican Savonarola in Florence in the late fifteenth century. The strength of the word would also be found in the realm of witchcraft and magic, for both are, after all, only words. How could such a world, where the image and the sound were absent, have failed to respond to the power and magic of the word?

This, then, was the Waldensians' world. It is easy to understand why they gave such importance to preaching, for what were the Poor of Lyons if not preachers? In the beginning, as we have seen, they were all charged to incite their fellows to be converted, by poverty in particular, so as to attain salvation. In its earliest years, Waldensianism was characterised as an itinerant preaching movement in which men and women alike were preachers. This helps explain the extent to which the Church was committed to defending its monopoly of the Word, not only so as to transmit the true message of God but to keep for itself the right to speak in public, which was a source of real power. Persecution meant that within the Poor of Lyons, preaching was gradually reserved for the leaders, masters and *barbes*. Their mission was altered by their clandestinity; they no longer sought to convert the masses but to maintain the true faith within their own little flock. It was to this end that the Brothers, dedicated to the Word, learned to read, speak in public and recite books of the New Testament by heart before setting off on their travels.

Let us return, then, to our two companions who had reached the village they were heading for. They knew of certain houses where believers lived. One of these, somewhat set apart from the others, could receive them; it had a bedroom with a fireplace and two beds, which were quite exceptional amenities in rural households at the time. But the sun had not yet gone down. They must await nightfall, so as to protect their hosts as much as possible. This enabled Pierre Griot to explain to the inquisitor who asked him why they had gone to this house rather than into the village: 'Because it was night when he arrived.' Having made their identity known to the host family, they were given food, and neighbours were alerted. It was quite an event in the dissenting community. A witness, Antoine Bourgue, questioned by the inquisitor in 1532, testified that a messenger had come for him saying that the uncles had arrived. 'Questioned about the time, said that it was at night.' The news thus spread, from house to house.

When night fell, when the faithful had gathered around the fireplace and the doors were safely locked, the meeting began in an atmosphere of congenial but fearful solidarity. Despite all their precautions, there was always a risk of betrayal. Pierre Griot affirmed that 'they have a secret amongst themselves which is that they never preach their doctrine except before those whom they know to be of their sect. And when they preach in a house, someone always keeps a lookout; and should someone arrive who is not from their sect, they stop preaching.' The night, the fire and the speeches impressed the faithful listeners during the gatherings that were both ritual and secret. This is confirmed by the 1488 Dauphinois trials. Philippe Pastor's wife, for example, described how 'when the *barbes* come they give a sermon in their house by night, by the fireside, and they get the Waldensian neighbours to come together to hear the said sermon'. It was a highly important time for the dissenting community gathered together to listen to the man they accepted as a master. We should not overlook the fact that he too was of the same stock. But he had been trained and he held a mission. He was qualified to speak the Word. The social promotion was considerable. The strength of the word was exemplified not only by the fact that he spoke in public to proclaim the Word of God but also by the absolution the Brothers granted to the penitent who came to confess to them. It was a formidable power that the Poor of Lyons denied to the Roman clergy and accorded to their masters. We do not know the form the sermon took, being oral. It was based, however, on the written word.

THE PRESTIGE OF THE WRITTEN WORD

The Brothers were not only speakers, they had also mastered the written word. From the earliest days of their movement, the Poor of Lyons took books with them on their evangelising missions. In the early fourteenth century, the inquisitor Bernard Gui described them as follows: 'Some of them can read, and sometimes they read what they say and preach, at other times use no books at all. This is naturally the case of those who cannot read; such men ensure they learn by heart.' The inquisitor's view may be rather dated, for it would appear that by this time all the Brothers were capable of reading. Raymond of Costa, for instance, interrogated in 1319 and 1320, owned three books: *The Holy Spirit*, *The Book of Esdras* and a third entitled *Discretis*. By the fifteenth century at least, the book is cited everywhere as one of the *barbe*'s habitual attributes. During his trial in 1494, Monet Rey, from Saint-Mamans near Valence, declared that he went one day to Beauregard, not far from there, at the invitation of a member of his family, in whose house he met two men; the elder began to read from the little books they carried with them. When Pierre Griot was captured in Lourmarin, books were equally found in his bags. He denied owning them before declaring that 'the books that had been found in a little white canvas bag were not his to tell the truth but he thinks they belong to a companion who is called Jeannet', his fellow *barbe*. That the Brothers should have books was striking within a totally illiterate population, and therefore memorable; it was also habitual, as Jean Bresse from Usseaux in the Cluson valley makes clear: 'The *barbes* always carry books.' Familiarity with the written word situated a man socially, distinguishing him from those around him. He was lettered, a clerk and probably a cleric. This was what Marguerite Lantelme from Sestrière understood: 'The *barbe* Simon carried books as if he were an ecclesiastic.' The choice of books, too, was of course revealing.

Before considering their contents, let us consider their appearance. First, do we need to remind ourselves that they were manuscripts? It took a good fifty years before the printing press, which originated on the middle Rhine in the 1450s, came into general use, and the Poor of Lyons did not use it. When they did finally accept the use of printing, they signed their own death warrant. The fact that dozens, even hundreds of manuscripts were thus being passed from preacher to preacher, periodically being seized and destroyed by the Inquisition and just as regularly copied out again, is an indication of just how attached the Waldensians were to them, and also how effective the copyists were at their work. The books were small, 'pocket-sized' opuscules. There is nothing surprising about this; they had to be easy to carry during the constant travels – and we know how heavy paper is – and also easy to conceal. A few escaped the eye of the inquisitor and have survived to this day. It is truly moving to be able to turn the pages of the five booklets which belonged to *barbes*, conserved at the library in Geneva, bearing in mind the distances they had covered, the adventures they had met with and the narrow escapes endured by these little, motionless witnesses which are so endearing, dumb and yet so eloquent. If the book could signal its owner's learning, it could also denounce him, throwing suspicion on him. It all depended on the type of book it was.

The language in which the book was written was a first indication of its type, irrespective of the contents. In the religious domain particularly, Latin was the only accepted language; used by Saint Jerome, the Church, science, law and the chancelleries, it was a guarantee of authenticity, a sign of truth marking the work as worthy of being written down. From the beginning, however, Vaudès dissociated himself from such an imperialist view of Latin. For a series of reasons which we have already considered, the Poor of Lyons preferred what is known as the 'vulgar' tongue, the one the people really used. This meant putting into writing a spoken language which often had no written form. It should be emphasised that this was no secondary phenomenon; rather, it was an innovatory cultural design. The vernacular tongues, previously considered less worthy, were being promoted to the status of a noble language by being written down and ranked equally with Latin. When documents give details about the *barbes'* books, they always record their being written in the local language. In Pragelato, at the end of the fifteenth century, a defendant made the following declaration to the inquisitors about the preachers: 'They carried a book written in French in which their sect is written and when they come to Waldensian houses they read this book written in the vernacular.' In their 1533 report, the royal commissioners from the Parlement of Provence described to the king how the *barbes* 'have some small books in French which contain their errors'. Their pastoral choice is self-evident. In order to be understood by the people, they had not only to speak their language but also to write it so that their flocks might understand the beautiful texts which were the key to their salvation. One of the manuscripts specifies that they were written '*per lo grossier poble e per la simpla gent*' (for the common people and for simple folk), in other words the farm labourers, shepherds and craftsmen who made up the diaspora of dissent. It was the vulgar tongue rather than the book itself which threw suspicion on the *barbe* who carried it.

If their form distinguished the Brothers' books, can the same be said of their contents? What did they contain? The titles of confiscated works are rarely specified, but a certain number of converging signs give us an idea of the kind of discourse they contained. It will come as no surprise to learn that at the heart of these travelling libraries were the holy texts. This had been the case since the earliest days of the movement. The inquisitor Stephen of Bourbon goes to some length to describe how Vaudès had the gospels and certain passages from the bible and from the Fathers translated. Walter Map, an English monk present at the Third Lateran Council in 1179, told in his *De nugis curialium distinctiones quinque* written before 1192 how the Waldensians, 'unlettered men from Lyons', had on this occasion presented the pope with a book written 'in the Gallic tongue'. The book contained the text and a commentary of the psalter, as well as several books from the Old and New Testament. One century later, Bernard Gui described in his manual how 'they have the gospels and the epistles in the vernacular usually and even in Latin since some of them understand it'.

Two hundred years on, the message of the bible was still of foremost importance in their written works. In 1494, Peyronette from Beauregard in the Valentinois recalled her first evening meeting with the *barbes:*

About twenty-five years ago, two strangers came to the house of Pierre Fournier, her husband, since deceased. They were dressed in grey and spoke, it seemed to her, Italian or Lombard and her said husband received them in his house for the love of God. While they were there, at a late hour, after supper, one of them began to read from a little book that he carried with him saying that in this book were written the Gospels and the commandments of the law, which he wanted to explain and make known to all those who were there.

Several centuries after Vaudès, the evangelical and biblical message was still at the heart of the Waldensians' mission. This message was at the core of the itinerant preachers' writings and their sermons.

The privileged position reserved for the Word of God is equally apparent in the training which the community organised for its preachers. As we saw above, this was clearly the case in the 1530s when two testimonies converge: the Morel report, an official, freely expressed document, and Pierre Griot's statement to the inquisitor which is less spontaneous but concrete and personal. Morel and Masson explain that the future *barbes* 'learn by heart all of Matthew and John and the chapters of all the epistles which are called canonical and a fair part of Paul'. This was not merely the theoretical view. Pierre Griot, who was still in training, told the inquisitor that the future *barbe* was made 'to study the New Testament for four or five years until he knew it all by heart, such as the gospel of St Matthew and of St John and the apostles Timothy and Titus and the epistles of St Peter, St John, St James and St Jude'. As far as he was concerned, he added a little later 'that he had spent two years studying St Matthew and the canonical epistles', which he indeed already knew by heart 'in his mother tongue, the Briançonnais dialect'. The Brothers' favourite works, in other words, were the gospels of Matthew and John, the letters of Paul known as the pastoral letters, and the epistles of Peter, John, James and Jude called the catholic or canonical epistles. We cannot fail to be struck by the converging testimonies from two totally different sources, given in completely opposing circumstances within two years. To dispel any remaining doubt concerning the *barbes*' bible-oriented, and especially New Testament-oriented religious culture, let us turn to the works that have survived from their library to be certain.

THE *BARBES*' BOOKS

More than two hundred manuscripts, often grouped or even bound together, have been identified as 'Waldensian' or linked to the Poor of Lyons and are conserved in about fifteen different libraries in Europe. They consist primarily of biblical extracts or, in a few rare unlinked cases, documents such as the one in Vienna transcribing the Bergamo meeting in 1218 and the Munich document. Three collections are particularly rich: those in the libraries of Cambridge (seven manuscripts), Dublin (six manuscripts) and Geneva (five manuscripts). Edouard Montet was the first to undertake a systematic study of the entire collection in 1885, analysing the evolution that can be traced within the corpus. As we saw above, all the documents came from the same half-century, so the evolution could not be inferred from their dates; across the ages, however, a form of stratification took place which the author broke down into four phases: 'Catholic' for the beginning in the twelfth and thirteenth centuries; then 'Vaudoise' in the poems, treatises and commentaries of *Pater Noster* and the Creed; next 'Taborite', a sign of the Hussite influence; and finally 'Protestant' for the very last writings. The homogeneous quality of the corpus is worth noting: all the manuscripts come from the same region in the upper valleys in the Alps (Cluson and Luserna valleys), were written as far as can be ascertained between 1450 and 1520 and most of them are in Romance, a form of Provençal. A few are in Latin but nearly all of them are in a tongue and a script that denote their voluntary archaism. Provençal, a spoken language only, had to be bound into a written form. In this way, a language form evolved for their religious celebrations and catechism. By being close to the spoken language, it could be perfectly understood by all, which was the preachers' principal concern from the earliest days.

The holy scriptures and the New Testament in particular occupy the central place in the Brothers' books. We have already seen the fervour with which the Poor of Lyons read the bible, memorising passages so as to imitate the life of the apostles and so attain eternal salvation. There should be no doubting the fact that biblical extracts represented the most frequently encountered texts amongst the preachers, each one probably owning a copy. If this was truly the case, it implies that a considerable number of copies existed, only a few of which have survived to this day. In the five copies known to us, the New Testament is considered as a whole. In his study of the Provençal and Waldensian bibles, published in 1889, Samuel Berger examined the five manuscripts. He even tried to establish their origins and various influences. The Old Testament, however, is never complete; the selected texts reveal the Brothers' particular religious sensibility. The Carpentras and Dublin bibles include Ecclesiastes, the Song of Solomon, the Wisdom of Solomon and Ecclesiasticus. The same orientation is reflected in the Cambridge and Grenoble bibles. Their liking for exemplary tales is clear in the choice of the sapiential books: Tobit, Job and 2 Maccabees. The faithful little flock who were forever persecuted doubtless saw themselves in the stories of a just man suffering for God.

As well as the canonical books, the Poor of Lyons added certain other, later books usually considered apocryphal or 'deuterocanonical' which they seem particularly attached to, such as *Pastor Hermas, La oracion de Manasesses* and the book of Esdras, a copy of which belonged to Raymond of Costa. Their typically medieval predilection denotes a genuine concern to interiorise their religion. Such readings attest the importance the Poor of Lyons gave to penance. *La oracion de Manasesses* (The Prayer of Manasseh) is a devastating appeal for divine mercy, an expression of sincere repentance, a penitential prayer given as food for thought for every believer plunged into present vicissitudes but promised eternal happiness. These sacred texts were further supplemented by books written by the Church Fathers. Writing about the Waldensian times, Stephen of Bourbon specified that, as well as certain biblical books, Vaudès had commissioned translations of the 'authorities of the saints' which Bernard Gui identifies more clearly as 'some maxims of St Augustine, Jerome, Ambrose and Gregory', in other words the four Fathers of the Latin Church whose dicta the Poor of Lyons called *sententiae*. None of the surviving manuscripts includes patristic books, with the sole exception of one in Cambridge entitled 'Sententiae of St Gregory'. Various references and allusions recurring throughout the treatises are a fair indication that readings and meditation based on the traditional writings of Latin Christianity were maintained in the Brothers' community.

The corpus is not just made up of holy scriptures, the apocrypha and the Church Fathers. It would be over-conscientious to analyse them all individually here or even to list them; there is no need either to follow Montet's example and distinguish various layers. Identifying the various types and situating the principal themes will suffice to give us an idea of the sort of pious literature they produced. In truth, we are not dealing so much with an original literature in terms of its contents as with rereadings of classical works, a selection from the mass available to them, or a different approach to such texts denoting their particular sensibility. This sensibility, which can be traced in all the manuscripts, derives from the ideal cherished by the Waldensians since the origins of their movement: the desire to live in accordance with the evangelical model and to meditate on the Sermon on the Mount (Matthew 5), a central text in the Waldensians' reflections, rather than debating doctrinal speculations. Their line of thought was moral rather than dogmatic, practical rather than speculative. Their approach was characterised above all by its pastoralism.

This tendency was expressed in several forms which we might call 'literary genres'. Eight poems, made up of more than 2,200 lines, were composed between the late fourteenth and the early sixteenth century. Fine examples of this production are *Lo Payre eternal*, *La Barca*, *Lo Novel Confort* and *Lo Novel Sermon*. All these writings reflect the Waldensians' religious world, but the most famous and probably the most frequently read in the community, appearing as it does in five manuscripts, was doubtless the *Nobla Leyçon*. This poem emphasises the persecution of the faithful flock and its masters, describing how the bad shepherds oppressed them. The most constant themes of the Waldensians' experience as a dissent can be found here:

But I dare to say, for it happens to be true, that all the popes there have been since Sylvester until the present one, and all the cardinals, and all the bishops, and all the priests, all these together do not have enough power to be able to forgive a single mortal sin; God alone can forgive, since no-one else can do so.

Another example, a striking summary of the Waldensian sensibility, runs as follows: 'If there are some who love and fear Jesus Christ, who wish not to malign others, nor to take oaths, nor to lie, nor commit adultery, nor kill, nor steal from another, nor seek vengeance, they say he is a Waldensian and worthy of punishment.' The *Nobla Leyçon* is thus a meditation on the destiny of mankind since the original sin. The man called for salvation operates of his own free will; it is up to him to answer the call addressed to him. But time is short, for the end of the world is drawing nearer. In this dramatic and sometimes apocalyptic atmosphere made up of both overwhelming anguish and rapturous hope, everyone has a mission to fill in the place accorded to them in the community: the pastors have to pray and announce the Word; the faithful have to repent and be converted. All these poems express a passionate devotion to the holy scriptures, particularly favouring readings from Matthew and John and evangelical passages to which they were especially partial: the Sermon on the Mount, the parables and the announcement of the Day of Judgement.

The sermons make up another group in which we find the same themes, the most frequently recurring of which being the call to repent and be converted. They are not intended to teach matters of catechism or theology which are studied elsewhere, but to inspire their listeners to think about their salvation. The manuscript *De la parolla de Dio* (On the Word of God) draws on Matthew 13: 3 ('Behold a sower went forth to sow') to develop a line of reflection on penitence based on the gospels. The 'Bestiary' (*De la propiota de las animanczas*) is more original, at least from our point of view, taking as it does a list of animals, and successively using their way of life and especially their image according to the mentality of the times to draw moral lessons from them. The dog, the pig and the lion serve as examples, but it is the eagle which offers the perfect image of the process of repentance. It flies towards the sun and burns its wings and eyes, goes to rub its beak on stone and then dives into a fountain of fresh water. Thus can a sinner be rejuvenated in the spiritual well of penitence, after a period of redemption: first comes contrition (the eye) when the believer regrets the evil he or she has done; then confession (the beak), when sins are recognised and admitted; finally satisfaction when sins have been expiated. These are the three stages in the sacramental rite. The sermon on Matthew 12: 36–7 emphasises the urgent nature of penitence, concerning idle words which will have to be accounted for on the day of judgement: 'Cry while you still have time, while your soul is with your body ... While you live, acquire the remedy for the future ... before you are engulfed by the depths.' Each sermon thus offers a commentary on the gospel.

The treatises, intended as works giving moral guidance, voice the same pastoral choices as the sermons. Here again, the Poor of Lyons retain their specificity, seeking to make Christian life in their era conform to that in the first communities in apostolic times. Both *Doctor* and *Las Tribulacions*, for example, renew the call to be converted and exhort penitence. *Somme le Roy* tackles the often delicate issues of marriage and the family, the latter being a fundamental unit in the society of the time, not only on a social level but also a religious level, for it ensured the survival and the transmission of the dissent. The first treatise considers their tribulations as the just wages of sin and as a beneficial opportunity for believers to examine their consciences; the second treatise on tribulations invites them to bear their persecutions patiently in imitation of Christ; in this way the believers will partake in the Saviour's Passion. It aims to exhort courage while their torment lasts. In the Cambridge manuscript this treatise is followed by the book of Job, the perfect example of the just man's suffering, by Tobit, the image of patience when put to the test and of unshakeable hope, and by Maccabees in which the Seven Brothers personify the heroism of the martyrs. It is clear that the treatise deals with the community of suffering believers. Have courage, it tells them, nothing is lost. Far from it. At the end of the path of earthly toil, they will be rewarded with eternity.

What we might call the group of letters is a more limited source. They are epistles sent by the community's leaders to the Brothers. They too emphasise the suffering endured by the Poor of Lyons. They make it very clear, however, that, to the authors' mind, this test which God has willed is a sign that they have been chosen by God and are loved by him; it also binds the community. The most revealing document in this respect is the letter certainly written between 1460 and 1500 from

Barthélemy Tertian, one of the rare *barbes* whose surname we know. His letter is an exhortation addressed to the diaspora of believers rather than to each devotee individually. It unites the elected people who will be saved in a vision that passes over the question of history; the Church of the apostles and the present community of farm labourers, shepherds and craftsmen are brought together beneath the eyes of God in the hope of eternal salvation. In all, the poems, sermons, treatises and epistles that were in secret circulation within the Romance group of the Poor of Lyons — for we indeed know much less about writings issuing from the Germanic wing — constitute a remarkably homogeneous ensemble. This homogeneity is first external, as we have seen, in terms of the date, the geographical origins and language used. It is also internal, as a result of the references, quotations, recurring themes, selected readings and pastoral choices which are expressed. The Brothers' library thus appears original; it cannot be confused either with traditional pious literature, despite frequent borrowings from this domain, or with works by other dissenting groups, although their influence too can be clearly traced.

ANOTHER CLERGY?

Before we can bring this overview of the Waldensians' oral and written culture to a close, one question remains outstanding. Had the masters not ended up becoming a clan of lettered men and inevitable cultural intermediaries — in other words, a new class of clerics — bearing in mind how they animated prayer meetings, preached the Word of God, studied the New Testament, learnt to read and write and always carried books with them? If this were the case, it would be a remarkable evolution indeed. Not that Vaudès and his companions were hostile to the learned classes *per se* or to classical written culture, but as time went by there was a growing feeling of wariness within the community towards school divinity, of hostility towards the habitual paths of learning with its vain speculative games and towards university ranks. The Austrian Inquisition in 1391 noted, amongst the declarations of Waldensians being questioned: 'It is a useless waste of time to dedicate oneself to study at the universities of Paris, Prague or Vienna in Austria.' For that matter, we do not know of one university-educated preacher, if we do not count Hussite Bohemia and the final period of the movement when we know of at least one former Dominican being made a *barbe*. There was thus no erudite man of letters, at least in the accepted sense of the term, amongst the Brothers. As we know, the *barbes* were recruited from the believers in the rural population and given special training which was not academic in the least. Does this mean they were ignorant?

Their enemies' testimonies would have us believe so. Bernard Gui wrote that 'some of them understand Latin; some can also read it'; which would imply that most of the Brothers were apparently illiterate. Two centuries later, Jean of Roma, the Dominican inquisitor, specified in his 1533 treatise against the Waldensians that 'The said preachers are largely ignorant and are letterless apart from one of their humanists. They are entirely barbarous to the extent that they fulfil the words of the gospel: if the blind lead the blind, both shall fall into the ditch' (Matthew 15: 14). The Roman clergy, however, tended all too often to debase the 'heretical' preachers and to vilify the heresiarchs who, being uneducated and untrained in any formal sense, inevitably misinterpreted the holy scriptures, spread false doctrines and led the poor, gullible people astray. The hierarchy traditionally apportioned the blame mostly among the preachers. The royal commissioners in their 1533 report on Provence also shared this position, as did the king's counsel Jacques Aubéry in his defence speech for the victims of the Luberon massacre before the Parlement of Paris in 1551. Should we too subscribe to this view?

First, it is important to situate the testimonies in their cultural context. A cleric or a man of letters at the end of the middle ages deemed any person who did not know Latin to be barbarous. This is the sense in which we should understand the term 'unlettered' which the inquisitors pinned to the Brothers. The very fact that any other language was qualified as 'vulgar' reveals the contempt that the learned circles reserved for everything that fell outside the domain of Latin. At the same time, we know of certain preachers who showed real learning. Friedrich Reiser learnt Latin and paid students to transcribe part of the bible for him. When he was arrested by the Inquisition in Strasbourg in 1458, he was in possession of several books and manuscripts: the holy scriptures, of course, but also treatises which he had had copied by masters, notably by his disciple Martin. He was condemned personally to throw into the fire those works which had fallen into the hands of the Inquisition. Reiser was incontestably a man of letters; his case was also atypical, as we have seen. In the west, however, certain *barbes* were just as educated as he was. Antoine Guérin, the hatter from Avignon, is perhaps not the best example. He was Pierre Griot's companion and attended the *barbes*' annual synod with him in 1532, but as a university-educated former Dominican who then became a Waldensian master, his case is quite exceptional. The deacon Raymond of Costa, however, was in possession of three books when he was arrested in 1319. During the twenty-four cross-examination sessions, he proved perfectly capable of entering into discussions with the bishop Jacques Fournier, the presiding judge. He draws on biblical quotations with discernment and has no special difficulty with Latin.

While there can be little doubting that certain masters had acquired true learning, it is nevertheless difficult to prove, for often the personality of the clandestine preachers, who had become masters of the art of dissimulation, remained obscure. When a Brother had the misfortune to be captured and forced to confess, we suspect that his case may have been an exceptional one from which little of any great value can be drawn about the preaching body as a whole. At the end of the fifteenth and the beginning of the sixteenth century, several testimonies concur about the existence of learned *barbes* such as Louis or Barthélemy or Stephen. But we know them only by their Christian names. The closing years of the dissent, however, reveal two more distinct figures. First, there was Jean Serre, the lame man from Murs in Provence. His family originally came from Piedmont and, like so many others, settled in Comtat Venaissin in the late fifteenth century. Pierre Griot referred to him for the first time during his trial in 1532, teaching us – and the inquisitor of course – that 'he had spent two years studying St Matthew and the canonical epistles under the doctrine and supervision of Jean Serre from Murs'. The inquisitorial net would then seem to have tightened around him. He was brought before the episcopal tribunal in Carpentras and questioned by the cardinal Jacques Sadolet who, indeed, found his replies perfectly orthodox and released him. We learn at this occasion that he owned a bible in Italian and a New Testament in French. Without knowing any more about this man, we should note that he was one of the *barbes'* training masters, he could read French and Italian and appears to be aware of the trend of thought in the German Reformation.

The figure of Georges Morel is even more telling. He was, as we know, sent by the synod of the *barbes* in 1530 with Pierre Masson as a delegate to Oecolampadius and Bucer. The nature of the consultations and discussions with the Reformers are suggested by the surviving collection of questions and answers in which the two *barbes*, but Morel in particular for he alone escaped police controls, demonstrate their learning. They appear as men capable of the most subtle discussions about faith and morality. The proliferation of biblical quotations shows them to be assiduous bible readers, which is hardly a surprise. But they have also read Erasmus and Luther, which is another matter, even if we do not know the language in which they studied these authors. Furthermore, the exchanges had to be in Latin, which was the only possible international language, for the reformers could not have understood the traditional Provençal spoken by the Romance branch of the Poor of Lyons. Not only do we have the collection of documents written in Latin, attesting the learning of certain *barbes*, we also have the translation into the Romance language that Georges Morel had to make so that it might be fully understood by his fellow *barbes*, proving that most of them at least did not understand Latin.

In this way, a contrast emerges within the college of *barbes* in terms of learning. Overall, the masters certainly did not know Latin, the language of law, science and religion. For this reason they were treated with a certain contempt by Roman clerics who had studied the humanities. It did indeed make them ignorant about all classical literature and many other riches, even in spiritual terms. It also protected them from vain, speculative and completely gratuitous inquiry, which was quite foreign to the Brothers' pastoral preoccupations, shaped as they were by their quest for the essential message of the holy scriptures, as they aspired to renunciation, the 'contempt of the world', and genuine poverty. What their enemies deemed to be ignorance, however, was in reality the result of a deliberate choice. The Poor of Lyons avoided the innumerable commentaries which dominated in the universities at the expense of the original text and oriented themselves in a completely different direction to that taken by school divinity. They abandoned sophistical explanations to get back to the holy scriptures themselves. Furthermore, we should not overlook the fact that these men could all read and write. The same could not be said for all the Roman clergy. This in itself meant their flocks considered them as 'ecclesiastics', for if the *barbes* appeared boorish to men of letters, they enjoyed the reputation of being learned amongst their people. Their believers could easily compare them with the parish priest and from such a comparison the *barbes* overall came off better by far. They were not dilettante latinists but ensured that their rural people could understand them; they had not read academic manuals but they knew the holy scriptures; their prestige was not based on a status imposed from outside but on a consensus confirmed wholeheartedly by everyone, as a result of the poor, worthy lives they led in the service of their flocks.

The Brothers' place within the Waldensian community thus appears very singular. They were not only men of the spoken word but of the written text. In a predominantly illiterate world, particularly in the countryside where almost without exception their believers lived, this fact alone set them apart from their fellows. Unlike other lettered circles, however, they did not form a caste or even a class. Their only real privilege, after all, consisted in being the first to be tracked down and persecuted. Furthermore, coming from the labouring families they served, the preaching body was constantly being renewed, even if the recruiting system was co-optative. The peasants acknowledged that the Brothers were of the same stock and they maintained close, permanent links with their origins. In particular, they did not adopt an artificial, esoteric and recondite language which would automatically distance them. If they enjoyed genuine consideration amidst their people, it was not as a result of the economic or social advantages they had been attributed but rather for the cultural duties they set themselves and for the knowledge they had acquired so that they might make it accessible to their people. In this respect, their role was essential in the Dauphiné when, after Cattaneo's crusade in 1487–8, court proceedings were opened, ending in a sentence of rehabilitation accorded by the king in 1509.

Their reputation was not solely due to their mastery of the written and spoken word, nor to the fact that these techniques were used for the benefit of the believers. It was also, perhaps primarily, a result of their being bearers of the Word and the Scriptures of God. They were 'theophors', those who bore God, since the bible was his Word. Their role was thus infused with some of the sacred character of their message, for we know the veneration surrounding the holy scriptures which were the absolute reference, the ultimate argument in the minds of the Poor of Christ. Their prestige was further reinforced by the power they held, unanimously accorded them by the believers, to hear confessions and grant divine forgiveness. But above all it was the life they led which earned them general respect, marked as it was by evangelical poverty, selflessness and accessibility as itinerants. Their exemplary behaviour bestowed authority and power on them and signalled their authenticity.

The Poor of Lyons did not, as some have maintained, constitute an oral people confronting a Catholic world founded on writing; theirs was not an egalitarian movement in a hierarchical society; nor was it a lay movement lost in a clerical world. As is often the case, this pattern does not conform to the truth, which was more subtle and multifarious. This is quite simply because life is not caricature but approximation, adaptation and influence. The Poor of Lyons resembled the world in which they lived but differed from it at the same time and it could not engulf them. This double-sided reality, resemblance and difference, shows up clearly in the leaders they chose: masters whom they welcomed in secret at their peril, *barbes* whom they hearkened to religiously, Brothers whom they supported financially. These men, who themselves were so like their flocks whose origins they shared and yet so different because of their status in the community, were remarkable cultural intermediaries. They were walking news bulletins, linking up the various regions of the diaspora as they trekked from one place to the next; they were public readers and writers bridging the illiterate countryside and the world of the written culture of books; they were bearers of the Word of God and as such set up the salutary contact between a tormented people and the expedient divine Word. The place held by the Waldensian preachers can come as no surprise. Their role was capital for it embraced the essential domains of geography for a scattered community, culture for an illiterate people and religion for believers dramatically reaching out for eternal salvation. The Brothers thus represented the living cement of a diaspora otherwise severely tried by centrifugal forces. Beyond this, they could, when it was necessary, act as authorised and efficient representatives of the community as a whole faced with the outside world. And so, when the Reformation began to spread through Europe, proposing new paths to salvation which were at the same time attractive and suspect in the eyes of the authorities, the *barbes* were quite naturally the first to be interested and to send missions out to probe the situation and find out more.

BIBLIOGRAPHY

Balmas, E. and Dal Corso, M., *I manoscritti valdesi di Ginevra*. Turin, 1977.
Berger, S., Les bibles provençales et vaudoises. *Romania* 18, 1889, pp. 353–424.
Dal Corso, M. and Borghi Cendrini, L., *Vertuz e altri scritti (manoscritto GE 206)*. Turin, 1984.
Degan Checchini, A., *Il vergier de cunsollacion e altri scritti (manoscritto GE 209)*. Turin, 1979.
Montet, E., *Histoire littéraire des vaudois du Piémont*. Paris, 1885.
Paravy, P., *De la chrétienté romaine à la Réforme en Dauphiné. Evêques, fidèles et déviants (vers 1340–vers 1530)*. 2 vols., Rome, 1993.
Raugei, A. M., *Bestiano valdese*. Florence, 1984.

8

THE SIXTEENTH CENTURY: THE END AS A WAY FORWARD?

Who could have imagined the repercussions that were to follow Luther's spark of inspiration in Wittenberg which became a protest and finally a movement of social and religious disobedience between 1517 and 1520? Neither the clerical class as a whole, nor the majority of political leaders took the trouble-making monk particularly seriously. When on 15 June 1520 pope Leo X issued the bull *Exsurge Domine* excommunicating Martin Luther, he believed he had settled the affair definitively. The Church, after all, had centuries of experience of dealing with schisms and heresy; this was the manner in which it traditionally eliminated its dissenters and enemies. Who had vied successfully with the Church? The immense and powerful normalising forces of ecclesiastical power, reinforced by the secular arm, had in time broken down all resistance and subdued even the most stalwart opponents. How could an Austin friar from Saxony possibly trouble Rome, even if he was a university professor? Even when, in answer to the pontiff's sentence, he burnt the bull of excommunication on a public square on 10 December 1520 with widespread local support – an act nevertheless of rare audacity – showing that he persisted in his schismatic position, the odds were still heavily against the subversive monk.

Even today, the causes of the Reformation are widely debated even if both theoretical and formal ecumenism ensure modern debates are far less rumbustious than they were before. The conditions of its success, however, are well established. An astonishing number of prevailing circumstances favoured the climate for change: the incomprehension and inflexibility of Rome; the recent upsurge in national self-consciousness among the Germanic people; widespread, increasingly pedantic religious zeal; Luther's particularly strong character; the sovereign princes' un-expected interest and support; the rapid diffusion of ideas thanks to technical advances in printing. After 1520, the year in which Luther's four major works were printed, the movement expanded steadily. The initial spark of inspiration which originated in a Wittenberg friary did not just spread to hearths in Saxony or even Germany but flared up until it threatened to engulf the whole continent. In the 1520s, and even more in the 1530s, the works of Martin Luther were printed, translated and circulated throughout Europe.

FIRST CONTACTS WITH THE REFORMATION

Even beyond the Germanic countries, the Reformation touched popu-lations everywhere, some of whom were merely interested, others wholeheartedly attracted. The Poor of Lyons were less likely than others to remain unmoved by the powerful call for religious reform, having already been so much influenced one century before by the Hussite movement, to the extent that the Bohemian Brothers had merged with the Unity of Czech Brethren. We can easily understand the interest the Reformation held for them if we consider the three founding pillars of reformist theology: justification by faith alone (*sola fide*); the priesthood of all believers, by which every person was entitled to examine the holy scriptures for himself; and the infallibility of the bible alone (*sola Scriptura*). The last two points were an exact echo of Vaudès's stand four centuries before. They were also fully in keeping with the tradition of Waldensian thought and practices as we have seen in the last two chapters. The two religious sensibilities thus shared a desire to engage fervently in the Word of God. Vaudès's movement, the older of the two, had stayed the course as best it could but had also tempered its demands over the centuries. The inspiration behind the Reformation was new and its initial impetus was still flourishing. Even before the new reformist trend had won over the northern Germanic countries, the Brothers felt the need to get to know it better.

The *barbes'* inquiries were justified. Did Luther, who was soon followed by a number of other evangelical apostles, really have anything new to say? How did his challenge differ from what the Poor of Lyons had been maintaining in word and deed for centuries? The very touchstone of Waldensian thought was, after all, the primacy of the holy scriptures and the Word of God made accessible to all by translation and preaching. However, when the *barbes* read the works by the Wittenberg reformer and learned of some of his positions, they remained perplexed. Luther's reading of the bible, for instance, did not correspond to theirs.

While he, as a good doctor of theology, explained the various levels of interpretation, the Waldensians limited themselves to a literal reading, refusing all interpretation. More serious still for them was the principle of *sola fides*, which was at the very core of Lutheran thought, for the Brothers believed firmly that people could aid their own salvation and remained attached to a whole series of rites and practices. The only solution was to make contact with the reformers and question them so as to have an opinion of them and make up their minds afterwards.

The first indication of contact between Luther and the Poor of Lyons dates back to 1523. At this time, the reformer wrote to the duke of Savoy to ask him to protect the 'Waldensians' in Piedmont who were his subjects. Otherwise, the few occasions on which he refers to them in his writings mostly concern Bohemia. In his letters, he touches on the Waldensian question three times, but only in passing, with the exception of a letter addressed in 1535 to 'Benedict Güb, from Boleslav, and to the Waldensian Brothers in Bohemia'. In this we learn that he and Philip Melanchthon had received two emissaries sent by the Czechs. He states that they were delighted to learn that children were baptised in Bohemia – which must be understood in the context of violent clashes with the Anabaptists – and that they, like the reformers themselves, recognised the sacraments of baptism and the eucharist. Were the envoys really Waldensians? Elsewhere, Luther refers more harshly to 'Picards' who would appear to have been Poor of Lyons, for this was another name by which they were sometimes known. The reformers' relations with them were thus extremely limited. The *barbes* contacted the reformers in 1526, although little is known about it. According to the historians Gerolamo Miolo in the sixteenth century and Pierre Gilles in the seventeenth century, the synod held in that year in Laux in the Cluson valley in Piedmont brought together 140 *barbes*. The assembly sent two of them, Guido from Calabria and Martin Gonin from Angrogna, to Switzerland and Germany to gather information. Gilles specifies that Gonin returned from Switzerland 'bearing a quantity of printed books of the Religion'. From this point on, at least, the better educated *barbes* could become acquainted with reformist thought in Latin, the others could do so in French or Italian. It was during this mission, in any case, that they made contact with Guillaume Farel, who was to establish and then maintain links between the Poor of Lyons and the Reformation as if within Reformation Europe the task had been assigned to him. His Dauphinois origins meant he was ideally suited to the task, as did his acquaintance with the Romance dialect. Farel, however, held opinions that were more inflexible than those of Luther, and as a result was further removed from the Brothers and their traditions. We know nothing else about the spread of reformist ideas in the Waldensian community in the second decade of the sixteenth century. Things changed, however, in the 1530s.

A CONSCIENCE-STRICKEN COMMUNITY

If the Poor of Lyons, and more particularly the preachers and leaders, were so strongly attracted by reformist tendencies, it was because the new trends coincided with an era during which, for some decades already no doubt, the Waldensians had been examining themselves; trouble and doubt had filtered through their ranks and what might be called an identity crisis had taken hold of the community as a whole. This is not just a hypothesis based on an *a posteriori* analysis of later events but a situation clearly evoked in the 1530 Morel–Masson report. Reading it, we notice how much the *barbes* appear to be hesitating over their beliefs – for again the testimony only concerns the western branch of the diaspora. They had been seized by the need both to reflect and to examine their consciences collectively. Their thoughts seem to run as follows: we alone have conserved, defended and passed on since our beginnings – which, let us recall, they sometimes dated as far back as apostolic times – the truth based on the gospel, but have we read the divine Word correctly? Their anguish over this matter was further amplified by their differences with the reformist outlook. The questions they appear to be asking are the following: what if, for centuries, we have been mistaken and have led our people astray? was evangelism, biblical literalism, the true path to salvation?

The questions were crucial, particularly as they implicitly acknow-ledged the *barbes'* own weakness. We saw above that the *barbes* were perfectly aware of the double game they were playing. Fear had forced them to dissimulate their preaching mission; the believers, moreover, had managed to conceal their convictions to such an extent that a real contradiction had arisen between the principles they proclaimed, derived from their literal reading of the gospel, and the way in which they applied them in their daily lives. If it had proved impossible to respect what they believed in theory to be the will of God, was it because of human weakness, persecution or as a result of misreading the bible? Who could answer the question better than these new prophets who, like Vaudès himself, were looking fixedly to the hereafter, inspired in thought and deed by the Word of God? These men, however, were wholly, or at best largely, unaware of the existence of the Poor of Lyons whose traditions had been kept alive by suffering. Furthermore, Luther, Melanchthon, Zwingli, Lambert, Bucer, Oecolampadius, Haller and later Calvin and the majority of reformers were former clerics and also urban dwellers, grounded in Latin and the scholastic methods of university training. They had nothing in common with the Waldensians and their deliberate, organised simplicity. What could they make of the boorish preachers serving a rural community? The question is all the more pertinent if we recall that the reformers were also men of the times whose vision of society was thus very hierarchical. They aimed to convert sovereigns and their courtiers, believing this to be the finest and easiest way to win popular support for their evangelical cause. Seen from this angle, what interest could the Poor of Lyons possibly hold for them?

The *barbes* were directed to Bucer and Oecolampadius, the reformers of Strasbourg and Basel, and their mission cannot fail to affect us and speak to us of their courage and intelligence. They could have drawn on their solid tradition dating back many hundreds of years, spoken superciliously of the persecutions that continued to be organised against them, seeking to impress the new preachers or even attempt to integrate the new dissenters into their diaspora, or at the very least they could have ignored them disdainfully. Nothing could be further from the truth. The Poor of Lyons put themselves into question and addressed the reformers with endearing humility. The reformers, whose origins and learning we have already alluded to, were certainly in the ascendant and must have been esteemed by the *barbes* not only for their culture, religious and otherwise, but also for their self-assurance resulting from their solid theological training. Even the most learned Brothers, as in the case of Georges Morel and Pierre Masson, were of no great weight compared to these men of God who were also humanists. Furthermore, the Reformation had been victorious in several states. The Poor of Lyons must have found this evangelical victory compelling after the centuries of suffering they had endured. Discussions were thus set up between the representatives of two cultural spheres who were so different they were nearly in opposition, yet so similar that they resembled unequal brothers. The ensuing dialogues are remarkable.

Let us summarise the situation. At the 1530 synod apparently held in Mérindol in Provence, the assembled *barbes* decided to send out two of their preachers, chosen from the most educated among them, capable of understanding Latin, the only common language possible between the Germanic reformers and the Romance-speaking Poor of Lyons, on a new, more specialised mission than that of 1526. Morel and Masson thus set out and met Oecolampadius in Basel and Bucer in Strasbourg with whom they exchanged ideas concerning their respective positions. On their return, Pierre Masson was captured, but Georges Morel returned to Provence, translated the debates into Romance and wrote an account of them for his colleagues. This document in two parts, Latin and

Romance, is now in Trinity College Library, Dublin and the Latin text
has been published by Valdo Vinay. Besides an exchange of letters, it
contains the questions (*peticions*) the Brothers asked the reformers,
followed by their individual replies. One hundred and ten folios of the
manuscript concern this essential material, the value of which is inestim-
able. It evokes all the points which caused difficulties, whether in terms
of doctrine or practice. The tone is clearly sincere and candid. A master
was speaking of his community, presenting it to his listeners who were
not even aware the Poor of Lyons existed. For this reason, the *barbes*' list
of questions, organised by Morel, respect the following pattern: these are
our beliefs, these are our practices, what do you think of them? The
delegates, who had read Erasmus and Luther, sought details, explanations
and comparisons related to their bible readings.

Morel and Masson wrote to Oecolampadius:

> It is our hope and our confident belief that the holy spirit will speak to us
> through you and enlighten us over numerous things which, because of our
> ignorance and our laziness, we doubt and also we do not know at all which is, I
> strongly fear, much to the detriment of us and our people whom we teach in a
> manner that is hardly competent.

The questions begin by presenting at some length the body of *barbes*,
who support and structure the community. It provides us too with a
remarkable source of information about the college of preachers which we
drew on above. There follows a reminder of their traditional refusal to
swear oaths, to kill and to bear judgement. In theological terms, their
position is in many respects close to the doctrine of the Roman Church.
They recognise 'free will', in other words the freedom people enjoy to
save themselves, or condemn themselves in the hereafter, and thus
recognise that 'good works' may work towards their salvation. They
retain the seven sacraments, and more particularly the transubstantiation of
the eucharist. As far as devotions are concerned, however, they had long
since distanced themselves from Roman practices. They do not accept the
cult of the Virgin and other saints, purgatory, suffrages for the dead, vigils
(on the eve of holy days), holy water, mass, abstinence (from meat and fats
on prescribed days) and indulgences. They hold the bible alone as their
reference on matters of faith and moral doctrine and read it literally. Such
is the picture of their community drawn up by the two *barbes*.

DIALOGUE AND DEBATE

Questions run between the lines of the letter to the Strasbourg reformer
from beginning to end, but the *barbes* addressed eleven direct questions

to him concerning matters 'which are most ambiguous and obscure for us'. These highlight the Brothers' particular concerns. The questions they were asking themselves and which they addressed directly to the reformers were as follows:

1. Should ranks of dignity be established amongst ministers of the Word, such as episcopacy, presbytery and deaconry?
2. Had God ordered authorities or magistrates to sentence murderers, thieves and delinquents to death or other punishments by which they might atone for their crimes?
3. Are civil laws and others invented by men valid in the eyes of God?
4. Is it licit to advise members of the community to kill false brethren who betray them and deliver the *barbes* to representatives of the Antichrist?
5. Is it licit for someone to take back himself those essential goods required for his survival which have been unjustly taken; is it licit for believers to go to law?
6. Should the inheritance of children who die intestate go to their mothers; if the mother then remarries, should the sons of the second husband inherit?
7. Is everything added to capital usury? Is all trade which earns money without labour sinful? Is every oath a mortal sin?
8. Are the doctrines of original, venial and mortal sins, and invincible and wilful ignorance valid?
9. Is it licit to weep for the dead?
10. Are all children, from any origin, who are not yet capable of reasoning saved by the grace of God and the passion of Christ? And conversely, are all those capable of reasoning who do not have faith in Christ condemned?
11. Must young people who seek and desire to live in celibacy take vows? Can marriage lawfully be contracted between blood relations of any degree, other than those evoked in Leviticus 18?

It is clear from this list that the Poor of Lyons' concerns bore upon concrete aspects of their practical life and difficulties resulting from their traditional biblicism. The most sensitive issue, however, at the root of the *barbes'* disquiet, arose from their doubts about the reformers' double position over free will and predestination. The debate between Catholics and reformers over this point was increasingly impassioned. The question was essential: can man aid his own salvation? Or, put another way, has he been predestined by God to salvation or damnation, making human will and human action powerless to alter God's will or to change his destiny? In 1524 Erasmus had published *Discourse on Free Will* (*De libero arbitrio*) to which Luther had replied sharply the following year in *The Will in Bondage* (*De servo arbitrio*). The debate is, of course, at the very heart of the Reformation. It was also the main stumbling block for the Poor of Lyons, who, as we have already seen, had traditionally set a high value on works, that is to say the whole repertoire of practices and pious rituals they observed in order to gain salvation. For this reason, Morel and Masson touch on the heart of the debate after the eleven questions. Although the passage is long, it is worth quoting, for it vividly evokes the perplexity in which they were living:

> Furthermore, nothing troubles our weakness, due, I admit, to our ignorance, more than what I have heard and read in Luther on free will and divine predestination. Indeed, we believe that God instils into each person a certain natural virtue, more to one and less to another however, as experience has clearly taught us that one man differs from the next and as the parable of the talents seems to indicate and as we have also seen by experience how in herbs, plants, stones and all other things there is its own natural energy put there by God, with which we can do much. So we believe that men can do something with the said virtue, especially when it is stimulated and incited by God as he himself has said: 'Behold I stand at the door and knock' and he who will not open with this instilled and stimulated virtue will, in the end, be treated according to his works. Otherwise, if this be wrong, I do not see how we can understand so many affirmative and negative precepts, such as Erasmus discusses. As for predestination, we believe that long, long before the creation of heaven and earth, the Almighty had foreseen how many would be saved or damned, and this because of their own fault, because they would not obey and observe the commandments. But if everything happens by necessity, as Luther says, and if those predestined to eternal life cannot be damned and vice versa, since divine predestination cannot fail to be realised, then what is the point of so many writings and preachers and healers of the body?

The *barbes* were profoundly troubled, for their attachment to good works was deeply rooted. They were ordained by the laying on of hands, they were celibate, they fasted, prayed and imposed penance on the believers whose confessions they had received. Alms still had special value in the eyes of the Poor of Lyons. Morel draws on this verse from Ecclesiasticus 3: 30, which he quotes in the *langue d'oc*: '*E enayma l'ayga steng lo fuoc, enaysi l'almona steng lo pecca*' ('Water will quench a flaming fire; and alms maketh an atonement for sins'). Morel returns to this obviously crucial issue in his nineteenth *peticion* addressed to Bucer, with a multitude of quotations from the holy scriptures recommending good deeds so as to attain eternal salvation, drawn from Matthew, Ecclesiasticus, Acts, Luke, John and Galatians. Morel concludes, '*De laqual cosa es vist esser segu cue la deo esser attribuy alcuna cosa a las obras*' ('As a consequence of which, it appears some value is to be attributed to works'). The letter ends with an entreaty: 'I beg that you be so kind as to reply particularly to these points.' The *barbe* sought an exegesis of the quoted texts and an indication of the biblical origins of the doctrine of justification by faith. In other words, Luther had not convinced him or, in all likelihood, his fellow *barbes*.

Oecolampadius' reply to the questions is short and succinct. His position is clear: he rejects free will as contrary to divine grace without going so far as to conclude that sin is necessary; he affirms predestination which is a mystery since God cannot be unjust. The reality he bids them to accept is that God alone can save; man alone is responsible for his damnation. Bucer proves more aware of the importance of the question and the extent of his audience's anxiety, for his answer covers thirteen hand-written pages. He replies by explaining the biblical passages which had been put forward, considering a literal reading to be insufficient. To his mind, interpretation is the key to their spiritual meaning. He too concludes by defending predestination. On this essential aspect of Christian life, the reformers took the opposite view to that cherished by the Poor of Lyons. In concrete terms, this led the Waldensians to re-examine practices established centuries before. The replies were brought back to the college of *barbes* and were very probably discussed at the 1531 synod. They must have thrown the college of Brothers into turmoil, with some members demanding they remain faithful to the past, and others turning their backs on former times to embrace new ideas that were set to ensure the victory of the gospel. In fact we know nothing of the annual meeting following the return of the delegates. On the other hand, we have a fair idea of what happened the year after.

COMMOTION AT THE SYNOD

While we know very little about all the other annual meetings of the *barbes*, we are fortunate enough to have Pierre Griot's direct account of the 1532 synod. When he reached Lourmarin in Provence, where he stayed for a few days before being arrested by the inquisitor Jean of Roma, he was returning from the Brothers' annual assembly. The young *barbe*, interrogated in November 1532, testified as follows: 'Similarly they gathered this last year in Piedmont, in the Luserna valley, in a place called Le Serre, where there are but ten or twelve houses ... And he who is speaking was this year in the said congregation.' We have no way of knowing how many members were present, nor where they were from. Pierre Griot, however, recalls certain figures amongst them. 'The current four are called Louis, the eldest, another is called Stephen, another Daniel and the fourth Luke.' Furthermore, the most well-known masters included 'John, Laurent, Georges and Jeannon'. These *barbes* remain particularly elusive for we do not even know their family names, but only their 'religious' names. Certain historians have attempted to lift the veil of mystery, identifying them as Louis Callier, Daniel of Valence and Georges Morel but this is pure conjecture.

The young Griot was equally impressed by other participants he met at his first synod, such as guest speakers or listeners. He recalls, 'this current year important clerics and doctors came to their congregation. The others included a black habit and a white habit; these were monks; two others were gentlemen from the region of Grenoble.' During the following cross-examination, the inquisitor asked him 'what these four disputants were called'. Griot replied 'The gentlemen were called Charles and Adam; the monks Augustin and Thomas.' Asked to give their ages he specified that the 'seculars', that is the laymen, were forty, as was Thomas; Augustin was about fifty. Who might these men have been, that were exterior to the community, yet, on this exceptional occasion, admitted to their debates during their official gathering? As far as the monks are concerned, it is curious that as members of the regular clergy they should have come in their clerical outfits; the testimony is, however, clear on this point. Thomas has until now remained the more anonymous of the two; his white habit may indicate that he was a Dominican. The second monk dressed in a black habit was possibly Augustin Maynard, the Piedmontese monk who preached for the Reformation in Cuneo. The laymen's identity is more certain. The man called Adam was in fact Antoine Saunier who had adopted the pseudonym, as a letter he wrote on 5 November 1532, signed 'your Adam', confirms. As for Charles, it would appear that he was really Guillaume Farel, although as far as I know, he never used this name. But he was a gentlemen from the Dauphiné, aged forty-three at the time. It comes as no surprise, in this case, to find him at the *barbes'* assembly for he was perhaps the only man in the reformist world to appreciate what the Waldensians' evolving attitude to the Reformation implied, and what it cost them.

As we have already seen, Farel represented the most rigorous trend in reformist thought – that which was most opposed to the ancestral ideas and practices of the Poor of Lyons. Discussions at the assembly looked set to be agitated, for the situation was already strained. For some years, troubled, divided *barbes* had been wondering whether they ought to maintain their traditional positions or whether they would not be better advised to join the huge tide of reform. The crucial point for what indeed proved a turbulent meeting was predictably the question of faith and works. Again, it is best to turn to Griot's account, as he explained to the inquisitor the way the debates had arisen, as he remembered them and as the court clerk recorded them, in the colourful French of the sixteenth century:

And a disputation was held between them about faith. The two monks said that faith alone was justification and the two others said that faith without works was dead. And on the contrary the monks said that works served no purpose for justification but were mere proofs of faith, and that works were just a superstition that had been invented and that God did not ask at all for these external works but only for man's heart. The monks also said, 'You are more concerned and troubled by your ceremonies and external works than those in the Roman Church' as if he meant that it was merely a waste of time and a useless burden to pay attention to these works and that they did not please God at all, for it prevented men from labouring and from doing temporal works. So that after the disputations of the said monks and gentlemen, the *barbes* remained quite scandalised because of what the said *barbes* are accustomed to, who persuade their people not to drink or eat or do anything without first praying to God.

They were scandalised too because the said monks told them they should not serve God but with their hearts and not in appearance since God did not ask for it. It thus appears that the said monks wished to make the world of the flesh into a world of the spirit. Moreover, the said monks and gentlemen disputed the sacrament of marriage. And since the said *barbes* promised God their poverty, chastity and obedience, the said monks said they were doing wrong to promise chastity and that they should all get married for St Paul said that he who teaches must be the husband of a single wife, and the same for the deacon. And so the said *barbes* were all scandalised, saying that it was not their custom to get married, and the others saying they were already old.

The quality of the statement, its naïvety, its genuine liveliness and its unique character should enable the reader to overlook the fact that it has been quoted at such length. It is irreplaceable in spite of the problems it creates. According to Pierre Griot, the monks were defending reformist ideas more than Saunier and Farel were. Had he muddled their words? This was possibly the case, for elsewhere during his trial, it is clear he had not fully understood the nature of the debates. What stands out clearly here is how impassioned the dialogue was as two religious cultures clashed over questions at the heart of the debate. What could it all lead to? The Poor of Lyons could reject justification by faith alone and, by doing so, reject the Reformation altogether. On the other hand, they could renounce their own past, thus turning their backs on what for four hundred years they had believed to be a faithful application of the holy scriptures, truly imitating the apostolic life, in intention at least if not in reality. The third, midway solution, was to retain those elements related to their particular religious sensibility from both their own traditions and from the Reformation, and to reject the rest, a solution which amounted to introducing reform within the community of the Poor of Lyons. Pierre Griot does not touch on this matter, but the Dublin manuscripts give us the answer.

RENUNCIATION

The conclusions reached by the synod of Chanforan, near the hamlet of
Le Serre, were drawn up in twenty articles, which were in fact
incorrectly numbered, the text of which has been published by Valdo
Vinay. It settled the differences between the Poor of Lyons and the
reformers, or at least brought the debate between them to a close.
Reference is made only to contentious issues; it is not a general statement
or a profession of faith. Only three articles concern their faith; the others
evoke matters of ecclesiastical discipline. The second conclusion, on faith
and works, is guarded: 'As for external works, which have not been
forbidden by God, man can do them or not do them, according to the
given conclusion, without sin.' In short, they established a compromise
by recognising that works were optional. On the contrary, the question
of predestination, which had provoked questions, confusion and doubt
amongst the *barbes*, was settled unequivocally in conclusions nineteen
and twenty: 'All those who have been and will be saved were pre-
elected before the creation of the world'; 'Those chosen to be saved
cannot failed to be saved ... He who establishes free will entirely denies
predestination and divine grace.' There is no midway solution here; it
was the inflexible reformist position which was adopted.

Similarly, as far as the sacraments were concerned, the Morel–Masson
report had stated that they believed in more than two of them, whereas
the Chanforan declaration deliberately comes into line with the reformist
position: 'On the question of sacraments, it is conclusive in the Scriptures
that Christ only left two sacramental signs; one of these is baptism, the
other the eucharist.' As far as the latter is concerned, which caused
dissension even within the Reformation, it is noteworthy that far from
adopting Luther's more moderate position (consubstantiation), the *barbes*
adopted the Zwinglian line of thought which was quite opposed to their
traditional stand (the presence of Christ in the gathering of believers), a
position Guillaume Farel had presented in his 1525 work *Summaire et
briefve déclaration*. As Vinay emphasised, the spiritual radicalism of these
conclusions 'obviously came not from Oecolampadius or Bucer but from
Farel who had dominated the synod of Chanforan'.

On a doctrinal level, the changes proved radical. On a moral level, in
terms of their daily practices, could the *barbes* maintain some part of their
venerable tradition which had forged a sensibility across generations of
believers and produced such astonishing masters? And was this what they
sought? The answer is clear if we examine the other conclusions drawn
up by the synod. There is little point analysing each decision individually; it will suffice to highlight those related to practices traditionally

honoured by the Poor of Lyons. Oaths are admitted; ministers are accorded the right to have private property; confession is rejected as are other pious practices such as prayers at set hours, prayers recited aloud, fasting on set days, the laying on of hands, kneeling and covering one's head. Establishing a virginal order is declared a 'diabolical doctrine'; marriage is forbidden to no-one; ministers of the Word are not to be transferred from one place to another. We can imagine how overwhelming such conclusions were. The Poor of Lyons were giving up what had been their particular spiritual essence, their common practices and their understanding of religious intelligence. Seen in this light, the occasion is astonishing in terms of dogma and moral principles, doctrine and practice.

The change of direction was further reinforced by what was truly an ideological transmutation. We saw above how selective the Waldensians' reading of the bible was, focusing particularly on books from the New Testament, namely Matthew, John, the canonical epistles and Paul's pastoral epistles. The Reformation, however, from Luther onwards, privileged other books, insisting particularly on Paul's more dogmatic writings such as the epistles to the Romans and the Galatians. This differing, if not conflicting, approach is apparent if we compare the Morel report and the reformers' replies. With regard to texts of reference, the synod of Chanforan again opted to follow the line of the Reformation. The conclusions drawn up by the synod cite the New Testament no less than nineteen times to justify the decisions being made. Paul is quoted nine times, three times from Romans. The increasing importance given to Paul is innovatory in the *barbes'* culture. Was their leaning towards this apostle of the gentiles merely lip service, signalling the growing importance of Farel? Or had the *barbes* really evolved so much over a few years, to the point of adopting a new reading of the bible, acquiring another religious culture and adhering to a new theology of salvation that had been unknown to them in former times? Whatever the answer, it is clear that the *barbes* had changed course quite radically. At Chanforan they renounced not only an essential part of the vision which had been perpetuated over centuries of dissent but also attitudes, behavioural patterns and rules on which their very lives had been based since Vaudès first voiced the cry of protest.

How were such astounding decisions made? How did the *barbes* come to break with their past so abruptly? Nothing is known, of course, about the manner in which voting was organised during synods. We can simply suppose that every *barbe* voted and that motions were carried by the absolute majority of votes, according to the traditional formula of the *'major et sanior pars'* (greatest and soundest part). Drawing on the manuscript of the conclusions, in which it is stated that the assembly was held in the presence of all the ministers and 'the people', certain historians have assumed this to mean decisions were made democratically, carried by the votes of all those present. I, however, am inclined for several reasons to believe that only the *barbes* voted. First, society in those times reasoned in terms of hierarchy. Second, as we have already seen, the Poor of Lyons organised their community in harmony with the prevailing mentality. It is most likely that the people were present only as onlookers, at least when voting took place. Moreover, the formula may conceivably have been merely formal, like that used by the ancient Romans under the empire even though it no longer corresponded to real practices, when decisions were made in the name of '*senatus populusque romanus*' (the senate and the people of Rome).

Whatever the case, the synod ended in upheaval. The discussions had been passionate and agitated. The *barbes* were not all of the same opinion and votes had certainly not been cast unanimously. Those who would not submit to majority rulings evoked their ancient customs, in the name of which they formed a sort of discontented party. Two such recalcitrants, Daniel of Valence and John of Molines, even decided to travel to Bohemia so as to expose the situation, their view of it at least, to the Czech Brothers. They presented themselves as delegates sent by their fellow *barbes*, calling the German Brothers to witness to the growing treason instigated by 'certain Swiss who are either scoffing at or corrupting the holy scriptures'. These were the terms used to describe Saunier and Farel. Their mission is documented by a letter signed by 'the Brothers and ministers preaching the gospel in Bohemia and Moravia' sent in return to their fellows in the west on 25 June 1533. The Czechs urged the *barbes* to be prudent, without taking sides over the heart of the debate. The appeal addressed by the *barbes* to their Czech brethren shows that, while relations may have been strained, links could be consolidated between the eastern and western communities, particularly during critical or decisive periods. We do not know how the letter was received at the following synod. It is certain, however, that the Chanforan conclusions were reasserted. In this way, the Poor of Lyons entered the vast movement of the Reformation, and more particularly into the French-speaking Swiss trend, at least on an official basis as decided by their leaders, and as far as their theoretical declarations were concerned.

A FRENCH BIBLE

Another important decision was made at Chanforan which is not evoked in the conclusions but is documented elsewhere: it was decided that they should print the bible. It can come as no surprise to learn that the Poor of Lyons showed such regard for the holy scriptures, so ingrained was this attitude in their community. It was furthermore what they shared most in common with the reformist world. Nor is there anything unusual in their decision to use the printing press, a new technique enabling documents to be diffused in greater numbers, more cheaply and more faithfully than had been the case for the manuscripts previously used by the *barbes*. We therefore might expect them to have printed a manuscript text already available within the community, in other words a bible in the *langue d'oc* used in the southern regions of the diaspora. This, however, was not the case. First, the versions used previously by the *barbes* were deemed inaccurate; it was decided that they should shun the Roman Church's traditional, authorised version in Latin, called the Vulgate, and to establish a new version drawn from Hebrew and Greek texts. Second, they chose not to use Romance, the language formerly used in all Waldensian texts, but Latin and French. This is stated clearly in a letter from Antoine Saunier to Guillaume Farel, signed 'your Adam', dated 5 November 1532, barely two months after the synod of Chanforan. On Saunier's advice, it had been settled that each page of the bible should be divided into two, unequally wide columns, the wider of the two bearing the French text, the narrower bearing the Latin text in smaller script. Farel was entrusted with revising the text.

The work, which appeared in 1535, includes a preface entitled *Apologie du translateur*, bearing witness to the origins of the undertaking. These are the opening lines, adapted in places to make them clearer to understand:

I remember quite well how you Cusemeth [Farel] and you Almeutes [Saunier], led by the spirit of God for those graces he has chosen to give you (concerning the understanding of the holy scriptures) set off three years ago to visit the Christian Churches, our good brothers. And when you had assembled (according to the custom) to confer and discuss the holy scriptures so that the people should always be instructed and taught in a holy way, between several fine speeches and saintly conferences, you declared that so many sects and heresies, troubles and tumults, were emerging in these times in the world, and this was because people did not know the Word of God; and seeing copies of the Old and New Testaments which were in our midst, written in the vernacular, copied out by hand in times long since past, we could not even remember when, which could only be of use to few people, you admonished all the other Brothers, for the honour of God and the good of all Christians who knew the French language, and so that they might rid themselves of any false doctrine that debases the truth, saying that it would be most expedient and necessary to purify the bible in French according to the Hebrew and Greek. Hearing this, our Brothers agreed

joyously and good-heartedly, doing their utmost in all ways so that this undertaking might be realised.

The result did not conform to decisions then made, which may come
as some surprise; the edition is even more surprising. The work prepared
by Pierre Robert, known as Olivétan, and printed by Pierre de Vingle,
known as the Picard, in Neuchâtel on 4 June 1535, apparently breaks
with books traditionally used by the *barbes*. These had been modestly
sized manuscripts adapted to suit their itinerant preaching mission. The
new publication was a large volume in folio made of 416 sheets of paper
that would be difficult to transport, measuring 24.5 x 34 cm. Previously
written in Provençal, it was now in French, once the Latin had been
eliminated. And yet the *barbes* had agreed to this. Furthermore, they
organised a collection amongst all the families of the diaspora to
contribute towards printing costs; in all, 800 gold écus were gathered and
sent to the Swiss publisher. In other words, the undertaking was financed
and approved by the Poor of Lyons, even though it appears, seen from
the outside, to be quite out of keeping with their former practices.

It is quite understandable that the *barbes* should have given up
manuscripts in favour of printed books; it is harder to explain why they
chose to give up their language. And for what reason did they agree to a
bilingual edition in Latin and French, before finally settling on a version
in French alone? We do not know how many Brothers used or even
understood French, but French speakers were in all likelihood a minority
among the Brothers and a rarity among their followers. Having opted for
the royal tongue, why also impose the cumbersome task of retranslating?
We can accept that the *barbes* were urged on by Saunier and Farel until
they felt they could not merely retain the French version published by
Lefèvre d'Etaples in 1530. But if a new version of the bible was needed
in French, why not translate the Waldensians' bible in Romance? The
decision to the contrary indicates the huge pressure of the reformers on
the college of preachers: the *barbes* had been led to believe that all
existing translations, their own included, were defective. These had all
drawn on the Latin texts and so, the 'Swiss' reasoned, a new translation
had to go back to the 'original' Hebrew and Greek texts. Their decision
amounts to a real cultural revolution as they agreed to abandon the
language spoken by their flocks, their venerable manuscripts and their
clandestine celebrations.

The format finally chosen is easier to justify if we recall that the
assembly in Chanforan had also called for an end to ministers' itinerant
missions and also to the double lives that were traditionally the lot of the
believers. The in-folio edition made dissimulation impossible and trans-

port difficult, thus encouraging community celebrations rather than individual or even family bible-reading. Its material and practical appearance in fact also concealed an ecclesiological vision, a conception of the community and how it should celebrate its faith. This is confirmed by the translated text itself. As we know, it was the work of Olivétan, Calvin's cousin. It is a well-known fact that a translation is never anodyne, rarely innocent and always revealing. As Bernard Roussel has shown, Olivétan apparently worked from a rabbinic bible. He played on three registers to work reformist ideas into his translation. First, he included notes in the margins pointing out certain leanings or injunctions such as participating in ceremonies held by the Church of Rome, for example. Second, he included an index in which it is clearly stated that free will (*libre arbitre*) is not a biblical expression. Such a mention is really quite remarkable and original, quoting as it does an expression which does not figure in the work. The fact that the author forgets to point out that the will in bondage (*serf arbitre*) is not a biblical reference either indicates how his approach is a deliberately slanted one. The third register is more subtle, for he plays on the translation itself. When a word in Hebrew corresponds to more than one word in French, his choice is never neutral. The vocabulary he uses reflects the theology he adheres to. The term 'priest' (*prêtre*) for example is rejected in favour of 'sacrificer' (*sacrificateur*). Olivétan's approach is iconoclastic: 'chalice' (*calice*) becomes 'hanap'. He also tends to avoid any charismatic or possible 'adventist' excesses. Roussel's conclusion sums this up well: 'This translation increased the pressure the French group were putting on the Waldensians, with the intention of confirming their clear adhesion to the Rhenish and Swiss Reformation.'

Olivétan's bible, these minor reservations notwithstanding, is a real landmark. To begin with, on a linguistic level, its importance as a sign of a cultural change is two-sided. At a time when French was still very variable, it fixed a language that could be understood by all francophones; it was also the first bible in French based on Hebrew and Greek. Furthermore, on a religious level, 'the translation, which profited from Calvin's observations, was in the following century to be updated by the pastor Martin, then by Osterwald; in this modernised version it was used by French-speaking Protestants until new editions came out in the nineteenth century', as Léonard wrote in 1961. This was the edition in which generations of French Protestants read the Word of God, often in secret, particularly during the arduous Wilderness period from 1685 to 1787, when the *religion prétendue reformée* was forbidden. Lastly, Olivétan's bible is a clear, concrete indication of the influence the 'Swiss' then had on the *barbes*. The Brothers were persuaded to agree to the new edition and to pay for it. We may, however, wonder whether events did not slip out of their control later.

The 800 écus paid for the printing is too high a sum to cover the 1535 bible alone. Gilmont estimates the sum as equivalent to the salary earned by a skilled worker in twenty years. Printing, however, would have taken ten fellow printers about four months. Does this mean that the *barbes* had also been cheated, or duped into financing other works without knowing it? The idea is abhorrent when we bear in mind that the collection which made possible the publication of the work, copies of which can still be found on the shelves of numerous libraries, came from the sheer hard work and commitment of such pious, laborious peasants as the Poor of Lyons. The undertaking proved furthermore to be a complete failure in commercial terms, which can hardly come as a surprise. The Poor of Lyons did not rush out to buy it. They had, after all, already paid for it. It was also in French, and its considerable size made it highly awkward to handle. So how was this work, referred to by some historians as the 'Waldensian' bible, really theirs? They had paid for it, which was no inconsiderable matter, but that was all. In 1561, twenty-five years after publication, a fair-sized stock of unsold volumes still remained in Neuchâtel, a certain number having already been transferred to Geneva. In 1670, nearly 150 years later, the Genevan booksellers J.-A. and S. de Tournes still listed it in their catalogue of available works.

It is certain, however, that the order to print was not imposed by the reformers but represented an official decision made at the *barbes*' annual meeting in 1532. It is equally certain that absolutely everything in Olivétan's bible runs counter to traditions formerly cherished by the Poor of Lyons. This both confirms and demonstrates how radically the *barbes* had evolved in terms of theology, moral issues and discipline. The most likely explanation is that the reformers, Farel and Saunier especially, had a clear project in mind as far as the future of the Poor of Lyons was concerned. Leaving aside the original political bodies which embraced the Reformation, it was quite rare to have a coherent, homogeneous, organised movement that was already committed to embracing the new path of salvation. How could the reformers not use this microcosm to help them establish a new, more faithful version of the holy scriptures, to finance the cost of printing and, through them, to spread the Word of God amongst the French-speaking populations who had so far proved rather disinclined to hear the true evangelical message? Lastly, it is more than likely that the *barbes* were somewhat overwhelmed by publishing concerns which were beyond them and grew out of their control, if ever they had had the passing urge to supervise it. They most probably had no idea of the consequences and repercussions that their rulings in Chanforan would have. They were certainly aware that they had instigated change, voting for transformations and new orientations. What they probably did not realise was that they had given up their own religious sensibility, their original culture and their ancestral past; in short, they had opted to lose their own identity.

FROM DECISION TO PRACTICE

The decisions reached in Chanforan represented the position held by the majority against a recalcitrant minority, as we saw in the move made by the two *barbes* to enlist support from their Czech counterparts. Since their initiative led nowhere, we may wonder what subsequently became of the opposition. Did they attempt to set up a dissent within the dissent, out of faithfulness to their traditions? Or did they finally resign themselves to the changes? There is no clear answer, although certain signs seem to indicate that it took a very long time before they were all in favour of them. Calvin disagreed with the *barbes* over the inevitable central and sensitive question of faith and works, as he explained in a letter to a young Czech theologian Matthew Cervenka, whom he had met in Strasbourg in 1540. Cervenka summed up the meeting as follows:

First, we evoked the question of the Waldensian Brothers living in the Swiss lands and elsewhere. We brought up the subject of two of them, one bearing the name of Daniel, the other John. The two men had, not so long ago, visited their Brothers in Bohemia. Calvin declared that he too belonged to the Waldensians, although he had distanced himself since disagreeing with them over religious matters. He spoke to me at length explaining why the separation had come about, particularly emphasising the fact that the Waldensians attribute too much to their own merits and do not accord sufficient importance to the article of justification by faith in Jesus Christ alone.

They were still weighed down by their venerable traditions. Eight years after the crucial synod, the *barbes* continued to endorse the Reformation half-heartedly. If we consider how far-reaching certain changes were, the Brothers' reluctance can come as no surprise.

If the *barbes*, who were in a position to bring about such changes, reacted in this way, what happened in the community as a whole? How revealing it would be to know what sort of welcome the *barbes* received when they set off on their missionary rounds in 1532–5, announcing the new measures to the families they visited: there would be no more secret meetings, no more confessing to *barbes*; they were no longer to attend mass in the parish church. In addition to these concrete matters – not to mention new theological positions about which they may well have understood very little – the community must have been perturbed by the disappearance of the preachers who were calling off their own mission. Having untiringly proclaimed the Word of God to their peers, preserved a fragile unity across a persecuted diaspora, protected the soul of a dissent committed to evangelical poverty and stayed the course over centuries of hardship and suffering, the spiritual leaders were now resigning. In the eyes of the believers, there can be little doubt that Chanforan represented not a transmutation but a rupture, if not a betrayal. The announcement must have been endlessly challenged and discussed, leaving no-one indifferent. The preachers were of course not abandoning their flocks altogether; their clandestine gatherings would henceforth be replaced by public worship, they were told; the community would be organised; their pastors would reside with them. But they could not say when such changes would come about. Moreover, if such settlements suited those countries which had hearkened to the gospel, where the sovereigns had publicly opted for the Reformation, what about the regions where the Poor of Lyons lived where hostility persisted? Hardly any trace remains of the anguish which ensued, easy as it might be to imagine.

There is only one testimony evoking the reactions of the Poor of Lyons on learning about the new word of the Reformation, and this is to be found in Antoine Saunier's letter to Farel on 5 November 1532. Saunier and Olivétan had stayed on in Piedmont to preach. The letter records how the reformers instructed the ministers and people of the Waldensian valleys; how everyone, with the exception of a few people of rank (*primores*), willingly attended their secret sermons, some followers even walking for two days to hear them speak. Does this imply the Poor of Lyons rallied enthusiastically and massively to the Reformation? It is indeed possible that the density of their settlement in those valleys made them easier to win over. But this does not inform us about the welcome reserved for the new ideas in the other regions of the diaspora, in the Dauphiné, Provence, Calabria and Apulia in particular. Nor is the matter entirely clear in Piedmont. When the *barbes* who subscribed to the new theses introduced the reformers into the community, the believers may have taken them for 'new *barbes*'. There is no reason to believe that Saunier's sermon really marked a new turning point; his word may well have caused no stir at all. With their 'donatist' approach, the Poor of Lyons were capable of great versatility, according to the situation. The reformers were good pedagogues and doubtless thought it better to avoid too much change. If we turn from Saunier's testimony – an exceptional case, which therefore reduces its importance – to consider not what people said, but how they behaved, it is no longer fitting to evoke change, but continuity.

In chapter 5, in which I attempted to portray religious practices within the Waldensian community, I drew on marriage contracts and wills that people in Provence habitually drew up in the presence of a notary, in whose archives such records have survived to this day. We need to turn again to these deeds to find out whether, in the years following Chanforan, there were any notable changes in people's behaviour, whether decisions made by those in command had any effect in practice, and when possible changes came about. Was the dogmatic rupture followed by immediate transformations in terms of the community's attitudes and mentality, or were alterations to be felt later on? That marriage contracts and wills can inform us on such matters may come as some surprise. It is certainly not the taking of oaths that can enlighten us, for, as we saw above, despite the fact that oaths were officially forbidden in any circumstances, the Poor of Lyons swore on oath quite as much as their Roman Catholic counterparts. At the most, the Chanforan synod left them feeling freer, for the first conclusion stated that 'It is licit for a Christian to take oaths.' On certain matters, the Reformation thus brought an end to the double life they had been living which, widespread and customary as it was, must have troubled their consciences. On other matters it confirmed ancestral habits, such as giving bread to the poor after the burial service, for example.

There were, however, practices which the Poor of Lyons had borrowed from their Roman Catholic contemporaries in order to resemble them more closely and so protect their own identity, which had come in time to be as traditional in their community as they were for Catholics. It was customary, as we saw, for the Poor of Lyons to order masses after their deaths to ensure the salvation of their souls; or to commend their souls not only to God but also the Virgin Mary or other saints named in the opening passages of wills; or again when drawing up a marriage contract to promise that the ceremony would be concluded 'before our holy mother, the Roman, catholic and apostolic Church'. Such engagements profoundly shocked the reformers, who believed they were thus dissimulating their faith, concealing the truth and making pacts with the Antichrist. To their minds, such diabolical practices had to stop. How did the Poor of Lyons living in Provence and elsewhere, who had officially joined the Reformation in 1532, react? Did they cease from the 1530s to request masses and to preface documents with Catholic declarations? Did they change the headings formerly used in notarial documents, which had suddenly become repulsive in their eyes? We have to admit that this was not the case. After 1532, the people in Provence blithely continued to get married before the holy Roman Church, to commend their souls to the saints and to request masses for the dead. This did not just go on into the 1530s and 1540s but also into the following decade. A study devoted to a period of twenty years in Provence establishes beyond a doubt that, as is the case elsewhere, a great gulf can separate decisions and their application. At most, the transformation of the community decreed by their leaders typically met with passive resistance from the people as a whole. In the end, however, the law was put into effect.

NEW PARISHES

Old habits gradually declined and new observances became discernible. The Poor of Lyons, or at least their leaders, began writing 'confessions of faith', something they had never before felt impelled to do. The Protestants, on the other hand, had from their earliest years felt the need to draw up and proclaim publicly the articles of their faith, the first such declaration being the famous Confession of Augsburg in 1530. This was not just intended to confront Catholics, but also to define trends within the reformed states themselves, each tending to produce its own text. In the same year, Bucer prepared his Tetrapolitan Confession signed by the towns of Strasbourg, Constance, Menningen and Lindau; Zwingli published his *Fidei ratio*. In 1532, Oswald Myconius, who succeeded Oecolampadius, drew up the Confession of Basel; the Confession of Geneva appeared in 1536. This practice, previously unknown to the Poor of Lyons, was taken up by them some time later. The first document of this kind to have survived from the Waldensian community has little in common with the equivalent reformist models. Signed by the 'community of Cabrières', in other words Cabrières-d'Avignon in the Comtat Venaissin, it was sent to the inquisitor Jean of Roma in 1533. The Poor of Christ from the region, who were troubled by the Dominican, wrote telling him that they were good Christians and sent as confirmation of this 'the faith and belief that we hold and believe in, a confession which must not be made through violence or torture but in freedom of spirit according to the faith that God gave by his grace to each of us'. The ensuing text is quite simply the Apostles' Creed, in French, transcribed in full. It is quite remarkable that when the Poor of Lyons felt compelled to make their faith public, which was a novelty for them, they found no better way than to present the traditional text of the Church, an approach radically different from that of the Protestants.

In the following years, the Provençal communities issued three more confessions. The first, dated 7 April 1541, was addressed to the Parlement of Provence by the Mérindol community which was threatened with destruction since a court decree had been published to that effect in the previous November. It was published by the Genevan printer Jean

Crespin in 1565. The other two confessions are more difficult to date; one is probably from 1541 or 1542, the other from 1544. Both documents conform totally to the Protestant model. The central theme is that of justification by faith. Similarly, they recognise only two sacraments, baptism and the Lord's Supper, thus adhering faithfully both to Reformation tenets and to the position adopted at Chanforan. There is nothing surprising about this if we recall how, in a letter of 25 April 1545 addressed to Farel, Calvin himself acknowledged having drawn up a profession requested by two delegates from Provence. This confession of faith was even presented to the king who, according to Calvin, was greatly angered by it. Calvin explained his reaction by claiming that the Provençal envoys had given a more forceful edge to it. Beyond the 1540s, the subsequent confession originated from the other side of the Alps. The historian Pierre Gilles stated in his *Histoire ecclésiastique des Eglises réformées*, published in 1644, that in 1556 the Piedmont reformists drew up a 'brief confession of their belief in which they declared what they believed'. The confession was addressed to the Parlement of Turin which had just issued a decree forbidding the reformed cult in the region of its jurisdiction. The document was divided into ten articles vindicating their orthodoxy and denouncing the errors of Roman doctrine. These documents, typical of the Reformation, thus make it clear that the new direction chosen at Chanforan continued to be followed, at least as far as the leaders were concerned. The Poor of Lyons were emerging from hiding and proclaiming their new faith.

Concrete signs attesting the Poor of Lyons' adhesion to the Reformation and confirming the theoretical position adopted at Chanforan, can be found from 1555 to 1560 onwards. The communities were henceforth parishes. In 1558, for example, in reply to Henry II, king of France, who had condemned the 1556 confession, the Piedmont reformists decided to organise themselves according to the presbytero-synodal model, adopting an ecclesiastical discipline along the lines of that applied by the Swiss Reformed Churches. In 1559 the first national synod of the Reformed Churches of France was held in Paris. The former Poor of Lyons who came from Provence and the Dauphiné, both provinces of the kingdom, did not differ in any way from their new co-religionists. The assembly adopted a profession of faith and a code of discipline established on the Genevan model which would hold for all the Churches of the kingdom. Furthermore, in the same year, following the treaty of Câteau-Cambrésis in which France gave up the region of Piedmont formerly under French control to the duchy of Savoy, the Piedmont Protestants sent the duke Emmanuel-Philibert an apologia and a confession, as drawn up by the Paris synod. It was also in those years that the first pastors arrived, particularly those trained in Geneva. The various trends within French Protestantism, from the pastors and deacons to the former members of the presbyterial council and the erstwhile Poor of Lyons, made up the 'remodelled churches'. This was the time when the first Protestant churches were being erected. For centuries, the Poor of Lyons had had no need of special places of prayer. The family home, or anywhere beneath the heavens for that matter, had sufficed, which suited their need for clandestinity. The first mention of such an edifice dates back to 1555 in Piedmont. In Provence, the first such Protestant church to be evoked is that in La Roque d'Anthéron in 1559. The diaspora had died; the era of the parishes had begun.

NEW PROTESTANTS

Which came first: institutional changes or radical modifications in behaviour? If new institutions could perhaps be passed off as the work of active pastors and missionaries, new attitudes, which were to develop into new habits, emerged within the community formerly called the Poor of Lyons. Again, notaries' registers in Provence provide us with the clearest indication of how behaviour evolved. Whereas Catholic deeds imperturbably retained the formula 'Before our holy mother the Church' in marriage contracts, the inscription was reworded by the former Poor of Christ from the 1560s to become 'as it is ordered', then 'as God by his holy Word has ordered' or even 'in holy congregation and assembly of Christians'. The traditional formula which had previously been maintained was officially rejected. A similar rupture can be traced in wills. First, they refused to make the sign of the cross which traditionally opened the testamentary proceedings. More revealing still, in notarial deeds registered between 1560 and 1564, the mention 'for the salvation of his soul', acknowledging the value of works and the existence of purgatory, is present in only 2 per cent of wills drawn up by the new reformists in the Luberon, compared to 28 per cent of Catholics; similarly only 26 per cent recommend the deceased to the Virgin and other saints as against 76 per cent of Catholics. From 1565, the formulas used are even more explicit, being unprecedented in the notaries' phraseology. They specify burial 'with no superstition as is the customary way amongst those of the Religion' or 'in the manner of those of the Religion, without obsequies' or again, the testator would request 'to be buried in the manner of the reformed religion', a request that was to become customary. The notary was thus obliged to take religious convictions into account, even if he himself was a Catholic. Indeed, the same notaries recorded Catholic and Protestant deeds.

This change represented a real cultural revolution. It is no easy matter adapting ancestral habits, particularly when, as was the case in the society at the time, one should venerate one's elders and when age, experience and example were values in themselves. Yet the Poor of Lyons gradually developed into Protestants, even in their most deep-rooted manner of thinking. The example of Lourmarin, a village situated at the southern foot of the Luberon in Provence, which had a largely Waldensian population in the sixteenth century, can serve to confirm what has been stated. As elsewhere, the believers became Protestants; their community became a reformed parish, the first register of baptisms to have been preserved dating back to 1563. Everyone is aware of how important the act of naming a child is, and also how the Reformation sought to mark its break with the past on this level too, encouraging its followers to select their descendants' Christian names from the Old Testament. Only 0.3 per cent of names I could find from the thousands of Provençal Poor of Christ baptised between 1460 and 1560 were Christian names of this type, limited to Daniel, Noah and Suzanne, which proves how little such considerations counted at the time. At the reformed church of Lourmarin between 1563 and 1570, however, 27 per cent of baptised children were given Old Testament names, including eleven Daniels, eight Isaacs, four Davids, thirty-nine Suzannes and seven Judiths. The onomastic evolution appears all the more abrupt if we bear in mind that none of the 772 adults – parents and godparents – choosing the names, had Old Testament names. If we consider how strong was the tradition of passing names within a family, we can appreciate how profound the cleft was between the two generations.

Changes in mental habits were not just limited to the naming of babies. The attitude to baptism itself evolved. The Roman Church had waged a secular campaign urging the baptism of the newly born as quickly as possible, the day after the child's birth at the latest. Congregations at large had hearkened to the message. Catholics were convinced that if their child, being tainted by original sin, should die before receiving the first sacrament, it could not be saved in the hereafter. This fear was deeply rooted in the mentality of the time. The Reformation, with its faith in predestination, dispelled the fear, and such haste with it. The baptism ceremony, representing the child's reception into the Christian community, was to be held before the assembled congregation on a Sunday or feast-day. The parish register kept by the priest from 1553 to 1558 indicates that the Poor of Lyons living in the region of Apt shared the local Catholic mentality, taking their children to be baptised within the twenty-four hours following a baby's birth in most cases, and at the latest within two days. In Lourmarin between 1563 and 1570, two-thirds of the 300 baptisms in the Protestant community were held on a Sunday. The remaining third can be explained by the troubled times which then reigned in Provence due to the wars of religion.

The behavioural changes were remarkable. There was nothing superficial in the Poor of Lyons' decision to shun the church that they had attended up until then to worship in the new Protestant church and to abandon the priest in favour of the pastor. Their choice touched on the very structure of the community and the mentality that had prevailed so far. The change of direction is documented very concretely, again by parish registers and notarial deeds. Two examples will suffice to make this clear. First, there is the case of Jean Roet from Lourmarin who in Mérindol on 25 April 1553 married Jeanne Serre from Gordes 'before our holy mother the Church'; their son Joseph, however, whose biblical name is characteristic, was baptised on 10 April 1564 at the Protestant church in Lourmarin. Second, there is the case of Jacques Michel from Apt and his wife Marguerite Bertholin. The priest from Apt baptised their son Raymond on 15 September 1557, whereas the baptism of their daughter Marie took place at the Protestant church in Lourmarin on 11 June 1564. The question is thus settled beyond a doubt. The Poor of Lyons became fully-fledged Protestants, not just in word but also in deed.

THE MEANING OF THEIR EXTINCTION

The Poor of Lyons had given up clandestinity and joined the group of reformed Churches, in accordance with the wishes of Morel and Masson, following the advice of Bucer in 1530 and the invitation extended to them by Farel and Saunier in 1532, and as Calvin had exhorted every true Christian to do. I have repeatedly emphasised the time which elapsed between the Chanforan synod and the first concrete signs of reform. During this necessary period, theoretical decisions were put into practice, former *barbes* and new pastors had to win the people's trust and the community as a whole had to grasp and accept decrees imposed upon them which to some extent changed their lives. The thirty-year period represented an entire generation, particularly at a time when life expectancy was so short. In other words, as the older generation, who were probably more attached to their ancestral past, disappeared, they made way for a younger generation brought up on reformed theology and moral doctrines, thus enabling the new ideas to penetrate the former Waldensian community. Thirty years may be long in terms of one person's life but set within the context of a movement dating back over the centuries, it is only a brief span. From this point of view, it is more fitting to speak of a break with the past rather than an evolution, particularly since the changes were so great, and the matters being renounced of such consequence. The Waldensian diaspora was swallowed up by the national Churches; former moral doctrines gave way to the new theology; the movement became a Church. The age of the *barbes* was over, replaced by that of the pastors; dissimulation, which had been an often unsatisfactory compromise, was ousted; the new era was one of opposition – the wars of religion had begun. From this time on, where there had formerly been the spiritual descendants of Vaudès, there would stand Protestant churches.

How had this been possible? The Reformation had succeeded in doing what the Roman Church had not managed to do either by reason or by force. Persecution had failed to eliminate the Poor of Lyons but they were won over by persuasion. As a result, the old 'Waldensian heresy' disappeared. The Poor of Lyons alone had survived into what are called modern times before being seduced – in every sense of the word – and enchanted by the Reformation. They turned to the Reformation, and vanished into its embrace. But if the Poor of Lyons espoused the Reformation, it was in part the responsibility of the Roman Church, which had formerly labelled every heretic a 'Waldensian', and then in the sixteenth century a 'Lutheran'. Failing to make elementary distinctions between dissents, it hunted down its enemies, referring to them all as 'Waldensian and Lutheran', as testified by the acts of the royal chancellery, decrees of the Parlement in Aix-en-Provence, inquisitorial trials and papal briefs issued against the Provençal deviants.

In this way, after a period of rapid evolution which began in around 1530, the Poor of Lyons became completely and unanimously Protestant in the 1560s. We might have expected them to constitute a relatively autonomous 'Waldensian' branch within the vast family of Protestantism which counted many others of this kind. This, however, was not the case. The Poor of Lyons were engulfed by the Reformation, whose every thesis they adopted, even those most in contradiction with their deep-rooted beliefs and practices; they aligned themselves unconditionally not only on a theological level but also in terms of ecclesiastical organisation. In the end, it was the Calvinist model which carried the day, as was the case for all the reformed movements in the kingdom of France. Two principal factors explain this outcome. The first is that, on an internal level, the project formed by the Swiss reformers concerning the Poor of Lyons, through whose agency they intended to win the kingdom over to the new ideas, coincided with the will of a certain number of *barbes* who believed that the future of their community lay in that direction. The second factor was external, deriving from the

Catholic Church's inability to distinguish Waldensians and Lutherans, whom it persecuted indiscriminately. The authorities' attitude incited dissenters to turn towards reformers whom they did not initially resemble on many points. Hence, in a curious but understandable manner, both reformers and the Roman Church refused to acknowledge the specificity of the Waldensian dissent. This meant that, paradoxically, the Catholic Church played a part in the Poor of Lyons' adhesion to, if not their total assimilation into, the Reformation.

BIBLIOGRAPHY

Cameron, E., *The Reformation of the Heretics. The Waldenses of the Alps, 1480–1580*. Oxford, 1984.
Gilmont, J.-F., La publication de la bible d'Olivétan. *Olivétan, traducteur de la Bible*, Colloque de Noyon, Paris, Cerf, 1987, pp. 31–7.
Léonard, E. G., *Histoire générale du protestantisme*. 3 vols., Paris, 1960–6; republished Paris, 1988.
Roussel, B., 'La bible d'Olivétan: La traduction du livre du prophète Habaquq'. *Etudes Théologiques et Religieuses* 4, 1982, pp. 537–57.
'Olivétan, corbeau enroué?' In *Olivétan, traducteur de la Bible*, ed. C. Casalis and B. Roussel. Paris, 1987, pp. 77–92.

9

EPILOGUE: THE WALDENSIAN CHURCH

Strictly speaking, the previous chapter narrated the end of the history of the Poor of Lyons and of Waldensianism. The reader should indeed have no reason to doubt that, by becoming Protestants, the Waldensians apparently preserved nothing of their former originality. Their religious sensibility became a dogma; what had amounted to a clandestine attachment to the Word of God, passed down through the generations within the family, developed into a means to propagate the gospel, which was at least what its destiny should have been; what was once a cluster of believers, tried and cherished by God, became a Church offering an alternative path to salvation in defiance of the Roman Church. The Waldensians' characteristic attachment to poverty, which had set them apart from their peers, was abandoned. In the west, the *barbes* represented both the frame and the lifeblood of the movement, despite its geographical fragmentation. Their importance, which had not escaped the inquisitors who questioned suspects directly on the matter, was such that the surest criterion by which to judge whether someone belonged to the sect was to establish whether he welcomed a preacher into his house. Until recent times, the inhabitants of the Waldensian valleys were indeed dubbed 'barbets' by their fellow Catholics in Piedmont. The Poor of Lyons were those who supported the *barbes*. On a practical level, as far as the community's organisation was concerned, when the bearers of the Word, mendicant and unmarried, gave up their itinerant preaching mission, it amounted to bringing Waldensianism itself to a close. Adhering to the Reformation indeed marked the death of the Waldensian dissent.

This may appear self-evident. It is certain that if the reader has grasped what was at the core of their movement, he or she will have understood that the Reformation was no more a continuation of the Waldensians' religious sensibility that it was for other medieval dissents, that of John Wyclif in England or Jan Hus in Bohemia, for example. These other dissents are not wholly comparable, of course, for two reasons. First, the Waldensian dissent was the only one to escape persecution as an organised group, surviving as a unity to join the Reformation in the sixteenth century. The second reason is that, even today, people claim to be descendants and successors of the Poor of Lyons. That the Waldensians subscribed massively to the Reformation is made abundantly clear by the Chanforan synod and its aftermath. But, as we know, they were renouncing traditions dating back centuries. It is, strictly speaking, incorrect to speak of the Waldensians beyond the 1560s. But, to return to the second objection raised above, men and women today continue to profess both their Protestant identity and their Waldensian heritage. It is in homage to their ancestors who were persecuted for their faith after the Reformation, particularly the tiny minority in Piedmont, first Savoyard, then Italian, who were for years a fragile, determined but solitary bastion defending reformist tenets in the Catholic, Italian peninsula, that I chose to add this epilogue. I repeat that as far as I am concerned, the history of the Poor of Lyons came to a close in Chanforan in 1532 as far as principles were concerned and on a behavioural level from the middle of the century onwards. The wars of religion which began in France in the spring of 1562 could not have been conceivable at the time of the Waldensian diaspora. The historian, however, must also bear in mind people's mentalities and issues about which they are sensitive. For this reason, we shall now consider briefly the landmarks over the past four centuries in the history of those who chose to call themselves 'Waldensians'. We can then conclude by considering how legitimate their claim is.

THE 'EXECUTION OF CABRIÈRES AND MÉRINDOL'

It would be quite incorrect to claim that persecution was the result of adhering to the Reformation. Suffering runs intermittently throughout the history of the Poor of Lyons, across centuries of trials, witch hunts and executions at the stake. In the sixteenth century, however, persecution developed both in terms of breadth and character. The princes who, for various reasons, eventually chose to remain faithful to Rome were troubled by upheaval in Germany growing from religious divisions but developing into political struggles. Sovereigns across Europe were haunted by the spectre of insurrection, rebellion and secession. One such monarch, Francis I of France, who was hardly a bigot or a staunch supporter of Rome, nevertheless observed what was happening across the Rhine and decided to enlist civil and religious authorities to hunt down heretics in his kingdom. Resulting inquiries revealed to the Provençal authorities not a few unlinked cases of 'Lutherans' as they had expected, but a well-developed, organised network long since anchored in more than thirty villages in the Luberon. They had stumbled upon the Poor of Lyons. A period of judicial manoeuvring and legal inertia ensued before the Parlement of Provence issued what is known as the Mérindol decree on 18 November 1540 against nineteen 'Waldensians and Lutherans' living in the village, ordering that the place itself be destroyed. For the first time, the courts were no longer attacking individuals, although heresy was defined as a personal crime, but an entire village. The suspects and the Mérindol community managed to have the judgement suspended for some years, although we do not know how. When the decree was finally enacted, however, it was all the more cruel for having been delayed.

A series of actions and coinciding factors gave rise to the massacre of the Waldensians in the Luberon in spring 1545. The pontifical chancellery was directly concerned since 'heretics' were living on lands in Comtat Venaissin, in Cabrières-d'Avignon in particular, and it therefore put increasing pressure on the French court to organise a common expedition. They finally reached an agreement. On 31 January 1545, the king ordered by letters-patent that the Mérindol decree be executed. It so happened that, since the count of Grignan, governor of Provence, was away on a mission in Germany, Jean Maynier, baron of Oppède, was responsible both for justice, as the president of the Parlement in Aix, and the police, as the absent governor's lieutenant. He therefore levied a popular army across the province, and added to it the ordinary troops of police; he also enlisted the support of 'the old Piedmont guard' as they crossed Provence on their way back from the Alps before they could set off for Marseilles where they were due to sail to England. He could also count on the support of troops levied in Comtat. The armed forces finally gathered together on 13 April, just after Easter which had fallen on the 5th that year.

A truly bloody week ensued, for the army advanced in formation, banners raised as if for battle, the troops convinced it was a crusade, when in reality they were pitted against bewildered groups of fugitive peasants. Nor did they limit their offensive to the village of Mérindol. Eleven villages were burnt or razed, the inhabitants shot, hunted down or imprisoned. Unmentionable atrocities were then committed by the unruly soldiery, followed by bands of pillagers who finished what the soldiers had begun. The lawyer Jacques Aubéry evoked the crimes in his

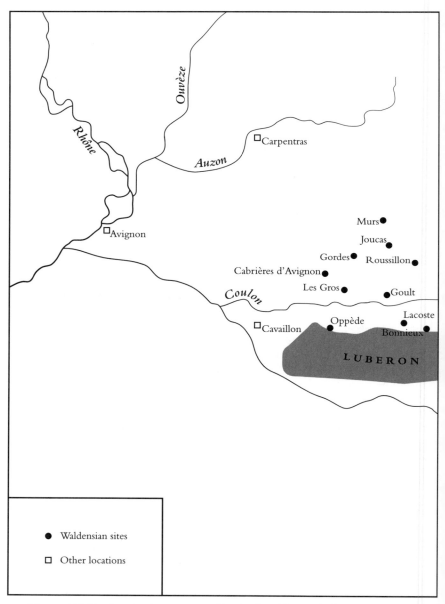

Map 2   Waldensian sites in 1532, according to the trial record of Pierre Griot

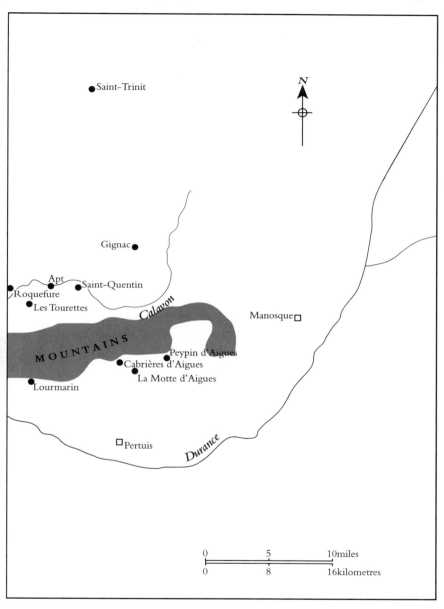

Saint-Trinit

N

Gignac

Apt
Roquefure
Les Tourettes
Saint-Quentin

Calavon

MOUNTAINS

Manosque

Peypin d'Aigues
Cabrières d'Aigues
La Motte d'Aigues
Lourmarin

Pertuis

Durance

| 0 | 5 | 10miles |
| 0 | 8 | 16kilometres |

defence speech given at the trial that followed, held in Paris six years later. Reading the account published in 1645 and reprinted in the 1980s still makes one shudder. The final toll, difficult as it is to make out, is sobering: 2,700 dead and 600 men sentenced to work on the galleys according to Aubéry, to which figures must be added the prisoners, orphans, widows, ruined families, exiles, particularly in Geneva where a group of bedraggled Provençals sought help in the following May, ruined crops, the countryside wrecked, and the surviving population hit by famine, trials and debts. The massacre, which was discussed across Europe, even reaching the ears of Charles V and the delegates arriving for the Council of Trent, was a bleak omen of conflicts soon to come during the so-called wars of religion.

What became known as the 'execution of Cabrières and Mérindol' was widely discussed not so much because of its cruelty, unquestionable as that was, but because of its miscarriage of justice and the extraordinary trial in which a sovereign court, the Parlement of Aix, was brought before another, equally sovereign court, the Parlement of Paris. If the fate of the heretical peasants hardly moved the iron-hearted populations in such times of adversity, there is nevertheless little doubt that the massacre hastened the Poor of Lyons' decision to embrace the Reformation, to which they had been committed to some extent for ten years already. None of the 'executed' villages was entirely abandoned, but the links which *émigrés* had forged with Geneva, where Calvin had been solidly and definitively settled since 1541, grew in strength from then on. The Provençal community ceased to be the Poor of Lyons, becoming Protestants who, in Mérindol from perhaps as early as 1545, celebrated the Last Supper in the Genevan manner. Likewise those who stayed in the Luberon or took refuge on the banks of the Leman broke with the ancestral custom of homogamy, henceforth choosing their spouses not only from within the Waldensian diaspora as had been the case before but from the Protestant community. The wars of religion (1562–98) completed the work which the 'execution' had begun. The former Poor of Christ living in Provence joined forces completely with the institutions and the framework of French Protestantism. They gave up their past entirely, and even their memories, with the sole exception of the 1545 massacre. From every other point of view, their Protestantism was the same as that everywhere else in France.

MASSACRE IN CALABRIA

The Poor of Lyons had several, fair-sized communities in the south of Italy, the southernmost tip of the diaspora. No-one has yet managed to determine the exact date of their settlement there, in the thirteenth or fourteenth century, for the history of these colonies is still unwritten, outside a few uneven studies limited to a particular period. But we can manage without such details. It is certain that, by the fifteenth century, considerable communities had been established in the region of Spoleto administered by the Holy See, and more particularly in Apulia, Manfredonia, Faeto, Celle, Motta and Monteleone as well as in Calabria, near Paola, in Montalto and La Guardia. As we saw above, whole families of Waldensians set off from Dauphiné and Cabrières-d'Avignon to settle in these regions in 1477. On many occasions, trials held in Piedmont and the Dauphiné in the second half of the fifteenth century indicate that the Alpine community maintained constant links with the Italian villages. They even situate the nucleus of the clandestine organisation in Italy. In 1532, Pierre Griot told the inquisitor 'that in truth the sect reigns principally in Calabria and in Apulia and preaches there almost in public'. Several leading preachers, such as Jean-Louis Pascal from Piedmont, had worked tirelessly in these regions to ensure that, as elsewhere within the diaspora, the Poor of Lyons should become true Protestants. Their mission was completed in 1560.

The supercilious administration of the kingdom of Naples, at the time under the control of the Catholic kings of Spain, suddenly discovered heretics on its lands. At the end of 1559, Jean-Antoine Anania, who was chaplain to Salvatore Spinelli, lord of La Guardia, became aware of the heretics' presence and notified the cardinal Alessandrino, a Dominican, a well-known inquisitor and the future pope Pius V. Alessandrino ordered that two Jesuits be sent to preach to the heretics and so convert them. Spinelli could not fail to be interested by what was happening in front of him; he had his own interests to look after, and the Pontifical Constitutions had made each lord responsible for the fight against heresy in his seigniory. Furthermore, in the absence of the cardinal archbishop of Cosenza, the town upon which the incriminated villages depended, cardinal Alessandrino incited the vicar-general of the diocese to take care of the situation. Jean-Louis Pascal was arrested and transferred to prison in Rome in January 1560 before being executed in front of the castle of Sant'Angelo. The duke of Alcala, the viceroy, urged the vicar-general to take action against the heretics in La Guardia.

The preachers first exercised their office in San Sisto, but in vain; they then attempted to intimidate the villagers. The inhabitants were horrified; some took refuge in their homes, some hid in the woods, others escaped to La Guardia. An atmosphere of insecurity reigned everywhere. Soldiers were assembled with the intention of taking San Sisto by force. The inhabitants requested permission to leave the neighbourhood with their essential belongings to go and live elsewhere. When this request was turned down, they declared that they were being forced to take up arms and embark on campaign. During one of their first expeditions, they were put to rout and their chief was killed. They joined forces with men from La Guardia and organised themselves better but were still defeated and dispersed a second time. Those who had stayed behind in the village saw an army of 600 infantrymen and 100 troopers approaching. Fugitives were hunted down mercilessly. Several weeks afterwards, poor, starving, homeless wretches were still being imprisoned by neighbours or soldiers who had taken up the Cross. Here again, it was seen as a crusade to protect the faith. When in September 1561 a new census was carried out in San Sisto to evaluate the demographic situation, in other words to re-evaluate taxes, the authorities discovered that many villagers had taken refuge in Montalto, La Guardia and the neighbouring towns of San Vincenzo and Vaccarizzo, all of whom were from families of fugitives or prisoners or those who had been killed or executed for being 'Lutherans'. As far as the survivors were concerned, the fiscal document specifies that a good number had already 'recanted'.

While these operations were being carried out, the governor of the province, the marquis of Bucchianico, set off at the beginning of June 1560 leading troops to La Guardia, following orders issued by the viceroy and confirmed by the arrival of the special commissioner, his brother-in-law. Salvatore Spinelli, lord of the village, was determined to show unlimited zeal when dealing with his obstinate vassals. The village was not easy to besiege, situated as it was on a hill and protected by fortifications. Spinelli resorted to trickery. He sent to the village about fifty prisoners with their warders, who were all faithful servants, claiming they had been sent to the prisons. Once inside the walls they seized control and called on their lord who was waiting outside with an army of 300 men. The ensuing carnage was merciless and indiscriminate, putting an end to the Protestants' resistance. The lord, who had sacrificed some of his subjects, was rewarded with a marquisate some years later; this was the origin of the marquisate of Fuscaldo. Seventy houses had been burnt down; devastation was widespread. According to Pierre Gilles, a certain number of villagers took refuge in the Alpine valleys, the home of their forefathers. The toll makes sombre reading, added as it is like a postscript to a letter from Placido di Sangro evoking the movements of the Turkish army:

Given the same day 14 June 1561. I send you the list of Lutherans of the two lands in Calabria, prisoners and dead:

Men aged 17 years and over	260
aged 10 to 17 years	50
Women aged 14 years and over	510
Pregnant women	29
Young children with their mothers	181
Young children aged 4 to 10 years	284
Killed and punished by law	60

It was too early to be a complete toll of casualties. The provisional total of 1,374, however, is already startling; that children figure on the list is equally so.

As a result of the reopening of the Council of Trent in 1562, which distracted individuals and religious authorities alike, the archbishop of Reggio was sent by the pope to the troubled areas to exercise power. He used his influence to secure the liberation of the prisoners, even accepting in certain cases that they be given a second chance to recant, which was contrary to all canonical rules. The law indeed stipulated that no forgiveness could be accorded to relapsed heretics. He did not, however, manage to convince the tax officers that they should give back goods confiscated for heresy. We have an idea of what the lives of the wretched villagers returning to their homes or to neighbouring localities must have been like by reading certain inscriptions in the census lists: 'Former owner but his goods are in the hands of the court ... journeyman when he can'. The conditions and punishments imposed on them were harsh, such as being forbidden to marry someone from their own community for twenty-five years. We cannot spend time here imagining what happened to the belongings of the prisoners, which were coveted and sought out by temporal lords and ecclesiastical authorities alike. Suffice it to say that those who were ruined by the incident were lucky to be alive.

As for Apulia, a letter from Naples dated 12 June 1561 specifies that four places there were equally 'infested with heretics'; these were most likely Monteleone, Monteacuto, Faeto and Celle, with Motta and Volturara. In this region, however, the affair was entrusted to the usual authorities in the dioceses. Moreover, the bishop of Bovino was Fernando of Anna, who was later formally suspected of subscribing to the principle of justification by faith. He proceeded calmly against 'heretics' in his diocese, although he still had to satisfy the temporal lords. He limited his actions to the most hot-headed and turbulent, otherwise accepting that people pay lip service to Catholic practices. In this way, the intervention of the Holy Office never became necessary. The understanding bishop could occasionally turn a blind eye, but he could not feign complete ignorance. He was still obliged to apply the Pontifical

Constitutions supervised by the cardinal Alessandrino, particularly from 1563 onwards when members of his diocese took refuge in Geneva. In other words, Apulia did not escape persecutions, but measures there were more tempered and, compared to what happened in Calabria at least, more humane. As a result, Protestantism was entirely eradicated in Calabria, whereas in Apulia inhabitants were gradually brought to recant. Some were even tempted to lead a double life for some time. Nearly thirty years later, former Protestants known as *Provenzani* who had recanted were either denounced or imprisoned for having continued to live in secret in keeping with reformist models. With time, however, the appropriately named Counter-Reformation gradually got the better of all the former Waldensians who had become Protestants. They, or at least their descendants, eventually joined the Tridentines.

What, then, can we conclude about this period in the 1560s just before what are known as the wars of religion broke out in France? The geographically far-flung boundaries of the Waldensian diaspora had been eliminated in different ways. In France, the Waldensians in Provence were labelled and treated as Lutherans. Not only did the bloody week in April 1545 sever all remaining links between them and the Roman Church; it also hastened them into embracing the reformist camp, the military terminology henceforth being most appropriate. There were no longer any Poor of Lyons in Provence, only Protestants. The same can be said for the Dauphinois Alps, to the extent that research recently carried out in the two provinces by Nicole Jacquier-Roux-Thévenet aiming to identify a certain Waldensian heritage in the customs, beliefs or mentalities of the populations descended from the Poor of Lyons came up with nothing whatsoever. There is, admittedly, a legendary source of sorts, but it has been strongly influenced by the Catholic environment and its story is much in keeping with that of other French Protestants. Calvinism had successfully smoothed over differences throughout France. The results in Italy were similar even though the method was different. The former Poor of Lyons also became known as 'Lutherans'; they were physically eliminated in Calabria and progressively assimilated in Apulia. At the dawn of the seventeenth century, there was no trace at all of reformist influence. There remained only family names and a particular dialect which to this day continue to attest the existence of the former dissent.

THE WALDENSIAN VALLEYS

Of the four occidental regions with the densest populations of Poor of Lyons who converted to Protestantism, only the Piedmont bastion remained intact. Emmanuel-Philibert, duke of Savoy, to whom the states were restored in 1559, was a subtle politician. His religious policy was two-sided: repression in the plains where, dispersed and few in number, Protestants lacked a common organisation; negotiation in the valleys where Protestants represented the vast majority of the population. A public disputation, like a verbal fencing match, took place in Ciabas d'Angrogna between the Jesuit Antonio Possevino and the pastor Scipione Lentolo in the presence of the count of Luserna who acted as arbiter. Some time later, Filippo of Raconiggi, a prince of royal blood, came to hear Lentolo's sermon. At court, duchess Marguerite, daughter of François I of France, was Protestant. Political considerations, however, took precedence over all others. In September 1560, the duke ordered count Costa della Trinità to reinstate Catholic order in the valleys. It was intended as a simple demonstration of authority to the obstinate peasants. The expedition developed into a fully fledged military campaign that was long and dangerous. A period of hesitancy gave way to conflict when the population was abandoned by leading figures who were prepared to negotiate, and urged on by certain ministers; they made ready to fight and resist. The traditional policy of non-violence was dropped as it had been in Calabria; obedience to the sovereign power was also forgotten. The attitude they adopted displeased Geneva, but the French quickly followed suit. A fair number of Piedmont Protestants, finding the situation inauspicious, chose exile, in Geneva in particular, as others before them had done.

The situation was novel: a group of armed peasants refusing to obey stood up to the troops of their legitimate lord. It resembled neither the war of the German peasants in 1525, nor the revolts that flared up sporadically in the countryside across Europe. The Piedmontese rebels wrote to the duke trying to explain that his authority was not in question, assuring him that they remained his loyal subjects; they were, they told him, acting in self-defence; they were not rebelling against their sovereign, but as Christians they were calling for the reform of the Church which the pope refused to grant. It was at this moment that in France, after the death of Francis II, Catherine de' Medici chose to negotiate with the Protestants and began preparations for the colloquium of Poissy. The Piedmont rebels thus received official support, sealed by an agreement signed on 21 January 1561 by their French co-religionists. The alliance made them conscious of their importance and their autonomy. On a theological level, they justified their action with references to the Old Testament; David and Goliath figured above all. The ministers supervising the rebels gave them the spiritual justification, the judicial reflection and even the tactical advice they needed.

From February 1561, when winter was far from over in the mountains, the Protestants took the offensive, plundering a church and burning down forts. The army, made up more of pillagers seeking booty than real soldiers, made little progress; Costa della Trinità was hardly acquainted with the terrain and had trouble estimating topographical difficulties; he let his troops disperse. The Protestants, on the other hand, frequently demonstrated their courage and daring; legend then took over to magnify their actions even more. The confrontations, which the pastors guided and watched over as their people followed ardently behind, became real liturgical celebrations; before and after each conflict, there were prayers and psalms were sung, thus recalling the Hussite battles and also prefiguring the French war of the Camisards 150 years later. Despite the arrival of the Dauphinois arquebusiers to reinforce their troops, the Protestant militia had secured no decisive victories by the end of the month of April. It was, admittedly, an exploit in itself to have held out for so long. Furthermore, the duke favoured an honourable, political solution and the duchess was equally inclined to such a settlement. An agreement was therefore signed at Cavour on 5 June 1561. The duke pardoned the rebels, remitted the war indemnity of 10,000 écus, confirmed all franchises and rights and authorised public worship in the most distant localities, Angrogna, Villesèche and Les Coppiers.

It was an original, and indeed unique agreement, completely disregarding the principle which had been generally adopted in 1555 to settle European conflicts, whereby subjects and sovereign should be of the same religion (*Cujus regio, ejus religio*). For the first time, a Catholic prince was abandoning the fight against heresy, a mission traditionally his responsibility, and tolerating dissent on his own lands. The agreement committed both the duke, who made concessions but did not capitulate, and the communities in the valleys. It defined the rules by which they had to live, which they had to respect, protect and defend. This gives us an idea of how original the Piedmont Protestants' situation was. Far from being wiped out like their fellows in Calabria, assimilated into Catholicism as had been the case in Apulia, or absorbed into the formal, national branch of Protestantism as in France, they were the only descendants of the former Waldensian diaspora to obtain official recognition. Their future and their history were assured by the Cavour agreement; they became synonymous with Italian Protestants.

To what extent, then, were the valleys still Waldensian? On a religious level, we have seen how, from 1558, the Piedmont reformists adopted an ecclesiastical organisation along Genevan lines. Shortly afterwards, they opted for the French-style synodal system, which followed the Calvinist model. Family traditions, however, were maintained and the Romance tongue, referred to as 'Waldensian' in these parts, continued to be used. In other words, the term 'Waldensian' lost its purely religious meaning. Its significance, which linguists would refer to as its semantic field, altered and broadened, to include a geographical connotation (the Waldensian valleys) and an ethnic connotation (the Waldensian population) which in the end also covered the religious field, for everyone was Protestant. Since the only Protestants in the Italian peninsula, surrounded on all sides by an arrogant, powerful Catholic Church, were the Piedmont descendants of the Waldensians, who were still living in the same valleys, it is easy to understand why the Reformed Church of Italy came to be known as the *Chiesa valdese*. It is also interesting to note that from then on, the term 'Waldensian' ceased to be pejorative as it had formerly been, not only in Catholic circles but also within the dissent itself. There were, in my view, two reasons for this. First, as we saw above, the meaning of the term itself had changed; it no longer referred to the Poor of Lyons or their descendants (evidenced by the fact that the term ceased to be used in France, even in the Luberon). Furthermore, it no longer denoted an ailing 'heresy' but a Church to be contended with – that of the Piedmont Protestants who appropriated and monopolised the term so that it henceforth referred to them and them alone. From that point on, when the Protestants in Piedmont heard the word 'Waldensian' they no longer felt insulted; on the contrary they were proud, it was the identity they claimed. It is surely fascinating, albeit perfectly logical, to note that the term, formerly avoided, was later proudly adopted, but only once it had lost its intrinsic religious connotation. This was made possible by rereading the Waldensians' past.

Protestant historians, in particular those from the valleys, understood and presented the history of the Poor of Lyons as that of a forerunner of the Reformation. To their minds, the Waldensians were Protestants before the term itself had been coined. From the sixteenth century onwards, there is an abundance of examples of this, so great was the need to seek and find ancestors, spiritual and otherwise, to rebut the accusation of novelty being levelled against the Reformation. A single example will suffice to illustrate this. When Pierre Gilles published his history book in Geneva in 1644, he entitled his work, *Histoire ecclésiastique des Eglises réformées ... autrefois appelées vaudoises* ('Ecclesiastical History of the Reformed Churches ... formerly called Waldensian'); in a way, even at the time, this amounted to a three-fold misinterpretation. First, the Poor of Lyons never constituted a Church; second, they always rejected what was then an abusive terminology; third, on a religious level, once they had become Protestants, they could strictly speaking no longer be considered to be Waldensians. A new edition of the work, issued in Pignerol in 1881, went even further. While the exact title was maintained inside, the cover very revealingly read, *Histoire ecclésiastique des Eglises vaudoises*. From a strictly emblematic point of view, the 'Reformation' had been pushed aside, which would imply that in Piedmont the term 'Waldensian' meant 'reformed'. In fact, the ethnic resonance of the term had grown stronger, so that using the word 'Waldensian' amounted to harnessing an entire heritage, including its religious connotation, which also meant deforming it, an indisputable manoeuvre which was psychologically understandable but scientifically regrettable. From then on, the other Reformed Churches called the Piedmont Protestants 'Waldensians' and, more striking still, the Piedmont community requested it.

UNCERTAIN TIMES

For a century, from about 1560 until 1660, the valleys were subjected to powerful and lasting pressure from the Catholic Reformation, which it is better to refer to here as the Counter-Reformation, so pronounced was the crusading spirit amongst those who sought to win back to the Roman Church those poor wretches who had erred into heresy and so compromised their salvation. The religious division was far from being accepted and no-one, from either side of the divide, could resign themselves to it. Everyone cherished the dream of Christ's seamless tunic, of a reunited Christendom. All, or nearly all, means were acceptable to attain this objective: a host of quotations from the holy scriptures; contradictory debates; lengthy theological demonstrations; polemical treatises; juridical quibbling, interminable drawing up of tracts; theatrical sermons, in a new era of missionary fervour; a new Inquisition heralded by denunciations and repression; weapons, finally, to overcome opposition where persuasion had failed. In short, it was an era of almost uninterrupted conflict. The wars of religion which broke out violently in France produced no more than distant echoes or secondary, marginal side-effects in the Alpine highlands. Apart from the astonishing campaign of the duke of Lesdiguières who advanced as far as Pignerol and Cavour in 1592, and Charles-Emmanuel's retaliation, during which he appropriated for himself the marquisate of Saluces, prompting a large-scale exile towards Protestant lands, the situation was balanced and stable, although perpetually uncertain. Henry IV's 1598 edict of Nantes put the seal on the situation in Piedmont.

Nearly the entire country, however, was shaken up by politico-religious strife. The Thirty Years War shook central Europe from 1618 until 1648, at which time Protestant Germany was saved by the intervention of Gustavus Adolphus, king of Protestant Sweden and by the support of cardinal Richelieu; on the other hand Austria, Hungary, Bohemia and Poland were definitively won over to Catholicism, and with them the former communities of the Poor of Lyons who had settled there. The 'Congregation for the Propagation of the Faith' set up in Rome in 1622 was entrusted with the double mission of spreading the faith and also rooting out heresy. In such a context, the Piedmont Protestants – whom we will henceforth refer to as Waldensians since it was the nomination they claimed, and the related misunderstanding has been elucidated – felt hounded, especially when the Most Christian King again captured Pignerol and the Cluson valley, making the Waldensian valleys into what amounted to a Savoyard enclave in France. The situation was further exacerbated by the complications of the duchy's administration with its constant verbal excesses in terms of threats, rules and reminders. A local small-scale tyrant Sebastiano Grazioli sought to impose his rule and issued a torrent of exactions before being suspended and imprisoned twenty years later. In spite of this inauspicious and troubling climate, the Waldensians maintained their organisation and forged closer links with Protestants elsewhere in Europe.

Controversies persisted in the valleys, particularly in writing. It was in such a context, with apologetics abounding, that the first three most important histories of the Waldensians were written. That by Jean-Paul Perrin was commissioned by the synod of the Dauphiné in 1603 and published in 1619; its lengthy title, according to the custom of the time, included a passage which I shall quote to illustrate the lasting confusion: *Histoire des vaudois divisée en trois parties. La première est leur origine ... La seconde contient l'histoire des vaudois appelés albigeois* ('History of the Waldensians divided into three parts. The first deals with their origins ... The second contains the history of the Waldensians known as Albigensians'). Pierre Gilles' work, which we referred to earlier, dates from 1644. Both books were published in Geneva. Twenty-five years later, in 1669, Jean Léger's work, entitled *Histoire générale des Eglises évangeliques des vallées du Piedmont ou vaudoises* ('A General History of the Evangelical or Waldensian Churches of Piedmont') was published in Leyden in the United Provinces. The three works make up the ideological foundations of official Waldensian historiography. They propounded the correct view that was to be held regarding the Waldensian past. It is not fitting here to offer a value judgement of these studies, which are incidentally remarkable. It will suffice to say that, as was always the case at the time, as was often the case later and is still sometimes the case now, history was not being written for itself but to serve a certain idea and a certain cause. In the same era, on the frontispiece of *Lucerna sacra*, the work by Valerio Grosso, there figured for the first time what was later to become the Waldensian emblem – which would be called a logo in the late twentieth century – a lighted candelabrum surrounded by stars with the motto *In tenebris lux* (In darkness, light). Since that era, a seventh star has been added to the original six, and the inscription has been changed to *Lux lucet in tenebris* (Light shines in the darkness) which is closer to the Genevan motto *Post tenebras lux* (After the darkness, light).

THE PIEDMONTESE EASTER

The reign of Louis XIV (1643–1715) coincides with the most crucial era in the history of the Piedmontese Waldensians. There was a multitude of reasons for this. It was an era of growing religious inflexibility, during which political rivalry – the incessant wars waged by the so-called Louis the Great – and religious opposition were often inseparable. It was an era in which absolutism prevailed, as a consequence of which the slightest resistance became intolerable to a sovereign who knew he was responsible before God for the thoughts and beliefs of his people. The Catholic counter-attack, both extensive and intensive, was frustrated by the few remaining outposts of resistance, particularly when they formed isolated Protestant enclaves. Furthermore, in spite of their being minority groups on a local scale, the inhabitants of such rebel settlements knew that, further afield, the victories of the Reformation had been conclusive, and that leaders whose power was firmly established could come to their rescue. It was also an era which maintained that tolerance was the result of indifference; consequently sectarianism dominated at both ends of the religious spectrum. Since the reign of Louis XIII, which came to an end in 1643, Reformed Churches in France had been under increasing pressure. Christine, regent of Savoy, was the sister of the king of France. In England, Charles I attempted to redefine the monarchy along French lines, Catholic and absolutist, and ended on the block in 1649. Cromwell's victory was also the victory of puritanism, thus restoring hope to Protestants everywhere. In Savoy, the regent Christine, Charles I's sister-in-law, also agreed to make Protestant dissenters in her lands toe the line.

The king of France signed the Grace of Alès in 1629 after the fall of La Rochelle. The defeated Protestants were accorded limited rights to hold their own services; the agreement abolished their famous strongholds, however, which had guaranteed their freedom but also constituted to a certain extent a state within a state, a situation that Richelieu had found intolerable. The royal commissioners drew on this edict to impose

Catholic services in Pragelato and the Cluson valley, administered by the Dauphiné, to restore ecclesiastical property to its former owners and reopen Catholic churches. The Jesuits, who spearheaded the Counter-Reformation, flocked to the region intending to convert the elite and the influential. In the other Waldensian valleys, which were dependent on the duke of Savoy, Protestants had to fight to ensure that the Cavour agreements continued to be respected. In economic terms, however, conditions in the mountains were increasingly harsh for the Waldensians; more and more families began to move down and settle in the plains. Incidents between authorities and rebels increased; goods were confiscated and convents were burnt. The Waldensians maintained their fight on a legal level, but the clashes soon escalated into armed conflict.

In 1655, on the orders of the marquis of Pianezza, the 4,000-strong army of the duchy, reinforced by the communal militia and Irish Catholics who had been persecuted on Cromwell's orders in their own country, were rallied for a new crusade against the deflated Waldensians. The latter sent out delegations and representatives to affirm their submission. In April, Pianezza ordered that the Waldensians house his troops, which amounted to forcing them to offer hospitality to those who came to pillage them. The Waldensians eventually had to accept. The military occupation of the Waldensian villages rapidly degenerated into a massacre which would appear to have been far from spontaneous. It became known as 'the Piedmontese Easter'; brutality, sadism, torture, slaughter and pillaging were widespread. Those who got away took to the hills; the soldiers, weighed down by booty, returned to the plains. On 3 May, Pianezza organised a ceremony to celebrate the Catholic reconquest, during which he had a cross erected 'as a sign of the faith and the might of his Royal Highness'. At this point the popular hero Josué Janavel emerged to organise a resistance movement that pursued the troops and avenged itself with equal violence. Fleeing Pianezza, the Waldensians made for the Cluson valley, in other words for France where the government had agreed to leave the border open. On 10 May, the Germanasca valley fell and Prali surrendered. Rewards were offered for the capture of all the Waldensian figureheads, including Janavel. In Turin cathedral, a lavish baroque celebration was held during which forty Waldensians and two pastors solemnly recanted. The Reformation had officially been overthrown; missionaries came rushing in to take over.

News of the massacre, however, had echoed throughout Protestant Europe and been received with cries of pity and indignation. Léger, the leader of the Waldensian Churches, known as the 'Moderator', had taken refuge in France since April and from there he transmitted information further afield. In early May, he wrote a vehement text announcing that the bastion of Waldensianism had fallen. He warned that the Catholic victories threatened the whole of Europe. In England, public indignation was running high. A national fast was observed in honour of the Piedmont martyrs. Milton composed his famous sonnet, 'On the Late Massacre in Piedmont':

> Avenge O Lord thy slaughter'd Saints, whose bones
> Lie, scatter'd on the Alpine mountains cold,
> Ev'n them who kept thy truth so pure of old
> When all our fathers worship't Stocks and Stones.
> Forget not: in thy book record their groans
> Who were thy Sheep and in their antient Fold
> Slayn by the bloody *Piedmontese* that roll'd
> Mother with Infant down the Rocks. Their moans
> The Vales redoubl'd to the Hills, and they,
> To Heav'n. Their martyr'd blood and ashes sow
> O'er all th'*Italian* fields where still doth sway
> The Triple Tyrant: that from these may grow
> A hundred-fold, who having learnt the way
> Early may fly the *Babylonian* wo.

Leaflets, publications, engravings, speeches and sermons evoked the event. The court of Savoy used diplomatic means to try to play down events. Sir Samuel Morland, a remarkable ambassador, was sent by England to make an official protest to the court in Turin on 25 May. A diplomatic incident was only just avoided. A group of Protestant peasants had been propelled to the forefront of the European political stage, suddenly acquiring unexpected importance. Cardinal Mazarin, the prime minister, intervened in person. Meanwhile, in the valleys, Janavel and Jahier organised an open Waldensian rebellion to strike back at what they considered to be occupying forces. A period of guerrilla warfare ensued. The count of Marolles replied by raiding the villages; the rebels retaliated in the same way. Janavel was injured; Jahier was ambushed and killed. Volunteers arrived from the Cluson valley; Huguenot officers took command of the rebels. On 26 July, they took La Tour and burnt down the convent. Unsure of whether they had the situation in hand, the court of Savoy chose to give in to diplomatic pressure and negotiate a settlement. The French ambassador acted as a mediator, while Swiss and English diplomats advised the Waldensian negotiators. The resulting edict, the 'Patents of Grace', represented the pardon accorded by the sovereign to his rebellious subjects. It aimed to calm public opinion across Europe. In fact, it only marked a time of respite.

The Catholic threat had not been defused. The slightest pretexts were seized by the ducal administration to justify disciplinary measures and confiscation of property and even to violate the edict. The Waldensians were subjected to constant pressure, a novel means by which to fight them. The leaders were first in line, and Léger the foremost target. Discontent eventually gave way to a renewal of armed conflict, which Savoy presented to the rest of Europe as proof of the Waldensians' typical insubordination. They were thus no longer seen as defenceless martyrs but as inveterate rebels. Janavel and his company harried the marquis of Fleury who was responsible for law and order. Léger was pursued and forced to go back into exile. But the villagers were generally weary of war, finding it a burden too great to bear. A turbulent synod took place, during which those in favour of negotiating a settlement were in a majority. Janavel was repudiated. A period of increasingly hard bargaining ensued in Turin in December 1663 and January 1664, arbitrated by Swiss envoys. It resulted in the publication of new 'Patents' the following February, confirming those of 1655. In addition, there figured an apparently trivial agreement stating that an emissary from the duchy should be present at synods. The Waldensian community emerged depleted from the conflict; deprived of its leaders, it would henceforth assemble only under strict surveillance. Certain leaders were in exile, such as Léger in Leyden where he wrote his *Histoire générale* to which we have already referred; and Janavel in Geneva where he published his *Instructions militaires*. The two testimonies are quite different but equally moving – a homage to the Waldensians paid by two of their own members.

THE DARK YEARS OF THE SUN KING

Although the Waldensian valleys were not entirely in France, they were not sheltered from the repercussions of French domestic policy. Since Louis XIV had installed his personal government in 1661, the edict of Nantes had been rigorously checked: everything that was not explicitly authorised was forbidden. Pressure gave way to repression; on a formal and legal level to begin with, it later became violent and brutal with the famous *dragonnades*, such as had already been experienced in Piedmont. The French Huguenots, and the Waldensians from the Cluson valley with them, were gradually eliminated. The climate had also changed outside France, for in England, when Charles II was restored to the throne, Catholicism too returned. The Most Christian King felt sufficiently strong in 1685 to sign the edict of Fontainebleau which revoked that of Nantes and forbade Protestantism on his lands. The Cluson valley was brought into line along with the rest of the kingdom, its inhabitants proportionately joining the biggest wave of exiles ever known in the *ancien régime*. A large-scale international research project launched in the 1980s estimated that between two and three hundred thousand Protestants left France to settle in various Protestant countries. The inhabitants of Pragelato made in the main for Hesse.

The Savoy Waldensians were soon also subjected to repression. In his edict of January 1686, the young duke Victor Amadeus II succumbed to the pressure of his uncle, Louis XIV, and ruled that in his duchy too the edict of Fontainebleau should be observed. A minority of Waldensians from the duchy recalled their recent past as *frondeurs* and sought to reawaken the zeal for armed resistance. Even their pastors and their Swiss allies recommended that the Waldensians go into exile, a solution forbidden by the edict of Fontainebleau but not evoked in the January edict. Marshal Catinat assembled his dragoons on the border. Protestant Europe kept silent. The Waldensians assembled on 12 March in Rocheplatte and it was decided that they should opt for exile until a pastor, Henri Arnaud, a figure who had so far kept a low profile but was henceforth to move to the foreground, made a fervent speech reminding them of the history of the Waldensians, the struggles faced by the people of God and the prophecies of the Apocalypse, the Beast of which he likened to Louis XIV. He exhorted them to take up arms for a short, decisive victory. In other words, he orchestrated a complete volte-face. The Waldensians chose to take up arms and resist; their last service was held on 21 March; then they awaited further events. A three-day siege was launched against them. Catinat's troops and the ducal forces, marching together, proved invincible. On 3 May 1686, the war was over.

The region was reconquered, but laid waste. About 2,000 people were killed, 8,500 taken prisoner. Everyone else recanted hastily. No sooner had the troops turned their backs than the rebels emerged from their hiding places; another round of guerrilla warfare began. The duke therefore ordained that the resistance fighters and their families could go into exile. The former Waldensian lands were immediately recolonised by Catholic peasants, but the task was delicate and met with little success. The prisoners' fate was more tragic, most of them dying in camps. Others were sold to Venetian or French galleys. The Swiss intervened on numerous occasions, trying to secure for the prisoners the right to exile, which the duke eventually granted in January 1687; the pastors, on the other hand, were excluded from this agreement. The long march of the Waldensian survivors then began, in the middle of winter from the Suza valley via the Mont Cenis pass and Savoy towards Switzerland. Of the 2,700 who had chosen exile, 2,490 managed to reach Geneva, thanks to the Swiss delegates who accompanied the sad convoy from beginning to end. In Geneva, the Waldensians were given a triumphant welcome, as long-lost family.

Religious refugees had been making for Geneva for nearly a century and a half, but in the years following the revocation of the edict of Nantes they arrived continuously, in vast groups. The people of Geneva were inundated. The Waldensians did not follow the path taken by their French co-religionists, who split up so as to settle down better; on the contrary, they clung together, never planning to put down roots in Swiss territory. They dreamt of returning to their valleys, and several abortive missions set out with this intent. The edict of Fontainebleau had had a poor reception in the courts across Europe. Not that sovereigns were shocked by the fact that a monarch should presume to impose his religion on his subjects, for this was quite commonplace, but they maintained that no-one could both forbid a religious confession and prevent its followers from going into exile, as Versailles was doing. A profoundly anti-French sentiment, that was generally kept subordinate to political interests, spread through Europe. In 1688 the Catholic king James II was dethroned in England, to be replaced by the Calvinist William of Orange, who was already Stadtholder of the United Provinces. The situation changed again and new alliances were forged. William III's envoys proposed a plan to the Waldensians which would enable them to return to their lands and open up an area of hostilities when Catinat's armies least expected them. The expedition was carefully organised in absolute secrecy to ensure its success; it planned to send doctors, officers, pastors and 1,000 men.

In mid-August 1689 another long march began, two years after the first, in the opposite direction this time, towards Piedmont; it was known as the 'Glorieuse rentrée'. It was a military expedition in the fullest sense of the term: they crossed Lake Leman by night; the 200-kilometre march was organised in obligatory stages, along infrequently used paths that were thus accessible only with difficulty. As the Waldensians travelled through each village, they took hostages as a guarantee of their security, only releasing them when they had crossed the region. The sick and the injured were left behind. The first skirmishes with French troops took place in Salbertrand in the Suza valley; the Waldensians were victorious. As they drew near, many Catholic colonists fled. The remarkable procession was headed by Henri Arnaud, a pastor and a general, armed with his bible and a sword. His troops were former *émigrés*, homesick peasants; they were also servants of the Lord invested with a special mission – that of proclaiming the Word of God in popish territory. On 11 September, the survivors proclaimed their faith in the famous oath which they pronounced in Sibaud. The event merits special emphasis. For the first and only time in the history of the Refuge, religious exiles were choosing not to submit but to hold their heads high again, to defy the all-powerful monarch and, taking up arms, to reconquer the country from which they had been expelled. Nowhere else can we find an example of such temerity. It was a military challenge to France, opening up a new centre of insurrection; it was an act of political bravado aimed at a power that claimed to be absolute; it was also an act of religious provocation directed at a Church which called itself 'Catholic', which means universal, but which was also determined to be unique.

CONFLICT, RESPITE AND LIBERATION

Despite Catinat's orders, the guerrilla attacks on the flank were not contained before winter came. The remaining 300 men in the expeditionary force were blocked in Balzigia, a village high up in the Germanasca valley. Arnaud appointed himself their religious and military leader. Although they suffered from the cold and from hunger, he managed for months to keep the ranks disciplined and to maintain foreign contacts. On 2 May 1690, there were signs that the battle for which the 300 bedraggled men had been preparing all winter was finally approaching. Singing the famous Psalm 68, which some twelve years later was to become the war-chant of the Camisards in the Cévennes, the Waldensians went down to confront 4,000 French dragoons waiting in battle formation. After two days of violent and bloody combat, a single square of Waldensians remained when night fell, sheltered on a rugged spur. Then, as a providential, heavy fog descended, they managed to cross the French lines. By morning, they were far away. Meanwhile, Victor-Amadeus II broke his former alliances and gave France up in favour of England and Austria. The Waldensians were safe. The pastors and the former exiles returned, the community began to come together again. The influence of the English was evident on most levels, including the definition of domestic policy. A synod of the Reformed Churches of Piedmont was held in Avigliana, near Turin, where a Protestant community grew up. Finally, the duke published an edict of tolerance, entitling the Waldensians to practise their own religion.

This bastion of Waldensianism was, however, no longer the locus of international struggle. Since recent developments elsewhere in Europe, it now only represented a Protestant enclave in Catholic lands. In the following twenty years, the Protestants in Piedmont would lose half their territory and more than half their numbers. In the treaty of Ryswick signed in 1697, the duchy of Savoy took possession of the Cluson valley. In a secret clause signed with France, the duke agreed to hound out all Protestants from the region. Yet another exodus began, for over 3,000 villagers and seven of the thirteen regular pastors, including Arnaud. This time, they made for Württemberg where they settled for many years, founding villages which they nostalgically named after their homelands: Pérouse, Pinache, names which still figure on maps and signposts in Germany today. Henri Arnaud died in Schoenenberg in 1721. At the beginning of the eighteenth century, however, the renewal of war against France led the duke of Savoy to show more tolerance towards the Protestants and they were again allowed to settle in the Cluson valley. The treaty of Utrecht in 1713 marked the beginning of a more repressive era, at the height of which, in 1730, a new edict forbidding the Protestant cult was issued. The Waldensians were again subjected to considerable religious pressure. The Dutch Huguenots then launched a collection to finance a large-scale educational programme in the valleys. Every Waldensian initiative inspired a Catholic counter-attack, even as far as this great programme was concerned. As Giorgio Tourn has said, the valleys had become a ghetto.

The vicissitudes endured by the Waldensian population during the French Revolution, the Empire and the Restoration are a clear indication that the Waldensian valleys were more French than Savoyard. Félix Neff profoundly shook them from their torpor in 1825 with his movement aptly named the 'Réveil' (Awakening), which in the valleys and beyond, particularly in neighbouring Dauphiné, stirred up religious divergences, denunciations and expulsions. At this point, a new figure arrived who was perhaps to leave the most lasting mark on the Waldensian community. It was Charles Beckwith, an Englishman, originally an Anglican, who had been strongly influenced by the 'Réveil'. He discovered the Waldensians after being injured at Waterloo and went to settle in the valleys where he remained until his death, dedicating his life to the community. Beckwith's decision and subsequent actions were motivated by his desire not only to organise and strengthen the Waldensian ghetto but also to expand well beyond the existing limits, down into Italy; in other words, he cherished a dream of evangelical victories, redefining the Waldensian initiative and mission. He launched his programme by founding schools in every village. In 1848, they numbered 169. In the year 1848 the whole of Europe was shaken by revolutions; it was also of considerable importance for Piedmont, and the Waldensians in particular. Charles Albert issued a statute on 8 February and letters-patent on 17 February. These expressly conferred civil and political rights on the Waldensians, ensuring their equality with all other subjects in their homeland, which had become the kingdom of Piedmont and Sardinia. They had still not been granted the freedom of conscience, but the news was enthusiastically welcomed in the valleys as a sign of their liberation, and due festivities were organised. Admittedly, more time was needed before the pronouncement of equality became a reality, but a page had definitively been turned in the sombre history of the Waldensians.

TO ITALY, AND INTO THE WORLD

Beckwith's vision was transmitted to the community and gradually put into practice. The synods revised the Waldensian Church discipline, the catechism and the psalter. They began to use Italian, they opened a theological school in La Tour where pastors were trained and set up their own publishing house. They had found a new lease of life. In the mid-nineteenth century, the Waldensian ghetto opened out. They first turned to Tuscany where pastors sent to learn Italian encountered energetic members of the Genevan Protestant colony. Just as inspiring was their meeting with Italian liberals who welcomed every new movement opposing religious intolerance, Catholic conservatism and political reaction in Italy. However, we know only too well how the immense optimism of the 1848 liberal revolutions ended in heavy-handed repression. By settling in Turin, the Waldensians expressed their desire to live in the heart of a capital where their activities spread to Valle d'Aosta, Alessandria and Genoa. They nevertheless failed to join with new Protestants to found a single reformed Church, the latter organising a Free Church. It is most likely that the Waldensians' feeling that they constituted a separate people, with their own history, sensibility and theology had something to do with this. As the Italian state expanded, so too did the activities of the Waldensians. Evangelists followed in the wake of the Italian army. Bearers of the Word multiplied, setting out across Italy distributing bibles and copies of the New Testament with renewed missionary zeal. In 1861 the department of theology was transferred to Florence, which had become the capital of the new kingdom of Italy. Then they reached Rome, which had since replaced Florence as capital. The Waldensians were not the sole evangelists, but their participation in this evangelical surge was on a large scale. A variety of Churches emerged once unity had proved unrealistic. The Waldensians, championed by the progressists, called for full freedom of worship and the separation of Churches and the state.

The turn of the century was a time of consolidation for the

Waldensian Church. By this time, it had a firmly established territory in Piedmont, where cohesion was social, psychological and religious. There was also a new diaspora of evangelical communities throughout Italy. Although their religious sensibility and their past were not the same, the Piedmont Waldensians had to open up to their far-flung parishes. Gradually their settlements developed as churches opened in Verona, Milan, Naples and Vittoria in Sicily. Towns and even villages in Mantua, Sicily and Elba had their own places of worship. Social institutions – schools, libraries, pedagogical and diaconal organisations – flourished, often as a result of local individual initiatives. The development served a clear purpose, in keeping with demands which had remained unchanged over the centuries: the Italian Protestants intended to show that the Catholic Church was not the Italian Church, but only one of many.

The next phase in the Waldensians' expansion, in which they went beyond the borders of Italy to the four corners of the earth, was motivated not by religious factors but by poverty. In the second half of the nineteenth century, an economic crisis resulting above all from an increase in the population, provoked a wave of emigration from Italy, and from Piedmont in particular. Waldensian associations were founded in Marseilles, Paris and Geneva, allowing homesick immigrants, who were also Protestants, aware that they formed a special reformed community, to come together. In 1856 three families from Villar Pellice arrived in Uruguay. A few years later, they founded the first 'Waldensian colony'. From here, people settled in the north of Uruguay and Argentina. The story of about one hundred families who set out from Rorà to the province of Chaco reads like an epic. Their pastors and their Protestant church ensured that the communities maintained their cohesion and their originality to the extent that the synod acknowledged that the seventeenth Waldensian Church, after that of Turin, was that of the *Colonia Valdese*. Finally, colonists arrived in the United States of America, from Italy and also from Uruguay. In North Carolina, they founded the colony of 'Valdese' which joined up with English-speaking Presbyterians. A new form of diaspora thus emerged, stretching from New York to South Africa. Even today, with their former language, their links with Piedmont and their religious specificity long since forgotten, place names and family names bear witness to the extraordinary history of a small but active Protestant population in Piedmont.

Now, at the end of the twentieth century, the Waldensian Church has an estimated population of 25,000 adults, which means some 45,000 followers altogether. There are eighteen parishes in the valleys, then those of Uruguay and the cities of Turin, Milan, Florence, Rome, Naples, Palerma and Montevideo. Each community of parishes is autonomous, run by a council of elders elected every five years. The synod is the general assembly of the Churches, bringing together an equal number of pastors and lay representatives. The synod holds two sessions a year: one in spring in Latin America; the other in summer in Piedmont. Pastors oversee the community; after a university education, they are appointed ministers for life. The Waldensian Church publishes several reviews and holds an annual history conference on Waldensianism and the Italian Reformation. While relations have improved between Waldensians and Catholics in our so-called ecumenical times, a number of misunderstandings have persisted, so great is the weight of history. The Roman Church had too long been accustomed to being triumphant and dominant; the Waldensians meanwhile found it hard to see themselves as anything other than a persecuted minority. But history goes on. We are all involved in writing, forming and nurturing it. As each day goes by, the present can be recorded, becoming tomorrow's past, future history. It is a great responsibility, commensurate with human dignity.

BIBLIOGRAPHY

Amabile, L., *Il santo officio della inquisizione in Napoli.* 2 vols., Naples, 1892; reprinted Soveria M.lli, 1987.
Armand-Hugon, A., *Storia dei valdesi*, vol. ii: *Dal sinodo di Chanforan al 1848.* Turin, 1974.
Armand-Hugon, A. and Rivoire, E. A., *Gli esiliati valdesi in Svizzera e Germania (1686–1690).* Torre Pellice, 1974.
Aubéry, J., *Histoire de l'exécution de Cabrières et de Mérindol.* Paris, 1645. Ed. G. Audisio, Mérindol, 1982; Paris, 1995.
Jacquier-Roux-Thévenet, N., 'De l'histoire à la légende: les régions vaudoises françaises'. Thèse de 3e cycle, 2 vols., Aix-en-Provence, 1986.
Kiefner, T., *Die Waldenser auf ihren Weg aus dem Val Cluson durch die Schweiz nach Deutschland, 1532–1755.* 4 vols., Göttingen, 1980–97.
Labrousse, E., *La révocation de l'édit de Nantes.* Geneva and Paris, 1985.
Magdelaine, M. and Von Thadden, R., *Le refuge huguenot.* Paris, 1985.
Pazè Beda, B. and Pazè, P., *Riforma e Cattolicesimo in val Pragelato: 1555–1685.* Pinerolo, 1975.
Tourn, G., *L'étonnante aventure d'un peuple-église.* Tournon and Turin, 1980.
Vinay, V., *Storia dei valdesi*, vol. iii: *Dal movimento evangelico italiano al movimento ecumenico (1848–1978).* Turin, 1980.

CONCLUSION

Discounting the epilogue which, for reasons I explained above, is not a direct continuation of the preceding chapters, this work has aimed above all to write a history which means, among other things, to surprise. It was never inevitable, predetermined or fated that the Waldensian movement should emerge, or be excluded by the Roman Church, or survive and expand, or again dissolve into the Reformation. To be astonished by past events and so to attempt to understand and explain them is the art, and the secret, of the historian. As far as possible, we have tried to trace the history of a minority, step by step. We have pinpointed in the community of the Poor of Lyons behavioural characteristics directly linked to their minority status. In stark contrast with their early missionary spirit, they came to keep themselves to themselves as evidenced by their endogamous, or homogamous, marriages where documents have survived to this effect. A warm sense of solidarity developed, as a limited number of people shared a universal message. They were self-assuredly aware that they alone had access to the truth, to the point that a real superiority complex developed as their minority status became the sign, the proof and the guarantee of the truth they held. They were a dissent; they were also a religious minority. They were defending the path to salvation on a doctrinal and a moral level. Their challenge was of consequence, particularly in a society where everything was religious and religion was everything. The dilemma facing the dissenters was crucial: they had to address their message of salvation to everyone; at the same time, only a small number could hearken to it and so be saved.

Christianity, however, offers a path to salvation via one person – Jesus

Christ: this is the Word of God. Like all other dissenting minorities, the
Poor of Lyons believed they should preach salvation and ensure that they
themselves were saved by returning to the holy scriptures. It was in the
name of the gospel, rediscovered and reread, that they evoked the
straight and narrow path to salvation, via poverty in particular. In the
name of the gospel they sought to correct a Church which had strayed
from its path and to recreate a real society of believers following the
model of the first apostolic community. Last of all, the minority dissent
was not only Christian but also clandestine. The official, established
Church persecuted them. And, as the gospels taught them, this persecution became the sign of their being chosen by God. This is not to say
they were content with it, but the arguments used against them were
subverted. There are numerous indications showing that they were no
more tolerant than their persecutors, for both were, after all, men of
their time, and they endured their suffering in the hope that they in turn
would be victorious one day. But as their situation persisted through the
centuries, the transmission of their message became dependent on their
survival, obliging them to adapt and organise. They were helped in this
by the fact that opposition was not absolute, positions were not always
well defined and opinions were often divided. For these reasons, the
Poor of Lyons remained reasonably faithful to their religious origins,
rarely considering the Roman Church as the new Babylon and funda-
mentally evil, spreading errors as well as vice. On the other hand, they
were always conscious of being sufficiently different from Christians
faithful to Rome, and even opposed to them on several issues, not to be
able to return collectively to the Catholic Church. Their ultimately
rather subtle position marks the profound, genuine originality of their
dissent, outside the fact that the internal coherence and rigid organisation
of their community enabled them to cross the centuries and arrive at the
outskirts of modern times.

Before bringing this study of the Poor of Lyons to a close, it is now
appropriate that we should not hedge the basic questions which have
surfaced in past years, often in impassioned debates. On the contrary, we
should tackle them directly, in keeping with the approach that I have
done my utmost to adopt from the beginning of this work. While doubts
persist and debates continue on many issues, there are, in my opinion,
three major lines of inquiry which deserve our attention. First, what
characterises the dissent, and indeed how exactly can it be qualified?
Second, is there a real continuity from its origins in Lyons through to the
Reformation? Last of all, in what terms should we refer to their
adherence to Lutheran and even Calvinist ideas? Each inquiry in fact
bears on the process of naming. Some might object that this is a

secondary considerations. I, however, maintain that it is essential. If we examine the questions closely, we can see that they touch on the three ages of every living organism, be it an individual, a group or a society: birth, life and death. Furthermore, as I explained above, naming means identifying, thus becoming an act which speaks volumes in terms of assessment, consciousness and appraisal. For these reasons, it would be not only a vain but also a somewhat frivolous approach to history that allowed questions to be elided and momentous answers to be underestimated.

A SECT OR A CHURCH?

The concept of a sect, which has never really had a good reputation, suggesting as it does a separation, has been considerably debased in our times, to the point of acquiring a clearly pejorative sense. In an age which preaches tolerance from all angles – admittedly not always practising what it preaches – the term 'sectarian' has become synonymous with 'intolerant' or even 'fanatical'. At the same time, in our increasingly secular times, the term 'Church' has lost much of its formerly positive resonance. To say one belongs to a Church tends today to mean that one is part of a clan or a cult. It is curious to see how the two words, 'sect' and 'Church', which etymologically and historically speaking were not merely separate notions but opposites, are now beginning to overlap in everyday vocabulary. In the past, the adversaries of the Poor of Lyons saw them as members of the 'Waldensian sect'. Nor is it impossible to find the word 'Church' applied to them; Bernard Gui, for example, wrote: 'They acknowledge a three-tiered hierarchy in their church' (*in sua ecclesia*). Since the Reformation, certain Protestant historians, themselves members of a Church, have referred similarly to the Poor of Lyons, projecting their retroactive vision on to the community as I showed above. We saw, for instance, how Gilles and Léger followed this trend in the seventeenth century. But modern times are no exception either, for Pastor Tourn chose as what he thought was an appropriate subtitle to his study of the Poor of Lyons and the Piedmont Waldensians, *L'étonnante aventure d'un peuple-église* ('The Astonishing Adventure of a People-Church'). As far as the Poor of Lyons themselves are concerned, they always rejected the word 'sect' but they never attributed to themselves the term 'Church' either. This does not make our work any easier. It is therefore fitting that in this work of history, we should pay attention to the matter before deciding whether one or other of the terms can continue to be applied to the Poor of Lyons.

The historian who devoted the most useful study to the matter was Ernst Troeltsch, whose work published in 1919 is still a necessary starting point for such an enquiry. Troeltsch divided Christian movements into four types: Church, sect, mysticism (*spiritualismus*) and Free Church. More recently, in 1977, Jean Séguy published a fine study of the Anabaptist-Mennonite congregations in France in which he drew on Troeltsch's categories, giving fuller data and making the concept more sophisticated. These two authors represent my points of reference in the analysis I would like to make here. In Ernst Troeltsch's opinion, the difference between a Church and a sect was that, while both derived from teachings in the New Testament, their vision of the 'law of nature' differed. A sect maintains that social inequality, the state, private property and so forth run counter to the law of nature. The Church-as-type, however, accepts and integrates such differences. The Church has gradually accepted the world, in other words giving society its religious seal of approval. For this reason, radicalism has been forced to the periphery. Marginalisation has taken two forms: the first is a maverick trend that is integrated within the Church as monasticism; the second is an independent trend which rejects the Church and the world; this is the characteristic of sects.

Seen from this angle, the Church is the type of religious movement or fellowship which, within certain limits, accepts the existing social order. It is an institution of salvation whose role is to bring all people into contact with the supernatural, aided in this by the state. It favours universality rather than intensity. On the other hand, the sect is a relatively restricted community that members join only after their conversion. The members aspire to inner perfection on an individual level; and direct, personal communion is actively encouraged between members. The Sermon on the Mount is the ideal charter of sectarian ethics, opposing as it does the world to the kingdom of God. The sect, unlike the Church, defends a non-sacerdotal form of Christianity. Sects frequently appeal to eschatology as they take the New Testament to be their permanent source of reference, dismissing the established Church as degenerate. The essential difference between the two is thus:

the opposition between the juridical bases of the Church and the sect. The Church is an institution of salvation. Its law derives from the fact that it is conscious of having been founded by Jesus Christ, whose hierarchy and sacraments it perpetuates. The sect is a fellowship of converts who have freely chosen to join. Its law is born from the pact that the believers have made amongst themselves, and that each has made with God (J. Séguy).

The opposition between sect and Church, analysed as types since reality is, of course, much less clear-cut, becomes problematic when the question of generations is evoked. In the strictest sense of the term, there is no sect, since it requires conversion, beyond the first generation. As soon as children are born 'into the sect' it ceases to be one, since personal conversion has not taken place. This approach is clearly over-simplified. As the sect endures, a new generation is born which requires education so that each new member too can be converted. In Jean Séguy's opinion:

> The sect is characterised by the fact that it considers a Church (in the theological sense of the term) as a community for which membership is contractual; it puts special emphasis on the need to be converted to gain admittance ... The sect continues to be a sect so long as it does not give up its requirement that followers should contract in.

Given this double definition, what should we conclude concerning the Poor of Lyons? Which religious type was theirs? The specific feature of a Church, of any kind, lies in the fact that it offers an alternative to the established Church. This is something which, unlike the Churches which developed during the Reformation, the Poor of Lyons never did, if we are to judge by the testimonies which have survived. The answer is thus clear: the term Church cannot be applied to the medieval Waldensians, or the Poor of Lyons. On the other hand, once they became Protestants, the term Church is appropriate. In other words, it is perfectly correct and legitimate to refer to the Piedmont Protestants as a Church from the sixteenth century until the present day. Does this imply that the Poor of Lyons who came before them were a sect? If the term is used in its sociological and religious sense, the answer is yes. The Poor of Lyons indeed never stopped believing that they belonged to the Church; nor did they abandon their belief that membership, which would ensure their salvation, was also contractual. This rejection of the world, and the emphasis on personal conversion, even if the notions were changed or played down in time, were permanent features throughout their history. If the term 'sect' can be emptied of its pejorative connotation and limited to the level of religious sociology, the Poor of Lyons really did form a Christian sect. Throughout this work, however, as the reader has doubtless noticed, I have avoided using the term 'sect' to avoid all confusion or misunderstanding, preferring instead the word 'movement' or 'dissent', even if it has the disadvantage of suggesting that the group was always a dynamic, unsettled fellowship of missionaries, which is not the case. Terminology betrays us. Who would still contest the strength of words?

RUPTURE OR CONTINUITY?

The other essential question, to which Merlo in particular drew attention, is whether or not there was real continuity in the Waldensian movement. In other words, were the Poor of Lyons as we saw them in the fourteenth, for example, or the sixteenth century truly the spiritual descendants of the first Waldensian group in the twelfth to the thirteenth century? By giving the same name to a wide variety of dissenters, are we too not victims or even perpetuators of the inquisitors' limited, dismissive vision? The problem was evoked earlier; let us now tackle it more fully. It is possible that dissenters who did not consider themselves to be Poor of Lyons, or even faithful Catholics were falsely suspected and accused of 'Waldensian heresy' and that they were even found guilty and executed, particularly when the term 'Waldensian', like 'Cathar' before and 'Lutheran' later, was used as a synonym for heretic. It has also been clearly proved that in certain times and places, such as fourteenth-century Piedmont for example, there have been periods of great flux in intellectual, religious and social terms, which troubles our Cartesian desire for order. Ideas were not always clear-cut and the line between orthodoxy and heterodoxy was sometimes vague, as was the boundary separating one dissenting trend from another, even if both were deemed 'heretical' by the ecclesiastical magistrates. The truth was that Christians anxious for salvation, avidly searching eternity and hankering after truth, did not think twice about crossing theoretical barriers of ideology. They were probably only half aware that such barriers existed.

The term 'Waldensian' is therefore not a suitable starting point for an inquiry concerning their real identity. Someone who judges merely by the label on a bottle risks being mistaken, if not poisoned. The contents too must be examined. Continuity in the community of the Poor of Lyons must be analysed in the most objective manner possible, by considering the affirmations and declarations made by members themselves about their beliefs and practices. This approach enables us to affirm that there was real continuity in the Waldensian sect, even allowing for nuances, exceptional cases and statements that were more or less forced upon certain defendants, as we saw above. This is not to deny that there were variations in belief and behaviour. Merlo even spoke of 'Waldensianisms' in the plural (*valdismi*). But in that case, should we not now speak of 'Protestantisms', 'orthodoxies' and 'Catholicisms' in the plural? The real question concerns where we should place the boundary. Up to what point was one still a Waldensian? When did one cease to belong to the movement? Indeed the question is equally valid for all religious societies, from the well-established to the most marginal.

That there was continuity in the Waldensian movement is borne out by the fact that throughout their existence we can trace a coherent, permanent, unyielding nucleus of thought that, to my mind, covers five distinct issues: on a doctrinal level, their attachment to poverty and their rejection of the death penalty, oaths and purgatory; on a disciplinary level, their efficient organisation of poor, itinerant preachers with a clear hierarchy amongst themselves, even if differences on a practical scale were discernible; on a social level, the diaspora and a pronounced rural identity maintained by their deliberate commitment to homogamy; on a cultural level, they had their own language, their own books and a network of cultural intermediaries perpetuating the spoken and written word; lastly, on a psychological level, they shared a collective memory and a sense of belonging to an old, minority community that had access to the truth. These five considerations enable us to confirm that it was the same sect which survived from the twelfth to the sixteenth century, despite their being persecuted and geographically dispersed. In fact, their astounding longevity across the centuries can only be explained by their strong, deep-rooted coherence and awareness that they were continuing a tradition. Their endurance was, after all, unique in the annals of medieval heresy, as I have pointed out before. Such considerations, however, make their commitment to the Reformation all the more astonishing.

TRANSMUTATION, CONVERSION OR SUICIDE?

Even if the exact circumstances are unclear, Vaudès's sudden burst of indignation fits in quite well with the religious context of the twelfth century. Similarly, the sect's development after being dismissed by the Church and its survival are not difficult to explain. What happened in the sixteenth century is far more puzzling. What explanation can we give, indeed what terms should we use concerning their decision to adopt reformist opinions? The question is in fact two-sided. Why did the Poor of Lyons give up their religious specificity? And why did they join the Reformation? It is important to make the distinction, even if it is somewhat formal. We can leave aside the notion of suicide from the outset. It is absolutely clear that the Poor of Lyons had no inclination to disappear, and it was certainly not their choice. At the same time, one fact remains undeniable; there can be no contesting the fact that Waldensianism came to an end at the synod of Chanforan in 1532 on paper and towards 1560 in practice. Almost without exception, every religious characteristic of the dissent – constituting its specificity in Europe both in the face of the Roman Church and the Churches of the Reformation – disappeared. Let me repeat that in religious terms: it was impossible to be Waldensian *and* Protestant at the same time. From this point of view, Waldensianism was swallowed up by the Reformation. It is appropriate to speak of the death of the sect.

It is indeed problematic to explain why a movement which had existed for almost four centuries came to disappear, when the most atrocious persecutions had failed to eliminate it. To my mind, and I am here voicing a hypothesis which deserves study and a line of research yet to be followed through, Waldensianism disappeared because it came to be, or to be considered as, useless. We have seen how Vaudès's original inspiration and the subsequent expansion of his movement derived from a double vocation of preaching and poverty in answer to the religious needs of the time. As years went by, however, preaching became the mission of a specialised body; it was also done in secret which is almost a contradiction in terms, a sort of evangelical aberration. As for poverty, it was not only abandoned by the members of the sect, becoming a feature just of the 'bearers of poverty', but by the sixteenth century what remained of poverty as a symbolic value and a commitment in principle acquired a negative connotation.

In the age of humanism, poverty and mendicity were seen to devalorise the human being. Furthermore, for upholders of the Reformation scrupulously rereading Old Testament texts, wealth and opulence could be signs of divine favour. If humanists and reformers alike considered that alms-giving could be useful and beneficial, they also believed it was a last resort and that mendicity should not be aided; work, in their eyes, bestowed dignity and value on the worker. Poverty was no longer seen as an evangelical value. What did the Poor of Lyons defend, besides this? Poverty was the core of their message, it was the very reason for which they had come into being. They were most likely unsuited to the new urban, commercial world which developed during the Renaissance; they were peasants who had doubtless forgotten that Vaudès and his fellows were townspeople. Perhaps the stubbornly rural community was ahead of its time, as it remained faithful to its conscience, rejected prevailing trends and doggedly chose to resist change. If Waldensianism stopped growing, it was because it had become archaic. If it disappeared in the sixteenth century, it was because it had become an anachronism.

But if Waldensianism was fated to disappear, why did it not just break apart and fade away? The fact is that it did not merely disappear but ceased to exist as an autonomous sect by becoming Protestants. Did some *barbes* at least realise that the synod of Chanforan amounted to a death warrant? Had they foreseen that by dissolving into a vast movement spreading throughout Europe they would paradoxically find a future for themselves? Will we ever know? What is beyond question is that some former members proclaimed a certain Waldensian heritage. This was not in Provence or central Europe where groups of the Poor of

Lyons merged completely with Protestantism, retaining none of their former characteristics, but in Piedmont. The former Poor of Lyons from Piedmont went on living in the same region, with the same family names, the same Romance dialect, cultivating the same past. When they became Protestants they retained considerable ethnic and social cohesiveness. Furthermore, on a religious level, they represented the southernmost outpost of Protestantism in Europe, perched in the middle of Catholic lands. Both their isolation, and the manner in which history tended to be written then, account for the ways in which some Piedmont people came to deform the past of the Poor of Lyons. It is surely revealing that the Waldensians found their first historians only when the Poor of Lyons had ceased to exist. It often happens that a reality begins to attract interest only once it no longer exists. Protestants descended from the Poor of Lyons made pre-Protestants of their forefathers even if these ancestors had always rejected the notion of the will in bondage; they promoted their forebears as champions of tolerance, an unforgivable anachronism, when they were really men and women of their time and consequently as intolerant as those who tortured them; they made them into heroes when in fact the wretched country folk were more often just martyrs which is more than enough in itself.

In this light we can understand why the title *Chiesa valdese* developed, even if in religious terms it is inappropriate twice over. In the first place, the Poor of Lyons never formed a Church. In the second place, the Church bearing that name today has none of the primary religious characteristics of the medieval movement which derived from Vaudès. In other words, still on a strictly religious level, before the sixteenth century the Waldensians had no Church; after this date, there were no more Waldensians since they had joined a Church. And yet, even today, the people of the Waldensian valleys in Piedmont have the deep-rooted, carefully maintained conviction that they are the descendants of the medieval Poor of Lyons. And so they are in terms of geography, and on an ethnic, linguistic and cultural level. But they are not their religious descendants. This being the case, how can we both defend the truth and show due respect to the Piedmont Protestants' legitimate heritage? My suggestion is that members of the Waldensian sect in the middle ages should be called the Poor of Lyons, thus reserving the term Waldensian for the Piedmont people who became Protestants and claimed this name for their Protestant Churches.

And so we come to the end of our historical itinerary which has been both a story and an argument, for every human adventure is built up around epic and enigma. It is a record of the Poor of Lyons' moving and appealing dissent, which in itself is worthy of our labours, but all the more worthwhile since at certain moments in its existence it touched on questions that still concern us directly. My readers will have doubtless understood my approach, even those who are not aware of the debates and quarrels that are more or less academic and not always as scientific as one might hope, but which, in the present volume are of no great importance. My aim was to extract what serious research has enabled us to consider as established – provisionally, of course, for there can be no last word in history – from what is probable, and especially from what is merely possible; I have sought to highlight those partially established results which deserve further discussion. This history has perhaps helped the Poor of Lyons to be better known, it has perhaps highlighted some aspect or other of these our distant and silent fellows, so that their secret, sometimes contradictory, ways might be understood and that through their hesitations and compromises we might come to love those who so resemble us. If this has been the case, the historian could ask for nothing better.

BIBLIOGRAPHY

Séguy, J., *Les assemblées anabaptistes-mennonites de France*. Paris and The Hague, 1977.
Troeltsch, E., *Die Soziallehren der christlichen Kirchen und Gruppen*. Tübingen, 1919.

BIBLIOGRAPHY

MANUSCRIPTS

Cambridge, University Library: Ms. Dd 3, 25–8. Proceedings against
  Waldensians from the diocese of Embrun (fifteenth–sixteenth centuries).
Carpentras, France, Inguimbertine Library: Ms. 8. Waldensian Bible.
Dublin, Trinity College Library: Ms. 259 (Morel report, 1530; Conclusions of
  Angrogna, 1532). Ms. 265, 266 (Waldensians from the diocese of Embrun,
  fifteenth–sixteenth centuries).
Gap, France, Archives départementales des Hautes Alpes: G 751. Persecutions
  against Waldensians from the diocese of Embrun, 1468–1502.
Geneva, University and Public Library: Ms. 206, 207, 208, 209, 209a. Barbes'
  books, fifteenth–sixteenth centuries.
Grenoble, France, Archives départementales de l'Isère: B 4350, B 4351.
  Proceedings against Waldensians from the Dauphiné, 1487–8.
Paris, Archives Nationales: Ms. Fr. 17 811. Proceedings against Waldensians,
  1495.

PRINTED SOURCES

Amati, G., 'Processus contra valdenses in Lombardia superiori, anno 1387'.
  Archivio Storico Italiano 37 (1865), 39 (1865).
Aubéry, J., Histoire de l'exécution de Cabrières et de Mérindol. Paris, 1645. Ed. G.
  Audisio, Mérindol, 1982; Paris, 1995.
Audisio, G., Le barbe et l'inquisiteur. Procès du barbe vaudois Pierre Griot par
  l'inquisiteur Jean de Roma (Apt, 1532). Aix-en-Provence, 1979.
  Procès-verbal d'un massacre. Les vaudois du Luberon (avril 1545). Aix-en-Provence,
  1992.
Dal Corso, M. and Borghi Cedrini, L., Vertuz e altri scritti (manoscritto GE 206).
  Turin, 1984.

Degan Checchini, A., *Il vergier de cunsollacion e altri scritti (manoscritto GE 209)*. Turin, 1979.

Durand of Huesca, *Liber antiheresis*, ed. K.-V. Selge. In *Die ersten Waldenser*, vol. ii. Berlin, 1967.

Duvernoy, J., *Le registre d'inquisition de Jacques Fournier (1318–1325)*. 3 vols., Toulouse, 1965.

Eymerich, N. and Peña, F., *Le manuel des inquisiteurs*, ed. L. Sala-Molins. Paris and The Hague, 1973.

Gonnet, G., *Enchiridion fontium valdensium*. 2 vols., Turin, 1958 and 1998.

Le confessioni di fede valdesi prima della Riforma. Turin, 1967.

Gui, B., *Manuel de l'inquisiteur*, ed. G. Mollat. 2 vols., Paris, 1926–7.

Kurze, D., *Quellen zur Ketzergeschichte Brandenburgs und Pommerns*. Berlin, 1975.

Miolo, G., *Historia breve e vera de gl'affari de i valdesi delle valli*, ed. E. Balmas. Turin 1971.

Patschovsky, A., *Quellen zur bömischen Inquisition im 14. Jahrhundert*. Weimar, 1979.

Patschovsky, A. and Selge, K.-V., 'Quellen zur Geschichte der Waldenser'. *Texte zur Kirchen und Theologie Geschichte* 18, 1973.

Raugei, A. M., *Bestiario valdese*. Florence, 1984.

Vinay, V., *Le confessioni di fede dei valdesi riformati*. Turin, 1975.

Weitzecker, G., 'Processo di un valdese nell'anno 1451'. *Rivista Cristiana*, 1881, pp. 363–7.

SECONDARY WORKS

Context or other religious movements

Amabile, L., *Il santo officio della inquisizione in Napoli*. 2 vols., Naples, 1892; reprinted Soveria M.lli, 1987.

Berthoud, G., 'Le solde des livres imprimés par Pierre de Vingle et les vaudois du Piémont'. *Musée Neuchâtelois*, 1980, pp. 74–9.

Cohn, N., *The Pursuit of Millennium*. London, 1957; republished 1970.

Comba, R., *La popolazione in Piemonte sul finire del Medio Evo. Ricerche di demografia storica*. Turin, 1977.

Dedieu, J.-P., *L'inquisition*. Paris, 1987.

Duverger, A., *La vauderie dans les états de Philippe le Bon*. Arras, 1885.

Gilmont, J.-F., 'La fabrication et la vente de la bible d'Olivétan'. *Musée Neuchâtelois* 4, 1985, pp. 213–24.

Labrousse, E., *La révocation de l'édit de Nantes*. Geneva and Paris, 1985.

Lambert, M. D., *Medieval Heresy*. London, 1977; reprinted Oxford, 1992.

Le Goff, J., *La naissance du purgatoire*. Paris, 1981.

Leff, G., *Heresy in the Later Middle Ages*. Manchester, 1967.

Léonard, E. G., *Histoire générale du protestantisme*. 3 vols., Paris, 1960–6; republished Paris, 1988.

Lerner, E. R., *The Heresy of the Free Spirit in the Later Middle Ages*. Berkeley, Los Angeles and London, 1972.

Macek, J., *Jean Hus et les traditions hussites*. Paris, 1973.

Magdelaine, M. and Von Thadden, R., *Le refuge huguenot*. Paris, 1985.

Molnár, A., *Jean Hus*. Paris and Lausanne, 1978.

Olivétan, traducteur de la Bible, ed. G. Casalis and B. Roussel. Paris, 1987.

Roussel, B., 'La bible d'Olivétan: la traduction du livre du prophète Habaquq'. *Etudes Théologiques et Religieuses* 4, 1982, pp. 537–57.

Schmitt, J.-C., *Mort d'une hérésie. L'Eglise et les clercs face aux béghards du Rhin supérieur du XIVe au XVe siècle*. Paris, 1978.

Séguy, J., *Les assemblées anabaptistes-mennonites de France*. Paris and The Hague, 1977.

Tapié, V.-L., *Une église tchèque au XVe siècle: l'Unité des Frères*. Paris, 1934.

Thouzellier, C., *Hérésie et hérétiques*. Rome, 1969.

Troeltsch, E., *Die Soziallehren der christlichen Kirchen und Gruppen*. Tübingen, 1919.

Yardeni, M., *Le refuge protestant*. Paris, 1985.

General history of the Waldensians

Allix, P., *Some Remarks upon the Ecclesiastical History of the Ancient Churches of Piedmont*. London, 1690.

Armand Hugon, A., *Storia dei valdesi*, vol. ii: *Dal sinodo di Chanforan al 1848*. Turin, 1974.

Gilles, P., *Histoire ecclésiastique des Eglises réformées, recueillies en quelques vallées de Piémont et circonvoisines, autrefois appelées Eglises vaudoises, de 1160 à 1643*. Geneva, 1644; republished in 2 vols., Pignerol, 1881.

Gonnet, J. and Molnár, A., *Les vaudois au Moyen Age*. Turin, 1974.

Léger, J., *Histoire générale des Eglises évangéliques des vallées du Piémont ou vaudoises*. Leiden, 1669.

Molnár, A., *Storia dei valdesi*, vol. i: *Dalle origini all'adesione alla Riforma*. Turin, 1974.

Monastier, A., *Histoire de l'Eglise vaudoise depuis son origine et des vaudois du Piémont jusqu'à nos jours*. Paris and Toulouse, 1847.

Muston, A., *L'Israël des Alpes. Première histoire complète des vaudois du Piémont et de leurs colonies*. 4 vols., Paris, 1851.

Perrin, J.-P., *Histoire des vaudois*. Geneva, 1619.

Tourn, G., *L'étonnante aventure d'un peuple-église*. Tournon and Turin, 1980.

Vinay, V., *Storia dei valdesi*, vol. iii: *Dal movimento evangelico italiano al movimento ecumenico (1848–1978)*. Turin, 1980.

The whole Waldensian diaspora

Armand Hugon, A. and Gonnet, G., *Bibliografia valdese*. Torre Pellice, 1953.

Balmas, E. and Dal Corso, M., *I manoscritti valdesi di Ginevra*. Turin, 1977.

Berger, S., 'Les bibles provençales et vaudoises'. *Romania* 18, 1889, pp. 353–424.

Biller, P., '*Curate infirmos*: The Medieval Waldensian Practice of Medicine'. *Studies in Church History* 19, 1982, Oxford, pp. 55–77.

'Medieval abhorrence of killing pre-*c.* 1400'. *Studies in Church History* 20, 1983, Oxford, pp. 129–46.

'*Multum jejunantes et se castigantes*: Medieval Waldensian Asceticism'. *Studies in Church History* 22, 1985, Oxford, pp. 215–28.

Cegna, R., *Fede ed etica valdese nel quattrocento*. Turin, 1982.

Merlo, G. G., *Valdesi e valdismi medievali*. Turin, 1984.

Montet, E., *Histoire littéraire des vaudois du Piémont*. Paris, 1885.

Schneider, M., *Europäisches Waldensertum im 13. und 14. Jahrhundert*. Berlin, 1981.

Selge, K.-V., *Die ersten Waldenser*. 2 vols., Berlin, 1967.

'La figura e l'opera di Valdez'. *Bollettino della Società di Studi Valdesi* 136, 1974, pp. 4–25.

I valdesi e l'Europa. Torre Pellice, 1982.

Les vaudois, des origines à leur fin (XIIe–XVIe siècle), ed. G. Audisio. Turin, 1990.

'Vaudois languedociens et Pauvres catholiques'. *Cahiers de Fanjeaux* 2, 1967.

Regional studies

Armand Hugon, A. and Rivoire, E. A., *Gli esiliati valdesi in Svizzera e Germania (1686–1690)*. Torre Pellice, 1974.

Audisio, G., *Les vaudois du Luberon. Une minorité en Provence (1460–1560)*. Mérindol, 1984.

Une grande migration alpine en Provence (1460–1560). Turin, 1989.

'Un exode vaudois organisé: Marseille–Naples (1477)'. In *Histoire et société. Mélanges G. Dubuy*. 4 vols., Aix-en-Provence, 1992, vol. I, pp. 198–208.

Cameron, E., *The Reformation of the Heretics. The Waldenses of the Alps, 1480–1580*. Oxford, 1984.

Chevalier, J., *Mémoire historique sur les hérésies en Dauphiné avant le XVIe siècle*. Valence, 1890.

De Michelis, C. G., *La valdesia di Novgorod*. Turin, 1993.

Fournier, P. F., 'Les vaudois en Auvergne vers la fin du XVe siècle d'après les interrogatoires de deux barbes'. *Bulletin Historique et Scientifique de l'Auvergne*, 1942, pp. 49–63.

Jacquier-Roux-Thévenet, N., 'De l'histoire à la légende: les régions vaudoises françaises'. Thèse de 3e cycle, 2 vols., Aix-en-Provence, 1986.

Kiefner, T., *Die Waldenser auf ihrem Weg aus dem Val Cluson durch die Schweiz nach Deutschland, 1532–1755*. 4 vols., Göttingen, 1980–97.

Marx, J., *L'inquisition en Dauphiné*. Paris, 1914; reprinted Marseilles, 1978.

Merlo, G. G., *Eretici e inquisitori nella società piemontese del Trecento*. Turin, 1977.

Molnár, A., 'Les vaudois en Bohême avant la révolution hussite'. *Bollettino della Società di Studi Valdesi* 116, 1964, pp. 3–17.

'Les vaudois et les hussites'. *Ibid.* 136, 1974, pp. 27–35.

Paravy, P., *De la chrétienté romaine à la Réforme en Dauphiné. Evêques, fidèles et déviants (vers 1340–vers 1530)*. 2 vols., Rome, 1993.

Pazè Beda, B. and Pazè, P., *Riforma e Cattolicesimo in val Pragelato: 1555–1685*. Pinerolo, 1975.

Thouzellier, C., *Catharisme et valdéisme en Languedoc à la fin du XIIe et au début du XIIIe siècle*. Paris, 1966; reprinted Brussels, 1969.

Utz Tremp K., 'Richard von Maggenberg und die Freiburger Waldenser (1399–1439)'. *Deutsches Archive für Erforschung des Mittelalters*, 1991, no. 1, pp. 509–57.

INDEX

Cambridge Medieval Textbooks